The Great Tower of Elfland

The
Great
Tower
of
Elfland

The Mythopoeic Worldview of
J. R. R. Tolkien, C. S. Lewis,
G. K. Chesterton, and
George MacDonald

 Zachary A. Rhone

The Kent State University Press

KENT, OHIO

For Maria, my companion on this journey

For Dad and Mom, my greatest supporters

For Charles, the Grey Wanderer whose staff nudged me
out the door to discover this path

Contents

Foreword

Colin Duriez

With any group of writers or artists, it is necessary to try to make sense of what holds together what almost inevitably is a disparate company of people, even if they are from the same social class or cultural background. This is true whether it is the Inklings, the Bloomsbury Group, the pre-Raphaelite Brotherhood, the Lake Poets, the Clapham Sect, the Blue-stockings Society of the mid-eighteenth century, or Dr. Johnson's Literary Club and The Scriblerus Club of the same century.

Zachary Rhone has masterfully responded to the untidy nature of groups in this study of the two most central members of the Inklings, and two significant writers who influenced them, with his reverse approach to the usual one, in moving from the particular to the general and abstract. This allows the capture of the creative and imaginative without abandoning a patterned and ordered intellectual structure to these four writers as seen in abstraction.

This study is an important addition to the as-yet modest number of books that have undertaken a study of writers notable for their connection with the Inklings or as important influences upon group members. I know of no previous book which so definitely explores the worldview of these four related writers as its main focus, rather than finding one or more characteristic and unifying themes, important as these may be. C. S. Lewis, in the early days of the circle, simply spoke of members of the Inklings (such as himself and his friend Tolkien) as sharing a tendency to write and Christianity. As Rhone makes clear, Lewis didn't see either his friendship with Tolkien or the Inklings group as an alliance of combatants consciously following a manifesto. I can imagine Lewis chuckling to himself as he might have conjured up mental pictures of his various friends in the club, as he called it. As a cheerful and combative debunker of overconfident errors of the modern age, it is easy, I think, to see how Lewis, at the center of the informal group, might be considered as such a combatant.

Dr. Rhone's purpose is to convincingly set out a worldview in common between two of the Inklings, C. S. Lewis and J. R. R. Tolkien, who were at the core of the Oxford literary group of friends whose association lasted through the thirties, forties, and fifties. For cultural and historical context, G. K. Chesterton and George MacDonald are explored in detail for their affinities with and strong influence upon the two writers particularly associated with the Inklings. Rhone's conclusion is that there is a shared and unified worldview between all four. In the process, he explores the whole idea of their worldview as a rich coherence of intellectual and imaginative elements, encompassing art, belief, social thought, theology, philosophy, and culture. Rhone concludes that it is "on the foundation of Christianity, that these authors perceive time, progress, science, and civilization and write with the hope of creating eucatastrophe and joy in the human spirit." He defines the worldview essentially as a mythopoeic (or myth-making) one, with all that this implies. The successful making of myth (in which all four participated) communicates deep truth through successful and convincing embodiment in literary art.

The book is marked by careful and attentive reading of the extensive works of the four authors and secondary works about them. As well as presenting new and little-known material, even familiar material (such as Tolkien's essay on *Beowulf*) contributes to a new understanding by treating it in an original and stimulating framework. For instance, as I mentioned, Rhone reverses the usual structure of introduction, exposition, and conclusion. Instead he proceeds in a creative, gestalt manner by exploring the main elements of the worldview the four writers have in common before gathering the pieces together into a full picture. This engages readers' imaginations as well as reasoning, allowing them to anticipate what the conclusion might be. The conclusion is then made concrete and definite by the powerful unifying image of an elven tower, indicating the overview, which includes the reasoned and the imaginative. Rhone in fact appropriates and modifies for his purpose J. R. R. Tolkien's famous image of the tower he used in the 1930s in his groundbreaking essay upon *Beowulf.*

An all-important feature of Rhone's book, in my view, is that it does what all proper learning should do: it opens doors and windows to further exploration, in this case, of the place of their worldview in the quality or essence that identifies individual members, two of whom are central to the Inklings. The implication, to my mind, is that the Inklings was larger in its significance than even the two most well-known members explored by Dr. Rhone—Lewis and Tolkien. Other members could be fruitfully studied for what I would hazard to call their Inklings-ness, in the light of Rhone's work in this book. An example of an Inkling member who would be illuminated by Rhone's insights is Owen Barfield. He could be looked at either in relation to Lewis or to Tolkien. In both instances Barfield's worldview, which he formed very early (evidenced in what he wrote in his twenties, *History in English Words* and *Poetic Diction*), is what had such an impact on the whole nature of their thinking and writing. Barfield returned from Oxford to live in London, before the Inklings as such came into being, to work in his father's law firm, forcing him to be an infrequent visitor to the circle. Yet there is an extraordinary impact of Barfield's worldview on both Tolkien and Lewis. It can be seen, for instance, in his characteristic notion about language as having an ancient semantic unity, implying a profound participation in the natural world on the part of our ancestors, a notion which became an integral part of both Lewis and Tolkien's deepest thinking.

Something that Lewis wrote about our changing human perception of the original universe, which is deeply indebted to Barfield, could in fact speak for Tolkien, and also for Chesterton and MacDonald, represented so well in Rhone's book: "The advance of knowledge gradually empties this rich and genial universe: first of its gods, then of its colours, smells, sounds and tastes, finally of solidity itself as solidity was originally imagined. . . . We, who have personified all other things, turn out to be ourselves personifications" (C. S. Lewis, "Preface" in D. E. Harding, *The Hierarchy of Heaven and Earth: A New Diagram of Man in the Universe* [London: Faber and Faber, 1952]).

Acknowledgments

I cannot go without first reverently acknowledging the work of those authors who provided the focus of this study: George MacDonald, G. K. Chesterton, C. S. Lewis, and J. R. R. Tolkien. I would like to thank the scholars who have gone before me and those who, I hope, will find my work helpful in their endeavors. My sincere gratitude extends to the many scholars with whom I have engaged at the C. S. Lewis and Friends Colloquium at Taylor University and the British J. R. R. Tolkien Society's conferences.

I offer my gratitude to those who reviewed my manuscript, in whole or in part, and those who provided guidance in my research: Charles Bressler, Colin Duriez, Bruce Edwards, Bonnie Gaarden, Don King, Chris Orchard, and the people at The Kent State University Press.

Many thanks to the Marion E. Wade Center at Wheaton College for the use of its resources and to Laura Schmidt, especially, for her help. I would also like to thank Linda Shaughnessy of AP Watt at United Agents LLP on behalf of The Royal Literary Fund for granting permission to use the unpublished G. K. Chesterton materials for this book.

I extend my sincere thanks to Craig Fusco Jr. for his artistry on the book cover.

Finally, I would like to thank my Lord and Savior for the blessing of this project and the blessing that I hope it will be to others. May it be one way in which I am an elf-friend.

Introduction

The Problem and the Purpose

For nearly thirty years, from 1933 to 1963, a self-dubbed literary group called "The Inklings" met weekly in Oxford, England, in C. S. Lewis's rooms at Magdalen College, the Eagle and Child pub (otherwise known as the Bird and Baby), and, later, the Lamb and Flag pub, among other places. The semiformal group consisted of Lewis, J. R. R. Tolkien, Charles Williams, Hugo Dyson, Robert "Humphrey" Havard, Owen Barfield, Warren H. Lewis, and Christopher R. Tolkien, along with others at different times and at any given meeting. They had no formal membership—only invitation by word of mouth. Aloud, the friends read texts to one another: Lewis's *Out of the Silent Planet*, Williams and Barfield's poetry, Tolkien's *The Hobbit*, and even The "New" Hobbit, later published under the title *The Lord of the Rings*. A round of bitter or tea by a warm fire kept conversation lively, even when critiques were at their sharpest. Jack and Tollers—as Lewis and Tolkien were called—and Williams, once he moved to Oxford, often met several times each week outside of the normal Inklings meetings on Thursday nights. Even when the Thursday night meetings ended in 1949, a smaller group continued to meet at the pubs until soon after Lewis's death in 1963, when the link that bound the chain together was lost (Carpenter, *Inklings* 252).

David Cecil, in 1955, would propose the possibility of an "Oxford School" having centered on fantasy, imagination, and Christianity, something echoed in Charles A. Brady's 1956 essay in *Books on Trial*, though

1

he adds Dorothy L. Sayers to the Tolkien, Lewis, and Williams's "Oxford Circle" (Zaleski and Zaleski 508–09). Not long after, in the early 1960s, John Wain, a member of the Inklings group since 1949 and a former pupil of Lewis, claimed that the Inklings had a unified worldview. Doctoral scholars and critics quickly assumed the validity of this premise. Marjorie Evelyn Wright's 1960 dissertation at the University of Illinois, "The Cosmic Kingdom of Myth: A Study in the Myth-Philosophy of Charles Williams, C. S. Lewis, and J. R. R. Tolkien," asserts a unified worldview of Williams, Lewis, and Tolkien, grounded in myth (11). Roger Sale's 1964 article "England's Parnassus: C. S. Lewis, Charles Williams, and J. R. R. Tolkien" in the *Hudson Review* and Charles Moorman's 1966 *The Precincts of Felicity: The Augustinian City of the Oxford Christians* claims, like Wain, that the Inklings were a collective—Moorman first dubbed the "Oxford Christians" to the Inklings, which Warnie resisted, as recorded in *Brothers and Friends* (Glyer 29). Lee Donald Rossi, in his 1972 dissertation at Cornell University, *The Politics of Fantasy: C. S. Lewis and J. R. R. Tolkien,* situates Lewis and Tolkien's unified opinion of social and cultural evolution as a result of their common Christianity and war experience (6). About the same time, scholars began to make connections between Inkling predecessors, as well. In Leo A. Hetzler's 1976 "George MacDonald and G. K. Chesterton," for example, he critiques theological elements in MacDonald and Chesterton's literature, building largely upon Chesterton's own criticism of MacDonald, to articulate a shared Christian mysticism. All of these works suggest that a rich tradition had begun in studying the unified worldview of the Inklings and those related to the group.

In 1978, however, when Humphrey Carpenter wrote the first major biography of the Inklings, he combated the critics who first presented the Inklings as a group with a unified worldview. Carpenter dedicates the entire chapter, "A Fox That Isn't There," to decry any theological or literary unity in the group: "'The Oxford Christians' does not seem to be a term which holds much real meaning. Nor does the idea that there was an *academic* viewpoint common to Lewis and his friends stand up at all well to examination" (*Inklings* 155). Generally, Carpenter diffuses similarities in Christian belief, literary criticism, views of myth, and writing style. To strengthen his argument, Carpenter recalls words of the Inklings, themselves, which suggest incongruity. Carpenter utilizes Lewis to fight against Wain. When Wain claims, "This was a circle of investigators, almost of incendiaries, meeting to urge one another on in the task of redirecting the whole current of contemporary art and life," Lewis responds, "The whole picture of myself as one forming a cabinet, or cell, or coven, is erroneous. Mr Wain has mistaken purely personal relationships for alliances" (qtd. in Carpenter, *Inklings* 160). The irony of Carpenter's pursuit, however, is that, after using Lewis to prove that Lewis was not some sort of leader in a literary movement, Carpenter then quickly turns to a letter by Tolkien in which he refers to the Inklings as "the Lewis séance" (171). Surprisingly, Carpenter wraps up the chapter with the following finale: "They were Lewis's friends: the group gathered round him, and in the end one does not have to look any further than Lewis to see why it came into being. He himself is the fox" (171). For a chapter which claims no unified worldview exists among the Inklings, which claims that no singular purpose or person guided the group, and which finally asserts that the Inklings were, in fact, centered around an individual who held certain interests, it appears that Carpenter truly has discovered the fox which he claims did not exist.

Nonetheless, critics have followed suit with Carpenter with very few exceptions. In 1979, Moorman tackles Lewis and Tolkien's fiction, claiming that *Narnia* carries a pattern of fall and redemption while *The Lord of the Rings* is something entirely different: "[A] basically pessimistic world of the sagas in which God does not intervene in human conflicts and in which the hero's or the society's struggle against evil culminates at best in a temporary victory achieved at tremendous cost. I would maintain that the two world-views, in spite of the shared Christianity of their authors, are opposed in kind and, furthermore, that it is impossible to construct an heroic poem—heroic, that is, in the traditional literary sense—that is at the same time Christian" (62).

According to Verlyn Flieger only five years after Carpenter's *Inklings*, Lewis's approach to Christianity was "based in logic" and fellow Inkling Williams's view focused on "mystical practice" while Tolkien's "Christianity is measured against experience and constantly put to the test" (*Splintered Light* xviii). In 2003, Brian Rosebury characterizes Tolkien as a "careful, single-minded literary artist whose work is essentially one great project" and Lewis as a "prolific and versatile man of letters whose work is always readable but not always carefully considered" (141); furthermore, G. K. Chesterton and Lewis "explicitly pressed the doctrinal point"—a "gadfly role" which Tolkien was not interested in playing (153). Marjorie Burns, in

2005, writes that Lewis's "effects and intent are not the same as Tolkien's," distancing these two authors' creative and philosophical perspectives (44). Martha C. Sammons dedicates an entire book, *War of the Fantasy Worlds: C.S. Lewis and J.R.R. Tolkien on Art and Imagination,* to a thesis which refutes unity in Lewis and Tolkien's mythopoeia: "Tolkien's and Lewis's views of art and imagination are not only central to understanding the themes, value, and relevance of their fantasy fiction but are also strikingly different" (x). Still, almost twenty-five years after Carpenter's claim, David C. Downing's 2012 article, "Sub-Creation or Smuggled Theology: Tolkien contra Lewis on Christian Fantasy," disavows unity between these two authors in light of their Catholic and Protestant doctrines, respectively, and differing views of practicing mythopoeia. Few scholars since the 1960s have even attempted to reconcile the seeming similarities among the Inklings, particularly Tolkien and Lewis. Carpenter's chapter appears to have entombed much scholarly consideration of its possibility.

I am not the first to recognize a problem in Carpenter's evaluation of the Inklings. Joe R. Christopher, in his biography of Lewis, remarks how Carpenter's chapter "proceeds to eliminate all of the things that the group had in common—because they differed on them in degree—until he is left with nothing but Lewis's gift for friendship" (171). The problem, certainly, is a matter of degree, for many scholars have affirmed specific agreements among Inklings and their predecessors. Several focused studies have analyzed a particular aspect of the Inklings—usually matters of shared interest in which Lewis and Tolkien's relationship is the most repeated point of discussion, whether because of their overwhelming literary successes or their intense, midlife friendship. Thus, in 2003's *Tolkien and C. S. Lewis: The Gift of Friendship,* Colin Duriez devoted considerable scholarship to the topsy-turvy Lewis-Tolkien friendship, focusing on life events and those literary parallels to experience. Few critics and biographers avoid discussing this relationship, and only one, since Wain, has attempted to focus on the scholarship emphasizing a unified perspective seemingly severed in the 1970s, although still resisting a claim of unified perspective. Diana Pavlac Glyer, upon quoting several Inklings who disavow any influence on one another, recalls similar literary groups—the Bloomsbury Group and the Transcendentalists, for example—who acknowledged mutual influence; accordingly, she explains that influence is inevitable when part of a writing group for reasons of audience (xvii–xviii). Glyer studies Inkling group dynamics: influence, resonance, challenging opposition, editorial challenges, collaboration, writing about one another, and creative similarities. Glyer's text lays the groundwork for further investigation as to how and why this group maintained a literary relationship for seventeen years (though reportedly ceasing as a writing group in 1949).

While her work is valuable, Glyer's attention to the group and its dynamics does not clearly target the worldviews of the Inklings but explains the effects of one author upon another, thereby only scratching the surface of their worldview. Her intent was to establish communal influence, and she does so effectively. Building on Pat Hargis's 1985 speech at Mythcon in which he claimed a collective interest among the Inklings in Christianity, myth, Romanticism, language, writing, education, and history, Glyer hesitates to posit a unified worldview but admits a unity in interests and influences (33–43). Hence, the worldviews, overall, are discussed not in terms of unity of perspective but in aspects of influence. Unities, in Inkling studies, appear most often in studies of two or, rarely, three authors, or in studies that compare Inkling members to their predecessors. As Christopher notes in 1987, the key Inkling players—Tolkien, Lewis, and Williams—agreed upon the significance of literature and the truth of Christianity, despite different emphases and literary tastes (60). Even Sammons's account of war between Lewis and Tolkien's fantasy and imagination seems to contradict the premise of her argument, for she notes several unities: writing should not be adapted in style for the audience (28, 30); morality is a key issue (35); sub-creation is a significant part of their purpose in writing (37); evil is twisted goodness of an ideal creation (59); they created Secondary Worlds which point to the Primary World's Creator (63); they had like traditions in literary criticism and Medieval philosophy (65, 74–97); they believed truth in the Secondary World is reflective of spiritual truth (66); MacDonald and Chesterton influenced them (xi, 71); fantasy glimpses at a joy of past, future, and eternity (115); *romance* is a term for their favorite fiction (117); the Secondary World requires a consistency like the Primary World (121); literature is a discussion of the human creature (143); they agreed on the advantages of fantasy literature, including recovery, escape, fulfillment of desires, myth, recombination of physical and supernatural worlds, consolation and eucatastrophe, and evangelium (165–91); and several more, from the presence of music in both Lewis and Tolkien's Secondary Worlds to a belief that pre-Christian pagan myths suggest Christian Truth (77, 180).[1]

Beyond the Lewis and Tolkien relationship, Brian Attebery's 2005 article, "High Church versus Broad Church: Christian Myth in George MacDonald and C. S. Lewis," discusses the partly shared, partly divided theological worldviews of George MacDonald and Lewis. In 2006, Donald T. Williams approaches Lewis, Tolkien, and G. K. Chesterton's shared Christian humanism—a helpful study but, at times, failing to connect each author at singular points. Alison Milbank, in 2009, evaluates some of the shared theological views of Tolkien and Chesterton while Carpenter's early *J. R. R. Tolkien: A Biography* and Tom Shippey's 2003 *The Road to Middle-earth* mention Tolkien's roots in MacDonald and William Morris as well as his Medieval sources, chronicled also by Burns, Flieger, and others. In 2015, Philip Zaleski and Carol Zaleski's biography of the Inklings (focusing primarily on Barfield, Lewis, Tolkien, and Williams), *The Fellowship*, confirms that, apart from their shared Christianity and location in twentieth-century Oxford, the group might appear as having "very little in common," though these shared parts play a critical part in their "cultural significance" (7, 12). Focusing on Lewis and Tolkien's forbearers, Hetzler critiques similar theological elements in MacDonald and Chesterton's literature, building largely upon Chesterton's own criticism of MacDonald. Again, two- and three-way studies abound on particular issues: faith, humanism, and literary interests. Lewis to Tolkien, Lewis to MacDonald, Tolkien to MacDonald, Tolkien to Chesterton, and Chesterton to MacDonald: despite the noted relationships, no one has yet been willing to connect the dots. No text ventures to uncover the unified worldview which was desecrated over three decades ago. The early observation of Inklings disunity—and, perhaps, rightly so for the group of thirty Inkling attendees—has encouraged a view of disparity rather than of unity even among a few authors in and around the Inklings.[2]

Through the following study, I will evince and substantiate the unified worldview that has been out of critical favor for over three decades. I will examine each of the individual relationships among Tolkien, Lewis, Chesterton, and MacDonald, utilizing both primary and secondary sources, to establish the primary elements of these authors' unified worldview. I am not positing that these authors were mimetic in their worldviews; certainly, they have differences in thoughts and opinions, but I am using Sigmund Freud's definition of a worldview, or *Weltanschauung*: "*Weltanschauung* is an intellectual construction which solves all the problems of our existence uniformly on the basis of one overriding hypothesis, which, accordingly, leaves no question unanswered and in which everything that interests us finds its fixed place" (783).[3] These authors share the same hypothesis, and from that hypothesis, problems of human existence are answered for them. As Duriez recounts, "Owen Barfield speculated, many years later, that what the whole Inklings 'had in common . . . was more like a world outlook, a Weltanschauung, than a doctrine" (*Tolkien and C. S. Lewis* 83). In response to the tradition of criticism which disavows a unified worldview, I propose to determine and to explain the essential elements of Tolkien, Lewis, Chesterton, and MacDonald's *Weltanschauung* and its overriding hypothesis.

A BRIEF BACKGROUND

The Tolkien, Lewis, Chesterton, and MacDonald schema is not trivial. In *Surprised by Joy,* Lewis recalls Ian Hay's claim that public school students who read George Bernard Shaw and G. K. Chesterton were as much in the minority as boys who secretly smoked (98). To no surprise, Lewis's secret echoes throughout his spiritual autobiography, often in dialogue with GKC's perspective, like the "natural growth" of religion Chesterton depicts in his *The Everlasting Man* (60); the reading of this text would help Lewis to see Christian history outlined for him in a way that made sense (*Surprised by Joy* 216). A rational and self-admittedly unemotional man, Lewis credits Chesterton as the first to break down his hard atheistic mentality. MacDonald, on the other hand, was the first to affect Lewis's creative mind toward Christianity. A coincidental selection of MacDonald's *Phantastes* from a bookstall at the train station would impact Lewis forever. In MacDonald, he discovered what had enchanted him in Thomas Malory, Edmund Spenser, William Morris, and W. B. Yeats, though he did not realize the Christian influence he had picked up along with *Phantastes* at the book stall (173, 175). MacDonald offered Lewis the first taste of pure *joy*—or, as Lewis defines the word, a joy which comes from a longing for joy. Several years later, after reading many of MacDonald's novels and sermons, Lewis provided a short anthology of significant passages in GMD's texts. In the Preface to the text, Lewis refers to MacDonald as "my master" (xxxvii), a sentiment echoed in Lewis's *The Great Divorce* in which GMD becomes the Virgil guide of his divine comedy—or, perhaps, divine tragedy. MacDonald had affected Lewis more than any writer, and Chesterton demonstrated more sense than all the authors of his time; Lewis only thought it a shame that both authors happened to advocate Christianity (*Surprised by Joy* 206).

If Chesterton and MacDonald had initiated a change in Lewis, then it was Tolkien who offered the next hand. Tolkien was both a Catholic and a philologist—two types of people Lewis was told never to trust (209). Carpenter, Glyer, and Duriez, among many others, have discussed the friendship between Lewis and Tolkien much further than may be covered or is even necessary in this brief summary, but it is important that Lewis and Tolkien had mutual influence on one another. Lewis's belief that everything, including the imagination, has the ability to reflect heavenly truth—not truth in its perfect form, but the image of it (161)—mimics Tolkien's idea of *mythopoeia*, cited in Carpenter as "reflecting a splintered fragment of the true light" (*Inklings* 43). Lewis, not long after hearing Tolkien's explanation of myth, admitted to a close friend that he had begun the final step toward Christianity.

Lewis was open to admitting Tolkien's influence on him; Tolkien, on the other hand, refuted any claims to Lewis's effect on him—as was known to Lewis. Although Lewis claimed that Tolkien either restarted a text from scratch or ignored criticism when it was given—for Tolkien accepted few of Lewis's suggestions for correction—Tolkien rewrote nearly every passage Lewis found troubling (Carpenter, *J. R. R. Tolkien: A Biography* 149). Shippey, in *The Road to Middle-earth*, remarks that, from Tolkien's early drafts to his later drafts, "the drafts suggest his critics sometimes had the right idea; they detected the finished work tendencies much more obvious in the medial stages, as also, on occasion and even more suggestively, motifs which remained forever buried to author and readers alike" (318). For example, in revision of *The Hobbit*, Tolkien admitted that his publisher's son, Rayner Unwin, agreed with Lewis in there being too much "hobbit talk"; Tolkien referred to Rayner and Lewis as "my two chief (and most well-disposed critics)" (*Letters* 36). Tolkien admits in his letters to constant need of Lewis and other Inklings' approbation to continue his work, going so far as to claim he would never have completed *The Lord of the Rings* had it not been for Lewis's push.[4] John Garth quotes Tolkien's fellow TCBS[5] member, Christopher Wiseman: "We believe in your work, we others, and recognise with pleasure our own finger in it" (253). Garth further claims that Lewis, who "rolled into one forceful personality" the roles of all TCBS members, "had become a closer friend to Tolkien than anyone since the heyday of the TCBS," and ironically, later in life, Tolkien appears to have distanced Lewis in the same way that he did Wiseman (282–83). Tolkien called Lewis a "great friend" who was "in close sympathy" with himself, and, with the Inklings, Tolkien can, at one meeting, remember little of what happened because they are such "like-minded friends" with "similar literary tastes"; he loved no sound more than the loud discussion that greeted him at the Bird and Baby, encouraging him to jump into the discourse (*Letters* 32, 102, 122, 129, 135).

Lewis was not alone in his valuing of Chesterton and MacDonald, for, according to Carpenter in his biography, Tolkien appreciated *The Princess and the Goblin* and *The Princess and Curdie* by MacDonald—with its fantastic kingdom and goblins under the mountains (30). Tolkien was asked to write a preface to MacDonald's *The Golden Key* and, in 1965, began the project. Unfortunately, Tolkien had difficulty enjoying MacDonald as he once did, comparing it to tasting a cake. He suggested that though the taste contains only a piece of fairyland, through maturity, that piece becomes a passport into the world of fairyland. Tolkien never finished the preface, but his metaphor of the cake became the novella *Smith of Wootton Major* (Carpenter, *J. R. R. Tolkien: A Biography* 244). Tolkien charged MacDonald with not only taking traditional tales and applying them to his fairy tales but also expressing power, beauty, and mystery—traits Tolkien had no problem adopting for his own writing ("On Fairy-Stories" 118).

In "On Fairy-Stories," Tolkien also cited Chestertonian fantasy and its *Mooreeffoc,* or the way in which boring or everyday things are seen from a new perspective (146). One might consider the simple Mooreeffoc of a small gardener whose continued sowing reaps the salvation of Middle-earth; Tolkien's effect was not always so different. Alison Milbank explains how Chesterton's "The Coloured Lands" demonstrates the theme of Mooreeffoc by a man who, in a magical way and thanks to a wizard, paints a world of colors that he loves only to find that it is the same world he disliked to begin with. Similarly, in Tolkien's "Leaf by Niggle," a painter paints one leaf in his lifetime but is given a vision of its completion in the afterlife (xiv). Tolkien read Chesterton's *Orthodoxy, The Ballad of the White Horse,* and would have been influenced by Lewis's praise of *The Everlasting Man. The Ballad of the White Horse,* says Milbank, tries to accomplish some of the same elements that Tolkien saw in *Beowulf,* for

Alfred is balancing between paganism and Christianity. A broken sword is the symbol of Alfred's coalition of Gael, Celt, Saxon, and Roman to defeat the Danish invaders—like Isildur and Aragorn's Narsil (x–xi). Despite how much Chesterton's epic reveals characteristics, themes, and motifs similar to *Beowulf,* Norse mythology, and even Tolkien's own mythology, Tolkien faulted GKC for knowing nothing of Northernness in his *Ballad of the White Horse* (*Letters* 92).

Perhaps this is the appropriate place to deal with some of the criticism which uses Tolkien's remarks to aid in the perceived divided worldview. Although in agreement with Lewis, Chesterton, and MacDonald about myth and fairy-story, Tolkien is a somewhat untrustworthy critic of literature if his criticism is to be reapplied to his own works, so much so that I venture to use the word *hypocrite.*[6] Clyde S. Kilby, likewise, attributes *contrasistency,* his term for consistent inconsistency, to Tolkien (Burns, *Perilous Realms* 3). His declaration that myth cannot be dissected and remain intact, for example, is "a claim that his own brilliant discussion of myth contradicts," observe Zaleski and Zaleski (216). Even such astute critics as Flieger and Shippey have noted the problems of Tolkien's evaluation of others' works, both past and contemporary. Flieger highlights Tolkien's criticism of Arthurian mythology, for instance, as "lavish, fantastical, incoherent, and repetitive" as well as "imperfectly naturalized," but, depending on the perceiver, says Flieger, Tolkien's mythology is guilty of the same faults (*Green Suns* 133–34). Similarly, Tolkien's claim to a lack of influence, particularly by Lewis and other Inklings, appears to be out of pride—if not so far as jealousy. George Sayer suggests that Tolkien may have been jealous of Lewis's productivity (Ward 9). Carpenter, in his biography of Tolkien, admits suspecting jealousy on Tolkien's part for Lewis's friendship with Williams (154). He also quotes passages of Tolkien's letters that admit Lewis received more publicity than Tolkien or others were comfortable with (155).[7] Additionally, Tolkien's success seems to have elevated either his taste or self-esteem or both, for after literary success, he claimed that he caught only a glimpse of Elfland through GMD's *The Golden Key* in a sort of disappointed way, and, as is aforementioned, he never completed the preface to MacDonald's book but published his own story from the analogy, *Smith of Wootton Major* (244). Despite Tolkien's repeated praise of Lewis as his greatest critic and the supporter responsible for Tolkien's publications, only four years after Lewis's death, Tolkien defensively wrote that in "very few places" did he find Lewis's critical observations "useful and just," even when he cut several passages of hobbit conversation due to Lewis's (and, later, Rayner Unwin's) suggestion: "I do not think the event has proved him right" (*Letters* 376). Still more, his pronounced distaste for Lewis's Christian didactic works does not necessarily appear to be due to the content, for some of Tolkien's epistolary remarks closely match Lewis's didactic in *Mere Christianity* and passages of *The Screwtape Letters*.[8] Tolkien's prideful response to the laboratory-isolated creation of his language is, perhaps, the only greater demonstration of his pride, refusing to admit much external influence, no matter how clear to the observer (e.g., see *Letters* 379–87 and the whole of Shippey's *The Road*). The only exception to his admissions of linguistic influence appear mostly in letters to his children or close friends, whom he seems to have trusted more than inquiring scholars and the public. Nonetheless, Tolkien was clearly influenced in literary, philosophical, spiritual, and linguistic spheres by others, including Lewis, Chesterton, and MacDonald. As biographers Zaleski and Zaleski suggest, he may have merely lacked the self-confidence of Lewis that can bear criticism—constructive or otherwise—leading him to desire only praise (239).

If we were to diagram the relationships of Tolkien, Lewis, Chesterton, and MacDonald, then we would have drawn lines by now among Lewis, Chesterton, and MacDonald; Tolkien and Lewis; and Tolkien, Chesterton, and MacDonald. There is also a line between Chesterton and MacDonald. MacDonald predates Chesterton's career, so MacDonald would have little chance to comment on a relationship with Chesterton; however, in 1901, one of the first articles Chesterton published in the *Daily News* was "George Macdonald [sic] and His Work" (Gabelman 2). In that article, Chesterton compares MacDonald to Blake as a forgotten "man of genius" who will hopefully be discovered again someday ("George Macdonald [sic] and His Work" 4). In his follow-up article only four years later titled "George Macdonald [sic]," the established Victorian critic does not hesitate to call MacDonald "one of the three or four greatest men of 19th century Britain," holding him in as high regard as Dickens, Hugo, Ruskin, and Thackeray (8). As Hetzler observes, Chesterton found MacDonald's fantasy to reveal the magic not only of fairyland but also of the real world (176). Chesterton appropriately describes his own father with MacDonaldian characteristics as "the Man with the Golden Key" and a magician capable of opening gates to goblin castles; he also recalls an uncle who argued about and agreed with

Browning and MacDonald (*Autobiography* 48, 50). It comes as no surprise, then, that MacDonald was the source of Chesterton's first Christian faith in childhood (172).

The Structure of the Argument

Admittedly, the work presented herein is offered in a nontraditional format; that is, tradition has the overarching thesis presented at the beginning, followed by the pieces in relation to and support of it. I have done so by claiming to argue and to present the unified worldview of MacDonald, Chesterton, Lewis, and Tolkien, but, on the contrary, I am not arguing the unifying principle first; rather, the unifying principle will come last. In terms of Gestalt principles, I will present the pieces in order to understand the whole instead of presenting the whole before analyzing the pieces.

I will begin by establishing these authors' view of language and meaning—how language is an inadequate signifier for the meaning behind it. Then, the literature and critical perspectives of the authors regarding this matter will be discussed at length because language and art are where these authors believe human meaning is first apparent; it is foundational to their viewpoints in each of the forthcoming chapters. Second, I will explain their humanistic perspective—what some have called *Christian humanism.* As they were concerned with language, this chapter provides a definition for what a *human* is in contrast to both the bestial and the divine. Furthermore, I will consider the state of humanity within the hierarchy of the universe, according to their view. Sequentially, as each human progresses on a journey through life, the third chapter discusses the literary theme of paths and roads as metaphors for the human journey. I will examine MacDonald, Chesterton, Lewis, and Tolkien's view of fate and free will, their belief that a companion for discipleship is needed along the road, and the signposts of virtues and morality needed along the way. Fourth, considering the idea of the individual human as a part of the collective, the common opinion may be that civilization facilitates evolution from the barbaric to a higher intelligence; however, these authors believe that science possesses no greater understanding than myth, and that civilization is no less barbaric than barbarism. The fourth chapter will also discuss what morality, then, looks like on a social level, beyond the individual. Finally, I will present the overriding hypothesis which guides their unified worldview: their Christian mythopoeia. Revisiting strands of the previous chapters, I will explain how, from their Christian beliefs and cultural contexts, a unified *Weltanschauung* was inevitable.

Unfortunately, in managing four authors, each with an extensive list of published and unpublished texts, I have not been able to include every written text. I tried to create a balance between breadth of texts and the essential nature of their worldview. I resisted reaching for other texts that would only cause me to add further explanation of the text rather than the principle under discussion. Additionally, as I am concerned with their shared mythopoeic worldview, I have generally avoided any fictional texts that may readily fall under the category of realism—Chesterton's Father Brown stories and MacDonald's Victorian Realism novels, for instance. I have also, for the most part, focused my reading to their prose, not because their poetry is insignificant but because it often takes an additional level of interpretation before it can be applied thematically. Certainly, MacDonald's Victorian Realism novels may emphasize his literary taste in the first chapter, Chesterton's published poetry may assist in explaining his humanism and the human journey in the second and third chapters, the histories of Tolkien's Middle-earth may aid in understanding his view of history and civilization in the fourth chapter, and Lewis's sermons may prove helpful in the final chapter, but I have been able to extract what is necessary from the texts utilized. To extend too far beyond the chosen texts would unnecessarily multiply, rather than add to, the length of this text and, I believe, cloud the essential issues under discussion.

Tolkien, in his "Beowulf: The Monsters and the Critics," complains that scholars have torn through *Beowulf* like those who might tear down a stone tower to examine the stone fragments. Some sought to uncover hidden or lost knowledge through carvings on the stones; others forgot about the stones and pursued coal or oil beneath the stone wreckage. They wonder why the tower was constructed from the maker's father's old stone house when the maker could have simply rebuilt the father's house. They failed to recognize that, from atop the tower, the maker could see the sea (7–8). Whether one sympathizes with Princess Irene or Curdie, Turnbull or MacIan, Edmund or Lucy, Sam or Frodo, we will begin this journey through language and literature, myth and fact, vice and virtue, humanism and materialism, being and becoming, and even belief and disbelief. We will examine the stones not for their source but for their purpose. We will try to rebuild the fallen tower constructed by Tolkien, Lewis, Chesterton, and MacDonald; we will try to climb the stairs of that tower. The string we follow will lead us through earth, sky, and madness, into the Perilous Realms, and even into the West, but each step will lead us to one overarching hypothesis—one unifying conclusion. We will attempt to stand atop that Great Tower of Elfland to see as these sub-creators saw the world.

Language and Literature

One of the initial and perhaps most general unities shared among Mac-Donald, Chesterton, Lewis, and Tolkien is their broad but overall unified perspective on language and literature. Because language and literature are the media through which humanism, existence, civilization, and all other aspects of life are discussed, it is important that we begin at the broadest level. The challenge, of course, is bringing the breadth to a unified point. As this chapter progresses, each point is intended to tie these authors' perspectives back to a simple but essential understanding of the universe: that something is behind, above, or further up and further in (to use McDonald and Lewis's metaphor) than what is initially present. This concept contains the following tenets: language, though simply used to communicate, signifies something or someone behind it and its creation; the best literature hints at truth beyond mere story; and the critic's every move should be to open oneself up to truth and seek it out. For these authors, there is always something behind the obvious, something to be discovered, pursued, contemplated. We will begin, then, with language, the building block of communication, which enables us to reach that truth.

THE AMBIGUITY OF LANGUAGE: FALLIBLE BUT POWERFUL

MacDonald, Chesterton, Lewis, and Tolkien are concerned with both the fallibility and the power of language. Linguists have repeatedly argued whether the signifier and signified are unified or they are arbitrarily assigned. In the former, each of these authors posit an original unification of signifier and signified, a Structuralist move that Jacques Derrida resists in his theory of arche-writing with its repeated "movement of the *sign-function* linking a content to an expression" (60); in the latter, the power of language is utilized by separating signifier and signified by having the signifier refer to a different signified or, perhaps, as Derrida suggests, by having no true signified but only a series of signifiers. The power, of course, comes from the one who assigns meaning: the God who created language or the politician who declares the meaning of a certain constitutional right.

MacDonald's most obvious concern for the separating power of language appears in his understanding of Christian biblical scripture. GMD believes in the fallibility of biblical authors who could misrepresent Christ's words (Reis 33). In a letter to a woman who asked if GMD had any of his "old faith" left, MacDonald responded firmly: "*But the common theory of the inspiration of the words, instead of the breathing of God's truth into the hearts and souls of those who wrote it, and who then did their best with it, is degrading and evil;* and they who hold it are in danger of worshipping the letter instead of living in the Spirit, of being idolaters of the Bible instead of disciples of Jesus" (qtd. in Greville MacDonald, *George MacDonald and His Wife* 373). For MacDonald, truth lies in the origination of language, and such origination cannot be reached completely by human authors or interpreters. He argued that Christ, of course, did not speak in Greek, and the translations made from it—as well as the Hebrew—add an additional accent to skew meaning (*Unspoken Sermons* 434). He writes in his *Unspoken Sermons* that, even if we are unable to interpret a passage of scripture clearly, "we cannot thus refuse the spirit and the truth of it, for those we could not have seen without being in the condition to recognize them as the mind of Christ" (46). Only when one reaches Heaven would she know how near she was to understanding the truth behind the words of scripture (434). Although GMD believes in the fallibility of language, he also believes in the infallibility of the truth behind language in scripture. Words only reach their full meaning when they are given directly from God; humanity's use of language is flawed because humans are flawed, "So the words of God cannot mean just the same as the words of man" (48). Thus, while human language may be flawed, in the way Derrida suggests, MacDonald hints at a true language of the divine which is perfect in its unity of signifier and signified. As he claims in "The Imagination," words are "born of the spirit and not of the flesh, born of the imagination and not of the understanding, and is henceforth submitted to new laws of growth and modification" (8). That is, they were pure before human corruption.

Nonetheless, MacDonald did not give up hope on words. His concerns about scriptural interpretation and refusal of orthodox doctrine in the late nineteenth century caused this minister to be deposed from his first and only church pulpit. Richard L. Reis argues that the most significant moment of MacDonald's life was his loss of a pulpit after being called into Christian ministry: "he felt that he had to find another medium through which to disseminate his essentially religious message, and he chose literature as that medium" (10). MacDonald's prolific literary pursuits may have elevated him to a high status in Victorian England and abroad, but as his son, Greville MacDonald, records, he was and is repeatedly dismissed by many readers for his preaching—though he felt he was serving a higher calling (375).[1] GMD sought to take the reader back to unity by stressing truth in his literature, no doubt, Reis notes, as a means of conveying what he felt divinely inspired to share (33). He did not want people to "word-worship" or to be "oppressed by words" (435) but desired that people understand words "for their full meaning" (48): that is, for the signified truth behind them. He desired to use language, corrupted by common use and misuse, in a poetic form that would bring words nearer to their original, pure, and distinctive meaning that was present in the imagination of God ("The Imagination" 8–9). There, he believes, humanity can find truth and meaning behind and beyond everyday use of language, "for if there be any truth in this region of things acknowledged at all . . . The work of the Higher must be discovered by the search of the Lower in degree which is yet similar in kind" (10–11).

Chesterton, likewise, worked "toward the redemption and restoration of language," according to Milbank, "since the greater the disjunction between conventional speech and the thing or idea itself, the more extreme the paradox and, most crucially, the larger the opening for analogical relation" (90). His use of paradox to understand truth often played on illogical assumptions or plurasignation. In *The Ball and the Cross,* GKC narrates, "Those who look at the matter most superficially regard paradox as something which belongs to jesting and light journalism. . . . But those who see and feel the fundamental fact of the matter know that paradox is a thing that belongs . . . to all vivid and violent practical crises of human living" (45). Paradox applies to the practical as much as to the linguistic. Indeed, words have, as MacDonald believed, lost sense in the original meaning, and sometimes those meanings can only be restored by understanding contradiction and paradox in their common human meaning. In Chesterton's *The Ball and the Cross*, Turnbull, an atheist, charges MacIan, a fierce Christian, with seeming "unable to understand the ordinary use of human language" (79). Although Turnbull does not clearly state what is intended by the ordinary use of human language, the intent is clear when his opponent, MacIan, argues, "Why shouldn't we quarrel about a word? What is the good of words if they aren't important enough to quarrel over? Why do we choose one word more than another if there isn't any difference between them? If you called a woman a chimpanzee instead of an angel, wouldn't there be a quarrel about a word?" (89–90). Clearly, a problem exists in the ordinary use of human language. As MacIan exemplifies in his argument within the story, there is no innate problem with the signifier *bloodshed,* as it signifies killing someone whether for war or as a just penalty; the problem occurs when the signified, killing someone, is under the signifier *murder,* which is unjust bloodshed (89, 92). Chesterton asserts that the simplicity of the ordinary use of human language—such as not specifying the kind of bloodshed—discourages reason and critical thought, and, as a result, meaning is lost (*Orthodoxy* 117–18). According to Milbank, "Like the symbolists, Chesterton sees language itself as material, and a poem as an object. The difference lies in the fact that he also sees language, like his revolutionary poet [Wilde], as an event" (89).

When the event occurs, then, the listener is placed in a position of interpretation. Chesterton, in *The Everlasting Man,* posits that language, though dynamic in signification, bears an underlying structure that is static. GKC comments on the inadequacy of language to convey meaning when he discusses the relationship between *taxes* and *pig.* Whereas some word associations do not seem correct, associating *taxes* with *pig* fits for some unknown, underlying reason—perhaps that taxes are made by pigs (66). These associations, for Chesterton, hint at an underlying signification beneath flawed human language; meaning, language's signifiers may go awry, but the signifieds do, in fact, exist beneath the surface, and listeners must do their best to understand the signified despite the fallibility of human language.

In line with GMD and GKC's understanding of language, Michael Ward highlights Lewis's view: "From one perspective, he has the highest possible view: language is a metaphysical reality with a transcendent origin. From another point of view, he sees that it is, in this sublunary world, subject to severe constraints" (151). Like MacDonald's expressed concern for the speaker—also observable in Chesterton's dichotomy of MacIan and Turnbull—Lewis understands how language is affected, depending on the speaker's spiritual state (143). In *Mere Christianity*, Lewis challenges the literalist readers of biblical scripture, noting that scriptural imagery of Heaven, such as harps, gold, and crowns, were intended to suggest the ecstasy, splendor, and preciousness of Heaven; otherwise, "People who take these symbols literally might as well think that when Christ told us to be like doves, He meant that we were to lay eggs" (114). Lewis believes that such literalist readings of language lead to misappropriation of symbol and meaning, of signifier and signified. In *The Screwtape Letters*, for instance, the demon adviser, Uncle Screwtape, advises his nephew, Wormwood, about the literalist value of language. These demons desire for humans to locate God in a certain part of the bedroom or within a certain sacred object; in this way, humans pray to the location or object—the human-made thing—instead of God as He is: "Not to what I think thou art but to what thou knowest thyself to be" (196–97). In other words, viewing human language as an end in itself—as a clear conveyance of truth—is misguided. The individual needs to understand not only the difference between signifier and signified but also the truth that may be behind or above the sign. As GKC and GMD suggest, looking beyond the sign begins with understanding the speaker, as Lewis notes in *The Screwtape Letters*,[2] and, accordingly, understanding the context.[3] Lewis found that, through careful attention to words and context, one could arrive at a better understanding of truth. For that reason, he found poetry "to be the continual effort to bring language back to the actual" (qtd. in Ward 151).

Tolkien, the most philological of the four, thrived on the ambiguities in language. The problematic nature of word and meaning led Tolkien through history and across languages to discover how words changed in meaning and form. As Ruth S. Noel asserts, a linguist is able to reconstruct culture because it is so integral to culture (3). Shippey recalls how Tolkien, however, had a particular interest in ambiguous words called "asterisk words," often Old English, without referents or with reconstructed forms and used rarely (sometimes only once) (*The Road* 20, 243).[4] For example, the word *elf* Tolkien drew from Old English *ælf*, Old High German *alp*, and, equivalently, Gothic *albs*—an asterisk word (57). Many of the names in Middle-earth are drafted from such mystery words, and the variations in meaning from one language or stage to another encouraged Tolkien's creative drive. Tolkien, for example, used the asterisk Germanic verb *smugan*, "to squeeze through a hole," and its Old English correlate *sméogan* (from a spell "wið sméogan wyrme, against the penetrating worm"), meaning "to inquire into" or, adjectivally, "subtle, crafty" (89). This asterisk word provided two villains for Tolkien: Smaug and Sméagol. It may be helpful to note that Tolkien's reapplication of linguistic mysteries did not add to confusion in language; on the contrary, Tolkien applied the words in ways that preserved what he believed to be the meaning of the asterisk word.

Like Lewis, Tolkien alludes to belief in the idea of a true language in which each signifier and signified are bound to one another (106, 114). Perhaps, for this reason, Tolkien suggests that phonetics have certain aesthetic properties that elicit effect, meaning, or even history—a science known as *Lautphonetik* (113–14). Such belief in a true language—a language like that described by MacDonald, Chesterton, and Lewis—echoes in Tolkien's Middle-earth, where creating languages was the basis for his fiction. Languages were not brought into the story for the purpose of the story; rather, the stories were made for purposes of languages (Tolkien, *Letters* 219). Hence, language begins in the heavenly realm with Eru Ilúvatar, the God of Middle-earth, and his Ainur, or angelic lords, who sing the world into idea until, at once, it comes into existence with the utterance of the copula by Ilúvatar: "Eä, the World that Is" (*Silmarillion* 20). Then, from the time the elves are born and onward, separation occurs in people, geography, and language, among other categories. Language, here, has a transcendent origin that becomes less unified as the world evolves and divides.

LITERARY PERSPECTIVE: MYTH AND FAIRY-STORY

Thus, in Tolkien's fictional world and in our Primary World, language, history, and, in effect, story are inexplicably joined at a root. Understanding how language connects with story is the next step in realizing the unified worldview of these authors. As Tolkien, in his "Valedictory Address," claims, language and literature are two heads of the same creature (230, 233). Lewis even points out in "The Empty Universe" that many theories have wrongly attempted to reduce all study that is not of a scientific discipline to being the offshoot of misleading signifiers in language (82). The nearest these authors get to such a theory is that something exists behind valuable literature in the way that something exists behind flawed human language. In the same way that true meaning exists beneath the surface of flawed human language—something in relation with the divine—these authors believe good literature also reaches to something beneath the surface: to deep truths. These truths are present in the literature they appreciated and, accordingly, created. Tolkien quotes Lewis in a 1955 letter to one of his fans: "If they won't write the kind of books we want to read, we shall have to write them ourselves; but it is very laborious" (*Letters* 209). Their words echo MacDonald's 1893 "The Fantastic Imagination," in which he claims, "I will but say some things helpful to the reading, in right-minded fashion, of such fairytales as I would wish to write, or care to read" (5).

And so they wrote what they read, sometimes including elements of what they read because deeper truths were present. Elizabeth Baird Hardy, for instance, believes Lewis's Jadis is a model of Spenser's Duessa (26); however, given Mr. Beaver's assertion that Jadis is a descendant of Lilith, I believe Lewis's source is more likely MacDonald's *Lilith*. Jadis's cold, pale beauty and child-snatching of Edmund matches the same deathly beauty and kidnapping of MacDonald's antagonist. Whether Duessa or Lilith, Lewis observed a deep truth inherent in the character he chose to adapt, a truth which Jung picks up on in his Theory of Archetypes. Robert A. Collins asserts that MacDonald's "archetypal figures" lead to the same conclusions as Jung some decades later, particularly the Shadow persona (8). Likewise, Flieger notes Tolkien's borrowing from Jung, particularly in "The Lost Road" and "The Notion Club Papers," for the collective unconscious and dream-memory passed from one generation of characters to successive others (*Green Suns and Faërie* 90). While accepted theories like Jung's Theory of Archetypes seek to probe beneath the surface of the human psyche for truth, these authors reach some of the same truths by delving into the depths of literature.

In this example, we observe that truth is passed ancestrally from Duessa and Lilith to Jadis like they are genetically passed through Jung's archetypes. In the same way, MacDonald, Chesterton, Lewis, and Tolkien believed truths evident in history are rediscovered and at times even made clearer in literature. It is no wonder that Tolkien found the blend of history and myth "irresistible" in Lewis's *Out of the Silent Planet* (*Letters* 33). In Tolkien's *Letters*, he discusses his adaptation of the Old English and Old Norse Miðgarðr as occurring at some point in the history of this universe, despite the geographical differences (220). Tolkien and Lewis's interest in history and myth is in agreement with myth-scholar Claude Levi-Strauss when he notes that "the simple opposition between mythology and history which we are accustomed to make—is not at all a clear-cut one, and that there is an intermediate level. Mythology is static, we find the same mythical elements combined over and over again, but they are in a closed system, let us say, in contradistinction with history, which is, of course, an open system" (40). Philip Ellis Wheelwright regards this blend of memory and imagination as the coalescence of *chronos* and *kairos,* "an interweaving not only of moment with moment, but of the transiency of moments with the permanency of that which sustains us in their passage" (20). The truths are, in a sense, a *kairos* event, recreated repeatedly in the chronology of history and its myths.

The shared element of history and myth, then, is deep truth. In order for these truths to be actualized, the Primary World of history and the Secondary World of myth need to have certain similarities. For this reason, the laws of the world are shared. Collins notes how the "spiritual and physical laws seem somehow interchangeable" in MacDonald's fantasy (10). MacDonald describes *law* in the fantasy realm as the means by which ideas are shaped into beauty to grow, out of which comes Truth, Imagination, and Fancy ("The Fantastic Imagination" 7).[5] Michael Mendelson follows the original subtitle of *Lilith,* "A Tale of the Seventh Dimension" to its source in Jacob Boehme, who finds "no distinction between body and spirit, the physical and the divine, the latter inhabiting the same space as the former" (30). Law, thus, facilitates function in a universe. Chesterton claims, "There is an enormous difference by the test of fairyland; which is the test of the imagination. You cannot *imagine* two and one not making three" (*Orthodoxy* 43). The word *law,* however, does not extend to occurrences by which science has determined a so-called law such as gravity. Chesterton offers the example of Newton's discovery of gravity; if an apple fell on Newton's nose, then it is as possible that it could have fallen on a nose it disliked more: "We have always in our fairy tales kept this sharp distinction between the science of mental relations, in which there really are laws, and the science of physical facts, in which there are no laws, but only weird repetitions" (43). In other words, the Secondary World shares laws with the Primary World that are necessary—that are clearly true; however, theoretical laws, such as gravity, are unnecessary, so fairyland is able to create a liminal space, where truth can play out without unnecessary constraints. Tolkien may have meticulously matched the orbiting of the sun and moon of Middle-earth to principles of celestial mapping, but a Silmaril, an orb encapsulating original light before the creation of the sun and the moon, may still be made a star by the astral journeying of Eärendil.[6] Lewis's Narnia may have gravity, as we understand it, but the world is not round, despite our scientific explanation of gravity needing a center.

These similarities between the real and the imaginative—what they love in literature—characterize their fantasy texts, which they utilize to convey truth. Chesterton explains that his ideas never quite make a story the way that he would like them to, but it is because he prefers to observe raw ideas, battling as they are rather than dressing up as something or someone that the ideas are not (*Autobiography* 282). As Peter J. Kreeft writes, "Myth and fantasy show us the significance of our lives, and, when done on a large and epic scale, of our history" (131). The twentieth century had much to offer in terms of fantasy authors whose tales display history in epic scale. Orwell, Golding, Vonnegut, Lewis, Tolkien, Le Guin, among others, are what Shippey calls "traumatised authors," writing into their literature the primary issues of the twentieth century, including industrialized warfare, the problem of evil, and humanism (*The Road* xvii, 329). Interestingly, they are all myth-makers, creators of, though sometimes tragic, fairytales. Unfortunately, fairy-stories have often been preconceived as children's stories. Tolkien claims that he writes not to address children but simply because he wants to write this kind of story (*Letters* 297). GMD would bear the same banner in "The Fantastic Imagination": "For my part, I do not write for children, but for the childlike whether of five, or fifty, or seventy-five" (7).[7]

It is important that we establish the nature of the fairytale which MacDonald, Chesterton, Lewis, and Tolkien favored. Tolkien provides a framework that we will use to discuss the main elements of the essential fairy-story for these authors, for this framework is necessary for eliciting what they believed to be higher truth. In "On Fairy-Stories," Tolkien claims that fairy-stories offer all of the following: Fantasy, Recovery, Escape, and Consolation (138). Fantasy, according to Tolkien, is a high, pure, and potent form of art which begins by "arresting strangeness" (139). Although the fantastic quality comes near to Victor Shklovsky's *defamiliarization,* this arresting of strangeness, or seeing things differently, is not purely linguistic, but the overall process leads one from a fallen perception to a redeemed one (Milbank 38–39). For this reason, Tolkien hints that *fantasy* includes both rational and mystic qualities (Shippey, *The Road* 50). Lewis, in *An Experiment in Criticism,* explains how *fantasy* is both a psychological and a literary term. As a psychological term, *fantasy* carries three meanings: the patient imaginatively constructs a pleasing reality by accident; a patient

constructs an imaginative reality which is "entertained incessantly," leading
to delusions of reality; and temporary indulgences of the mind that are
"subordinated to more effective and outgoing activities," such as a daydream
(50–51). Psychological fantasy does not function effectively with literature,
according to Lewis, because it promotes what he calls "castle-building," or
daydream wish fulfillment[8] (52). Castle-building ignores the presence of the
reader in the text because they demand ordinariness and basic laws like
gravity, when fairy-stories do not require them (54–55). Chesterton may
clarify Lewis's sentiment when he observes that one kind of fantasy (castle-
building) fancies an enjoyable idea only (*Everlasting Man* 108); in literature,
on the contrary, *fantasy* refers to any story which includes "impossibles and
preternaturals" (Lewis, *An Experiment* 50). These impossibilities allow the
reader to observe the reality of terror and beauty, for terror and beauty, experienced in the Secondary World, reach the reader in the Primary World
and, as Chesterton argues, extend into the spiritual realm by touching the
human soul (*Everlasting Man* 108). Hence, Latin myth multiplied gods to
bring them closer to humanity and Greek myths' gods expanded, contrarily,
away from humanity. Chesterton claims these mythologies are a kind of
fairytale told by the fireside or in a child's nursery because they are tales
about the world around the listener, even about the things near to them in
their home (*Everlasting Man* 142). For MacDonald in *Lilith*, a simple library
becomes a gateway to fairyland, to death, and, ultimately, to new life for Mr.
Vane—the real can rattle the soul. Fairy-story fantasy defamiliarizes the
real—not necessarily linguistically—for the reader to engage in something
and someplace new, which is transformational. This *enchantment,* says
Tolkien, creates a Secondary World where the creator and the perceiver can
both enter satisfactorily. The *enchantment* is purely from the desires and
purposes of the artist, a magic which produces, even if in a fictional world,
an alternative reality to the Primary World ("On Fairy-Stories" 143).

Second, the fairy-story offers a specific aspect of fantasy: *recovery,* "which
includes return and renewal of health" and is the "regaining of a clear view"
(146). Alister McGrath notes, for instance, that reading, for Lewis, should
force the reader to return to the primary world a changed person (188). Milbank claims that the *recovery* includes bringing reason back to fantasy and
joining childlike rationality with wonder (147). More complete is MacDonald's explanation in his *Unspoken Sermons:* "The truth *of a thing,* then, is the
blossom of it, the thing it is made for, the topmost stone set on with rejoic-
ing; truth in a man's imagination is the power to recognize this truth of a

thing; and wherever, in anything that God has made, in the glory of it, be it sky or flower or human face, we see the glory of God, there a true imagination is beholding a truth of God" (469).[9] Tolkien exemplifies this defamiliarization-turned-wonder with *Mooreeffoc*, or Chestertonian fantasy—a term drawn from Dickens who saw *coffee room* backward on the inner side of a glass door ("On Fairy-Stories" 146). Chesterton says that, when a person has reached an extreme degree of blindness to the wonder of imagination, he will not be able to look at something in reality with wonder until he sees the world as something never seen before nor part of this world (*Everlasting Man* 15). Chesterton offers the example of a man on a horse. The scene is only spectacular if the viewer imagines that the horse is being ridden for the first time—"then it is as magnificent as St. George and the dragon" (15–16).[10] Tolkien first found his love of words in his wonder of the simple things like trees, bread, and fire ("On Fairy-Stories" 147). Lewis calls this moment of restoration an experience of the *numinous*, when something special and awe-inspiring is communicated (*An Experiment in Criticism* 44).

Third, *escape* works as a sort of wish fulfillment in fairy-stories (Tolkien, "On Fairy-Stories" 147–53).[11] In his well-known *Anatomy of Criticism* in 1957, Northrope Frye terms *escape* as *displacement* in his theory of myths (136), an understanding that is taken all too often as a negative characteristic of fantasy literature. Accordingly, both Tolkien and Lewis target common concerns about fantasy writing as "escapism" (Tolkien, "On Fairy-Stories" 148; Lewis, *An Experiment in Criticism* 61). Escape through fantasy texts is tainted with a scorn by the populace, as if the author and reader are evading the Primary World. On the contrary, these authors feel that the Secondary, fantasy world is as real as the Primary World because it can show truths much like the material Primary World.[12] Lewis asserts that all reading is escape, but the concern is what one escapes to: castle-building, play, or art (68–69). The concern behind escape appears to be a matter not of the escape but of people's perception that the escape is into a childish realm.[13] Lewis claims, "Most of the great fantasies and fairy-tales were not addressed to children at all, but to everyone," before deferring to Tolkien's "On Fairy-Stories" for a full explanation (70). Quite simply, Tolkien says that, yes, fairy-stories offer escape from many things, but these escapes are ways to engage the individual's interests and humanity's deepest concerns, from travel (Tolkien finds the Bifröst more interesting than Platform 4 at Bletchley Station) to evil and ugliness to death (149–53). As Lewis claims, a book which appears to be realistic is one that is more likely to deceive its reader because the reader finds the book in the realm of possibility; the romantic author whose text admits it is fantasy is the one which clearly will not deceive its reader, for it presents its fiction honestly (*An Experiment in Criticism* 67). In short, *escape* is engagement—escape from the Primary World's dealings to engagement with them in fairyland. During World War I, Tolkien took to extrapolating experiences into other forms such as Morgoth, Orcs, and Eldalie (*Letters* 85). Likewise, death is the source, according to Tolkien, of MacDonald's inspiration for fairy-stories—the real-life challenge which GMD escaped to engage with ("On Fairy-Stories" 153). As Chesterton asserts, his greatest philosophical experience began in the nursery, where he learned fairytales, those things that "I believed most then, the things I believe most now"; for Chesterton, "Fairyland is nothing but the sunny country of common sense. It is not earth that judges heaven, but heaven that judges earth; so for me at least it was not earth that criticised elfland, but elfland that criticised the earth" (*Orthodoxy* 41).

Last, *consolation* is "the joy of the happy ending" (Tolkien, "On Fairy-Stories" 153). Chesterton writes, "In the fairy tale an incomprehensible happiness rests upon an incomprehensible condition" (*Orthodoxy* 48). Consolation is the resolution of these conditions. MacDonald believed that the author and teacher's duty is to have a happy ending because good must prevail (Reis 47). Tolkien explains that, while tragedy may be the highest form of drama, the *eucatastrophic* tale is the highest and truest form of the fairytale. *Eucatastrophe* is the highest form of consolation:

> [T]he good catastrophe, the sudden joyous 'turn' (for there is no true end to any fairy-tale): this joy which is one of the things which fairy-stories can produce supremely well, is not essentially 'escapist', nor 'fugitive'. . . . It does not deny the existence of dyscatastrophe, of sorrow and failure: the possibility of these is necessary to the joy of deliverance; it denies (in the face of much evidence, if you will) universal final defeat and in so far is *evangelium*, giving a fleeting glimpse of Joy, Joy beyond the walls of the world, poignant as grief. ("On Fairy-Stories" 153)

For example, in Lewis's *That Hideous Strength*, the N.I.C.E. group has channeled the devil and is preparing to take over the world at all costs. At a particular moment when the group is fully assembled, the miraculous occurs: the bear, Mr. Bultitude,[14] had lost his senses, wandered into the N.I.C.E. home at Belbury, and in a rage, tore many in the group to pieces (344–47).

The massacre here may be grievous, but through the slaughter, the world experiences Tolkien's "sudden turn of events" and "the joy of deliverance" because final defeat has been, for the moment, derailed.

Elements of the Primary World, thus, comprise the fairy-story's environment, and the story is constructed in such a manner that the reader is led to escape into that fantasy realm, which leads, finally, to the consolation of a happy ending. It has been easy, in fantasy stories like Sir Thomas More's *Utopia* or Swift's *Gulliver's Travels,* to assume allegory; however, MacDonald, Chesterton, Lewis, and Tolkien each resisted the allegorical label on myth and fairy-story.[15] Allegorical interpretations of Tolkien's works, in fact, infuriated him (e.g., Sauron is Hitler; Saruman in the Shire is postwar labor government) (Rosebury 159). Tolkien would agree entirely with Chesterton in *The Everlasting Man* that "Myths are not allegories" (104) and MacDonald in "The Fantastic Imagination" that "A fairytale is not an allegory. There may be allegory in it, but it is not an allegory" (7–8). Allegories, in creating a one-to-one correlation between Primary and Secondary Worlds, cannot very well evidence deep truth, which is, for them, the greatest purpose of literature. The problem, however, is that myths and fairy-stories, at times, contain allegories, and there's the rub.

Tolkien demonstrates the clearest resistance to allegory, as he declares that no symbolism or intentional allegory exists in the story of Middle-earth (*Letters* 262).[16] Regardless of clear symbolic points and even of obvious allegorical texts such as "Leaf by Niggle," Tolkien repeatedly denounced the presence of allegory and, in effect, symbolism in his work due to a strong distaste of allegorical texts (though he admittedly needed to use allegorical language to explain mythopoeia[17]). Sméagol, for example, whose name means "burrowing, worming in" in Old English, obtains his power by murdering Déagol, whose name means "secret" (Noel 63).[18] Both names function allegorically in *The Lord of the Rings.* Déagol is the secret by which Sméagol acquires the Ring—which, in effect, leads him to burrow into the cave Bilbo discovers him in. Gollum's power is the sum of suppressing, murdering, and eventually forgetting a dark secret. Likewise, Shippey, in *The Road,* explains how "Leaf by Niggle" is a clear allegory of life, heavily laden with Tolkien's feelings about his own journey (43). Richard L. Purtill explains that Tolkien's "Leaf by Niggle" is a purgatorial story about death. Purtill believes Tolkien resists the term *allegory,* arguing for myth, instead, because Niggle is not the embodiment of a single vice or virtue; however, as Purtill notes, "this is a very narrow interpretation of allegory: not all allegories feature personified vices and virtues" (24). As Novalis's theory on the nature of the fairytale claims, fairytales are dreamlike with coherence, nature must express the spiritual world, and the spiritual world must be similar to the real world; it is no surprise that MacDonald included his theory in a three-paragraph epigraph to *Phantastes* (Hein 153–54). These authors' resistance to the label of *allegory*, narrowly defined, is justified in the genre's general inability to convey deep truth; however, their mythos certainly contains allegory in the broader sense.

Theoretical Implications

Theory, as the literary person knows today, is the lens by which one interprets text. From Russian Formalism and New Criticism to Reader-Oriented/Response Criticism, Structuralism to Deconstruction, Feminism to African American Criticism, among others, aspiring literature students are indoctrinated with theoretical viewpoints, and they *must* use them. MacDonald, several decades before any of these criticisms would reach prominence, claims, "A spirit of criticism for the sake of distinguishing only, or, far worse, for the sake of having one's opinion ready upon demand, is not merely repulsive to all true thinkers, but is, in itself, destructive of all thinking" ("The Imagination" 39–40). Duriez, in *Tolkien and C. S. Lewis: The Gift of Friendship,* notes that Oxford circles became acquainted with new psychology in the 1920s, from Freud to I. A. Richard's psychoanalytic approach to literature in 1924's *Principles of Literary Criticism* and 1929's *Practical Criticism, a Study of Literary Judgment* (28–29). Lewis, in *The Abolition of Man,* claims that "Dr [sic] Richards, who first seriously tackled the problem of badness in literature, failed, I think, to do it" (698). Perhaps the most aware of contemporary literary criticism, Lewis feared what Matthew Arnold prophesied—that literature would replace religion in that all texts would become sacred and, as a result, be interpreted and expounded upon, like an advertisement from the seventeenth century placed under the scrutiny of a critical scholar who finds "the most profound ambiguities and social criticisms" that are clearly not present ("Unreal Estates" 149–50). On the contrary, Lewis asserts that "The true aim of literary studies is to lift the student out of his provincialism by making him 'the spectator', if not of all, yet of much, 'time and existence'" ("Is English Doomed?" 29). As MacDonald encourages, a friend will "discourage indiscriminate reading" of any book available, but the friend also "knows that if a book is worth reading at all, it is worth reading well" ("The Imagination" 39). Because of the resistance to standardized criticism, instead of presenting an holistic concept for approaching a text critically, I have decided to offer a set of concerns shared by MacDonald, Chesterton, Lewis, and Tolkien that help one to "read well": the innate value of the text; language and its implications; art; the artist's perspective; historical and cultural context; audience; classification of genre and purpose; myth; mystery; adventure and discovery; and discovery of truth. Each of these concerns continues the key element of their worldview that there is something "farther in, higher up than the seven dimensions, the ten senses," for the artist's responsibility is to create art that speaks to the audience, and it is the reader's responsibility to allow the art to take them "further up and further in" (MacDonald, *Lilith* 231; Lewis, *The Last Battle* 761).

The concern for the innate value of the text begins where Lewis left off on the problem of criticism—that critics too often see what is not even present in the text. Tolkien disapproved of critics on the whole for their imitative, malicious blabbering ("Beowulf: The Monsters and the Critics" 12; Shippey, *The Road* 27). Chesterton, in *The Everlasting Man,* claims that "Criticism is only words about words . . ." (209). D. Williams notes how postmodern Deconstructionists reduce story to sign, literature to philosophy, truth to power, and history to race, class, and gender, making literature something of a war between class and gender where white males are the enemy (46–47). For this reason, perhaps, MacDonald's critical lectures were more summary and opinion of the narrative than what we understand as criticism. As Chesterton admits, "I have never taken my books seriously; but I take my opinions quite seriously" (*Autobiography* 113). Tolkien wrote to Lewis, seemingly apologizing for a comment he made at an Inkling meeting, admits that he is not a critic, does not want to be one, and declares that, although he is capable, at times, of performing criticism, he is not naturally a critical person (*Letters* 126). These authors resisted what was occurring in the early- to mid-twentieth century with critics who attempted to create strict theoretical frameworks for criticism. Certainly, they were in the opposite opinion of Frye's belief that criticism is an art form which makes art speak because art cannot speak on its own (3–4).[19] Lewis, thus, asserts that the conjunction of reader and text should occur spontaneously without being spoiled by critical theories and their baggage (*An Experiment* 129). The only qualification needed in order to approach the text is to understand what it is—that is, to ascertain the purpose (*A Preface to Paradise Lost* 1). For this reason, Lewis resists the understanding of texts simply as texts of a genre—too much baggage comes by studying genre, alone (*An Experiment in Criticism* 5). Rather, with the reader's understanding of a text's genre, the text should be allowed to speak for itself—not solely as how the text fits into the genre. As Bruce L. Edwards Jr. asserts, "Rather than force writers and texts into the privileged categories of contemporary literary theory, he sought the grounds for appreciating the literary artifact *in situ*" ("Toward a Rhetoric of Nineteenth-Century Fantasy Criticism" 70). Lewis does not believe that all literature should be viewed for its ability to reveal truths about life or as an aid to transforming culture—not that literature cannot do these things, but these should not be understood as the purpose of all literature. The text, on the other hand, should be treated "as an end in itself" (*An Experiment* 130). Edwards observes that Lewis, like Chesterton, believed that "debris" needed to be removed from the reader's point of view in order to see the text for itself (72): as "*Logos* (something said) and *Poiema* (something made)" (Lewis, *An Experiment* 82, 132; *A Preface* 2). Essentially, the text must first be understood simply as a text, an end in itself, before it can be seen to reveal a deeper truth beyond the text (though not all texts reveal deeper truth). The working definition of a *critic*, therefore, may be defined as the following, which Tolkien, despite his resilience, exemplifies all too well: "He is, in a word, to have the character which MacDonald attributed to God, and Chesterton, following him, to the critic; that of being 'easy to please, but hard to satisfy,'" for the critic is responsible only to observe what was said and what was made (*An Experiment* 120).

If literature is to be, in part, *logos* for these authors, then, concomitantly, GMD, GKC, CSL, and JRRT would have a concern for language and its implications. Building on their shared view that language is fallible but powerful, MacDonald explains, "Words are live things that may be variously employed to various ends. They can convey a scientific fact, or throw a shadow of her child's dream on the heart of a mother. They are things to put together like the pieces of a dissected map, or to arrange like the notes on a stave" ("The Fantastic Imagination" 8). Words are a puzzle, then, or a kind of tool for revealing meaning. As Shippey points out, the Old Norse word *sjónhverfing* means "aversion of the sight," an equivalent of the Scottish word *glamour*, meaning a species of witchcraft that deceives the eyes and, furthermore, a corrupted word form of the modern English *gram-*

mar, which parallels the Old English *gramarye:* "occult learning, magic, necromancy" (*The Road* 52); in other words, grammar as we know it in English is grounded philologically in magic, mystery, and spell-binding. In *Miracles,* Lewis argues the validity of human reason, as demonstrated via language. The word *because,* for instance, can be used to denote cause and effect as well as "Ground and Consequent"; while the former indicates a relationship between events, the latter signifies a relationship between belief and assertion. Lewis, thus, asserts that human thoughts are as valid as events because of their analogous relationship (314). Likewise, events must be reduced to cognitive processes because events are only understood by perception. Both uses of *because,* then, find their grounds in knowledge—in the mind and not in the physical world (316). All thoughts, then, become "merely subjective events, not apprehensions of objective truth" (317). Ultimately, Lewis concludes that the divide between perception and reality is a false divide under the presupposition of naturalism (i.e., the world is a self-revolving process of nature, untouched by metaphysics). All understanding of reality may be reduced to the act of knowing, a Kantian principle foundational even in the worldviews of Derrida and Foucault. Like Derrida, Lewis—and his colleagues in this text—note the irrevocable relationship between epistemology and language, but unlike Derrida, they believe that language, though flawed, can be a signifier of deeper truth. "Seeing it could not give life," says MacDonald, "the letter should not be throned with power to kill; it should be but the handmaid to open the door of truth to the mind that was *of* the truth" (*Unspoken Sermons* 435). Tolkien would claim that language is "a disease of mythology"[20] ("On Fairy-Stories" 122). He makes his claim clear in "A Secret Vice," where he explains the entanglement of personal and traditional aspects in language (211). No doubt, as mythology is created by individuals, these linguistic aspects would only help language to evolve and disburse into new languages. If myths are a means of conveying truth (as will be further discussed later), then, according to Chesterton, "The power even in the myths of savages is like the power in the metaphors of poets" (*Everlasting Man* 105).

Literature is the art of language,[21] appreciated by these authors as well as other art forms, so the third theoretical concern is a concern for art. According to Lewis, all art requires that the perceiver surrenders before the piece to allow the senses and mind to receive; the critic must lose herself in the work of art to receive it and not use it (*An Experiment* 19). One of Tolkien's complaints with traditional readings of *Beowulf* is that the text has been studied for facts, and the art, itself, has been largely ignored ("Be-owulf: The Monsters" 5). Commenting on Lewis, Tolkien, and Chester-ton's concern for art, D. Williams notes that art is the signature of humans because it is what separates humanity most from other animals (21), for humanity has had art long before it has had a recorded history—at least one legible to modern eyes; it is the sign, says Chesterton, that what we often call "primitive" and "prehistoric" were, in fact, human civilizations (*Everlasting Man* 43). Some art arouses emotion—others, imagination—and the viewer must allow the text—the art—to speak for one to fully enjoy it (Lewis, *An Experiment* 23–24). Only when the critic has surrendered to the *logos* and *poiema* of the text can the critic begin to see, if it is present, a deeper truth, for art has an ability to deepen the significance of subject matter, as Tolkien believed of the "word-music" of poetry ("A Secret Vice" 218). These authors were concerned with art in its various forms, explicat-ing only that "A genuine work of art must mean many things; the truer its art, the more things it will mean" (MacDonald, "The Fantastic Imagi-nation" 7), but one thing is certain: the truest art, according to MacDon-ald, Chesterton, Lewis, and Tolkien, is one which elicits truth. When one paints true art on Earth, that person is able to see parts of Heaven on Earth (Lewis, *Great Divorce* 510). In that glimpse, we are able to find some of the most powerful epiphanies: "We have all forgotten what we really are. . . . All that we call spirit and art and ecstacy only means that for one awful in-stance we remember that we forget" (Chesterton, *Orthodoxy* 46). As Lewis posits, the art needs to be placed higher in concern than the critic. Other-wise, the critic becomes too self-focused to allow the art to work on him, and as a result, he sees only himself in the art. Once the self is surrendered, he thinks more clearly and sees from a new perspective (*An Experiment* 85), not unlike recovery in a fairy-story.

   This art, however, must have an artist. We may recall the compound of *logos* and *poiema,* something made and something said (Lewis, *An Experi-ment* 82, 132; *A Preface* 2); in order to have something made and something said, we must first have someone to make and say it.[22] Hence, in addition to the concern for art, these authors held a concern for the artist's view, espe-cially as it is communicated through his or her art. By allowing the artist to speak, truths behind the text may be reached by artist and critic, alike. Tolk-ien wrote to Lewis that criticism hinders a writer who has something per-sonal to say, offering the example of a tightrope walker who simply needs practice, not to develop a "theory of equilibrium" (*Letters* 126).[23] The artistic perspective is different than the person who deals solely with facts and theories. MacDonald posits that the poet, in expressing the visual exterior, has an "infinitely deeper" understanding of truths than the scientist because the scientist sees only components; the poet sees the purpose (*Unspoken Sermons* 452–53). He demonstrates his theory by considering an analysis of a flower by both a scientist and a poet. The scientist will explain parts, operation, and how the parts and operation provide life to the flower; the poet, on the other hand, listens for what the flower has to say to her: "The truth of the flower, is not the facts about it, be they correct as ideal science itself, but the shining, glowing, gladdening, patient thing throned on its stalk—the compeller of smile and tear from child and prophet" (465). Lewis argues that one needs to step into the creation of the artist without any set prejudices, and due to the open-minded approach, one is able to understand the artist's view, whether liked or disliked. While the narrative, order, or principles of design may have nothing to do with the artist's "*Weltanschauung*," one cannot appreciate the sculpture fully without considering the sculptor's "view of life." The idea, says Lewis, is not to attempt to change our view of the world but to enter fully into the worldview of the artist, and sometimes, as a result, our view of the world is changed (*An Experiment* 83–84). Only by listening to the text and to the artist's perspective can the critic possibly enter into further-in, higher-up truths.

Obviously, a text does not exist in a vacuum, so truths cannot always be reached readily by *logos* and *poiema* alone. The artist, the text, and the critic, of course, all exist within their own contexts, another concern shared by these authors. MacDonald cared little for the correctness of a translation, "except it bring us something deeper, or at least some fresher insight" into what was meant by the words (*Unspoken Sermons* 454). In order to understand the deeper insight, sometimes the translation must understand the linguistic and cultural, among other, contexts. Authorial intention relies on the concern for context. Tolkien would read and critique ancient texts in a way which elucidated truths about language, history, and belief (Shippey, *The Road* 48). For this reason, Lewis valued literary historians such as W. P. Ker and Oliver Elton, who placed the text within its historical context, revealing the setting and demands of the time period (*An Experiment* 121). Christopher notes Lewis's critical approach in *A Preface*, in that Lewis believes the critic needs to be aware of the "principle concerns" of the time period when the text was written (40). In "De Audiendis Poetis," Lewis asserts that sometimes the critic needs to journey outside of the text in order to approach it well-prepared (1). Hence, according to Duriez, Lewis's historical work sought to improve textual interpretation as well as improve one's perspective of historic culture (*Tolkien and C. S. Lewis* 152). What we know of history is the result of combining various perspectives of events, people, and places, traditionally communicated via text (I use the term broadly). Text, culture, and history are, then, transactionally connected. Chesterton, in *The Everlasting Man,* asserts that, as long as humanity ignores the many subjective perspectives of history, what he calls "the inside of history," art will always offer something that the study of history cannot; the fiction of art may very well be more true than so-called fact because the art of the storyteller inside of history conveys truths and reality that an objective study neglects (139). The subjective side of sixteenth-century England may have been lost, according to Lewis, when the term *renaissance* is used as "an imaginary entity responsible for everything the speaker likes in the fifteenth and sixteenth centuries" instead of the "revival of learning" that the term actually means. Certainly, study in this time yielded a revival of learning, but subjective study of many texts in the fifteenth and sixteenth centuries reveals that only certain humanists were aware of living in what Lewis terms *renascentia* (*English Literature* 55). Subjective study of the poem, likewise, helps the critic to better understand history, and likewise, history, then, aids in the understanding of poems. Although Tolkien would resist providing his own biographical information because he doubted its "relevance to criticism" (*Letters* 257), Tolkien, in "Beowulf: The Monsters and the Critics," writes that he is interested in how the author feels and perceives the world; history is only important to him as it is necessary for understanding the view of the author and poem (20). In doing so, however, Tolkien examined culture in a Foucauldian archaeological manner, concluding that *Beowulf* embodies a relationship between old and new, thought and emotion—here, specifically, the contact between the old, heroic Norse mythology, and the new, virtuous Christianity in England (20–21). Art and history, therefore, transact in the subjective perspective of the viewer to recover a better understanding of both art and history. By understanding such contexts, the critic is better equipped to examine texts for the truths deeper than surface narrative and even to be impacted by the art.

If art is to have an effect on the viewer, so much so that the viewer gains a better understanding of history and the art, then it is clear these authors were concerned with the audience, as well. T. S. Eliot argued that good contemporary poets are the only "jury of judgement" in *A Note on the Verse of*

John Milton; Lewis points out the irony: no one can be a critic if no one can declare the best contemporary poets so that there may be critics (*A Preface* 9–10). It is, perhaps, no surprise that on p. 216 in Lewis's copy of Matthew Arnold's *Essays in Criticism,* the text is underlined: "the great art of criticism is to get oneself out of the way and to let humanity decide."[24] In *An Experiment in Criticism,* Lewis observes that literary criticism typically deals with the evaluation of texts; inversely, he would like to discuss the types of audiences, or readers, by the texts they read and the way in which the texts are read (1).[25] For this concern, MacDonald subtitled *Phantastes* "A Faerie Romance," a fairy-story for an adult audience. It is not to be read as a childish fairytale, though children may read it, but, as Reis notes, as a work of adult symbolic prose (87). Tolkien learned the hard way when he published *The Hobbit.* Flieger argues that Tolkien lessened his concern for audience in writing *The Hobbit* to pondering the relationship between children and fairy-stories in "On Fairy-Stories" to writing *The Lord of the Rings* (*Green Suns and Faërie* 63). In other words, these authors' concern for the audience is from their perspective as artists. The artist must consider the audience of his or her artistic piece in order to understand how to convey, via *logos* and *poiema,* deeper truth than what is seen at face value. In a 1961 letter, Tolkien admits making a mistake by trying to meet the children audience's intellect halfway, which appeared pointless for stupid readers and damaging to gifted readers, for, when he wrote *The Hobbit,* he had not yet broken free of the general opinion that fairytales are for children only (*Letters* 310). A fine line, then, must be walked by the artist who needs to have concern for her audience, but she must not meet the audience half-way; rather, the author need only be concerned with how she can convey her perspective effectively—not by dumbing it down or raising its diction. The artist must decide how best to get the audience to meet her perspective—and, hopefully, the underlying truth. MacDonald and Tolkien's concern for the audience requires the reader to step into the world of the artist—into the artist's view that they value so much. Lewis comments, in *The Abolition of Man,* that the responsibility of a modern-day teacher is not to reduce the information given but to provide more information to the unaware, because, when the unaware students are faced with the real world, they will not be prepared (699).[26] Insofar as the educator should not reduce the force of the teaching to meet the student halfway, it is not the responsibility of the artist to taper the work to the audience's varying tastes; contrarily, the audience must choose to like art according to their taste.[27] Tolkien "deplored" W. H.

Auden's assertion that *The Lord of the Rings* is a measure of "literary taste," insinuating that each reader has a right to his or her own tastes, a claim Tolkien would use in his defense when he admitted dislike of another's work (*Letters* 229). In receiving negative critiques from publisher reviewers, Tolkien responded that a gap exists between the tastes of reviewers and of readers, and he felt that he understood the tastes of simple readers, like himself, fairly well (304). As Lewis recapitulates from Aristotle's *Ethica Nicomachea*, education's purpose is to help the reader discover what he likes and dislikes (*The Abolition* 700). Criticism of the work is very much about the audience's taste and experience. Chesterton admits that his biography on Browning was about "love, liberty, poetry, my own views on God and religion . . . , and various theories of my own about optimism and pessimism," but the biographical elements of Browning were few and "nearly all wrong. But there is something buried somewhere in the book; though I think it is rather my boyhood than Browning biography" (*Autobiography* 103).

The concern for audience has two implications: the direct implication that the audience has different tastes, as described above, and the consequential implication that texts have certain purposes and genres, the concern now under discussion. As we have hinted earlier, not all texts convey deep truths; some are intended for entertainment only. Lewis resists the elitism that is sometimes a part of literary criticism, which privileges one reader or one text over another and argues that different people have not only different tastes but also different purposes for reading—in the same way texts have been purposed by their authors for different tastes and purposes (*An Experiment* 5–8). The concern for genre and purpose is not to attempt to decide how a text fits into a genre in the way Frye does with his archetypal mythos. As MacDonald explains in "The Fantastic Imagination," he resists offering a definition for the fairytale genre because it is too broad and too abstract; instead, he is concerned with instructing the reader on how to approach the genre (5). Understanding the genre and purpose can be helpful in allowing the text to speak to the reader and, therefore, reveal anything that may be beneath the surface of the narrative. Tolkien, for instance, in "Beowulf: The Monsters and the Critics," asserts that *Beowulf* is not an epic or a lay, as has been ascribed to the poem, for no words from Greek or other standard literatures apply. Thus, he proceeds to define the poem as an heroic-elegiac poem (31). For Tolkien, a concern was, no doubt, for the cultural and historical trajectory associated with genres, which is why he disregards the Greek terminology. John R. Holmes recalls two Old English terms for elegies with which Tolkien would have been familiar: *sarcwide,* the common Old English word for an elegy, meaning *sorrow-speech,* and *dustsceawung,* an Old English elegy reflecting on an old civilization, including those who built it and used it only once (46–47). These Old English terms may give us a key into understanding the genre association Tolkien made with *Beowulf* and why he interprets it in terms of loss, sorrow, and pagan heroism. Chesterton, too, notes how one genre and purpose achieves a different aim than another. Fairytales, for instance, start with a normal person in a world full of strangeness and mystery; twentieth-century psychological novels, however, make the protagonist strange and mysterious while the world is normal: "Hence the fiercest adventures fail to affect him adequately, and the book is monotonous" (*Orthodoxy* 8). While the fairytale is intended to convey sanity in the protagonist, the modern psychological novel, by nature, makes the sanity of the protagonist questionable. Poetry, similarly, has a certain effect that prose cannot create. The poet "deals with the outer show of things, which outer show is infinitely deeper in its relation to truth, as well as more practically useful, than the analysis of science," according to MacDonald (*Unspoken Sermons* 452); while the novel looks at humanity from many angles, claims Chesterton, the poet looks at it from one ("George Macdonald [sic] and His Work" 5); for Lewis, modern poetry attempts to mean something as well as to exist as a work of art, saying what prose cannot say in the same way. Like Eliot, he finds summary a heresy for any genre, and Tolkien finds a prose translation of any poem "an abuse" (Lewis, *An Experiment* 41–42, 92; Tolkien, "On Translating *Beowulf*" 49). Clearly, these authors believe the poetic genre—like Coleridge, Sir Philip Sydney, John Dryden, and Percy Bysshe Shelley—typically signals to the reader that something deeper will be expressed, something that not only is but also means.

Of the genres, myth is of especial concern for these authors, as we have mentioned already.[28] Myth, because of its connections to history and the search for something greater, is the genre of choice for MacDonald, Chesterton, Lewis, and Tolkien. Frank McConnell claims that *myth* comes from Greek *muthos* meaning "word," "story," or "tale" (7). In *An Experiment in Criticism,* Lewis explains that the mythic story has particular characteristics:

- It is "extra-literary," meaning the story has relationships to stories, persons, or events outside of the text (43).

- The narrative is not reliant upon suspense or surprise (43).
- Readers are unlikely to "project ourselves at all strongly onto the characters," though one may recognize "profound relevance" to real human life (44).[29]
- Myth is fantastic, dealing with the impossible and preternatural (44).
- Myth is always grave; "Comic myth . . . is impossible" (44).
- And, the reader's experience "is not only grave but awe-inspiring. We feel it to be numinous" (44).[30]

In summary, each of these characteristics demonstrates how myth is defined by its effect on the individual rather than by characteristics of plot, style, or form as with other genres. Lewis admits that he is concerned with how myth affects the imagination through experiencing them, "contemplated but not believed, dissociated from ritual, held up before the fully waking imagination of the logical mind," though he admits plenty occurs beneath the surface of the human imagination—but unobservably so (45). Attebery elevates MacDonald's myths because he "forces us to rethink myths and our relationship to them rather than simply to accept them as given . . . [which] asks us to investigate and re-inhabit the myths that formed us . . ." (16). Myth, then, is experiential, even historical. When Tolkien claims that history and myth share a resemblance because they are composed of the same elements, he echoes what Chesterton claims in *The Everlasting Man*—that a historical imagination is not possible without a mythological imagination (Chesterton, *The Everlasting Man* 69; Tolkien, "On Fairy-Stories" 127).[31] Myth, for these authors, is the most powerful of genres because it is historical, in a sense, and a genre innately affective on the reader to reveal something more.

Myth, and the numinous in particular, lead these authors to an expressed concern for mystery. Flieger, in "Myth, Mysticism, and Magic," claims, "The essence of myth is to be inexplicable in rational terms. The less it yields itself to analysis, the more mythopoeic it is, and the more effective and compelling it becomes" (45). Accordingly, in "The Logic of Fantasy and the Crisis of Closure in *Lilith*," Colin Manlove presents five different, and at times contradictory, interpretations that can be drawn from the text of MacDonald's *Lilith*. Ambiguity and mystery have driven the literary canon to modern literary studies. Tolkien claims that the fairy-story may be a means of conveying mystery, what he claims MacDonald attempted in *The Golden Key* and *Lilith* ("On Fairy-Stories" 125). He argues, in his

Letters, that there should be an element of mystery in detailing a mythical age; a story should leave many things unexplained, including enigmas like Tom Bombadil in his own work (174).[32] Bombadil has been a pinnacle of mystery in Tolkien studies, each scholar theorizing about what he means, is, or does, some unsure if Tolkien meant any more by him than intentional mystery. As Chesterton declares, "As long as you have mystery you have health; when you destroy mystery you create morbidity" (*Orthodoxy* 20). Tolkien decried "scientification," or the need to have storial devices explained scientifically (*Letters* 274). Lewis's nemesis, Prof. J. B. S. Haldane, criticizes Lewis's sci-fi trilogy for lacking scientific accuracy of outer space and grumbles at the scientific necromancy of a severed head kept alive in *That Hideous Strength* (16).[33] Lewis, in "A Reply to Professor Haldane," explains that he was writing fiction and needed enough astronomy as necessary to create willing suspension of disbelief. He was, in no way, attempting to satisfy a real scientist (71). Lewis attempted to create myth's mystery and wonder via a willing suspension of disbelief—what Chesterton found so precious in childhood (*Autobiography* 46).

The mystery and wonder lead to the next concern: a concern for adventure and discovery. This concern is the gateway from the previous concerns—of the text, the artist, the context, and approach, for instance—to whatever truth may be further in or higher up. As Kreeft notes, Tolkien found his creation of Middle-earth to be as much of a discovery as it was a creation (128). In Middle-earth, Tolkien placed a people whose imagination was very small, dressed as "rustic English people"; these are the half-sized humans known as hobbits (qtd. in Carpenter, *J. R. R. Tolkien: A Biography* 180). It is as if Tolkien was commenting that the imagination is half of what makes a human, a human. Without a sense of imagination and adventure, the latter of which is prohibited by hobbit culture, humanity is reduced to half of its potential.[34] The effect of aroused imagination and emotion that reading the *poiema* has on the reader, Lewis contends, allows the reader to escape into the perspective of others, to see as the author sees—like a whole world of adventure and discovery opens before the reader (*An Experiment* 134–37). MacDonald believes, "The best thing you [as an author] can do for your fellow, next to rousing his conscience, is—not to give him things to think about, but to wake things up that are in him; or say, to make him think things for himself" ("The Fantastic Imagination" 9). That is why Chesterton argues that the old fairytales are so powerful, because the normal hero's adventures are startling in a mad world (*Orthodoxy* 8). These authors value fairyland so much because it is a land of wonder, rather than information, where they are naught but an adventurer discovering or trespassing in a new world (Tolkien, "On Fairy-Stories" 109). Safety, says Lewis in *The Great Divorce*, or the feeling of safety are fine for the present, but they have no benefit for the future (474). As these theoretical concerns were practical to these authors, they believed it was a responsibility of every individual to discover the adventure in her life. Chesterton, for instance, while on his honeymoon, felt like he met with a friend inside a fairytale as he stood beneath the sign for the White Horse in Ipswich, an image which later led him to write the epic *The Ballad of the White Horse* (*Autobiography* 44). There, at Ipswich and on his honeymoon, GKC bought a pistol simply because he felt himself in one of his youthful adventures and needed to protect his wife from the pirates in the Norfolk Broads where they stayed, for, wrote Chesterton, many people in the region still carried Danish names (45).

Finally, their concern for adventure and discovery leads to the concern which has been the focus of the entire chapter: the concern for the discovery of further-in, deeper, higher-up, and transcendent truth. As Frank McConnell states, "*All* storytelling is didactic" (4). According to Carpenter, Lewis and Tolkien annoyed many of their friends by arguing that the only truth is found in literature (*J. R. R. Tolkien: A Biography* 121). The literary *logos* allows the reader to get something out of the text, to discover something from the point of view of the author—not necessarily "affectational or moral or intellectual . . . [but] has something in common with all three" (Lewis, *An Experiment* 138). This truth is not the kind of truth proven by scientific or historical fact, asserts MacDonald, for it is a truth in regard "for higher things" (*Unspoken Sermons* 459, 462). Hence, in Chesterton's unpublished "The Psychological Man," he disavows the pursuits of psychology over the late nineteenth and early twentieth century: "But it can be better expressed by saying that, in this last period, the Mind was studying the Mind, instead of studying the Truth" (2). The mystic, claims Chesterton, knows that truth exists behind what is visible with the eyes—something "that imagination is a sort of incantation that can call it up" (*Everlasting Man* 105). Michael Mendelson cites Vane's journey in *Lilith* from the Primary to Secondary worlds through the library as an example of the discovery of truth via literature and imagination, calling this portal the "bibliographic door" (27–28). The imagination, so far discussed, needs some clarity, since it is the key to the discovery of truth for these authors.[35] Mendelson traces Tolkien's reading of Primary and Secondary Worlds, the use of law in the fictive world, and the distinction between Fancy and Imagination in "On Fairy-Stories" to MacDonald's "The Fantastic Imagination" (22–23), which, I may add, is evident as well in Chesterton's *Orthodoxy*[36]; furthermore, these authors clearly drew upon Coleridge's *Biographia Literaria.*[37] The Primary Imagination is God's creative ability, as seen through the human mind, and the highest degree of imagination; the Secondary Imagination is humanity's attempt to create a world as God created the Primary World and is a degree lower than the Primary Imagination; and fancy, or psychological fantasy, is combining a sense of reality with imaginative ideas, the least of the three imaginative levels. Out of the imagination, "Myth and fairy-story must, as all art, reflect and contain in solution elements of moral and religious truth (or error), but not explicit, not in the known form of the primary 'real' world" (Tolkien, *Letters* 144).[38] Although not all myths and fairy-stories contain the same amount or form of truth, "Truth is truth, whether from the lips of Jesus or Balaam" (MacDonald, *Unspoken Sermons* 69).

MacDonald, Chesterton, Lewis, and Tolkien's concerns all deal with relationships—of person, language, place, culture, art, and even divinity—to what is beneath the surface. These relationships are central to the person— the person always in relation to the others, to their art, and ultimately in relation to the transcendental. That is, art, created by humans, reveals to humans truth that is further in and higher up than the material art itself. Their view of language and art, while specific in its view that something is hidden from the surface, extends to areas well beyond language and art: to history and culture. The relationship of the seemingly disconnected categories herein discussed is evidently grounded in their relentless pursuit of higher truth. We have begun in the broadest category of thought: how the earthly signifies the transcendental via art, how the artist transmits these significations, and how the critic is to approach art to discover deep truth. Now that we have examined some of the principal elements of their perspective—meaning their view of art, language, and how each hint at something beyond the signifier—we must shift from looking at the general relationship of these elements—art, human, and transcendental truth—to the center of the relationship: the human being.

All That Is Human

According to MacDonald, Chesterton, Lewis, and Tolkien, the best literature uses language to reflect deep truths beneath the surface of signifier and story. Our focus must now shift from the broader category of communication to those the communication concerns, for as we discussed in the previous chapter, both the artist and the audience matter. In this chapter, we will build upon the mysteries behind language and literature to examine the mysteries of the human being—to discover what is "further in" beneath the surface of the individual and what is "higher up" than humanity in the hierarchy of created beings.

In line with the hierarchy subscribed to by the four authors, Lee Oser classifies Tolkien and Chesterton, along with Eliot, as Christian humanists. Oser defines *Christian humanism* as a revitalization of the significance of humanity and human reason which prevents the corrupting of power by political and religious institutions by conserving the "radical middle between secularism and theocracy" (5). Humanism has a complicated history because the lineage is believed to begin anywhere from the ancient Greeks and Romans, according to Matthew Arnold's ideas of liberal humanism (study of Greek and Roman antiquity), to Auguste Comte's positivism (social evolution), to the humanness of Christ (6–7). In any of these historical views, *humanism,* essentially, refers to the significances of humanity and human reason. Oser, however, notes how, in the twentieth century, humanity became less *animal rationale* (reasoning animal) or *animal rationis capax* (animal capable of reason) and more, simply, animal (10–11).[1] In *Orthodoxy,* Chesterton claims that "Nature is not our mother: Nature is our sister" (105). Under the biblical precepts of Creation, Chesterton posits that humans are, like nature, children of the Christian God. Chesterton couples men with nature in *The Everlasting Man,* claiming that Earth contains many unusual plants and animals, but none more unusual than "men of science" (23). Although a comical observation, Chesterton asserts that humans are part of the animal kingdom—a portion of nature—but adds the important caveat that humans are a unique form of animal, one to be set apart from the rest of nature. "We can be proud of her beauty," Chesterton writes, "since we have the same father; but she has no authority over us; we have to admire, but not to imitate" (*Orthodoxy* 105).

Distinctly Human

Thus, humans are a unique type of nature and unlike all other animals. In a paradoxical statement for which Chesterton is often recognized, he notes the irony of the human animal: "the more we really look at man as an animal, the less he will look like one," for "we do *not* fit in to the world. I had tried to be happy by telling myself that man is an animal, like any other which sought its meat from God. But now I really was happy, for I had learnt that man is a monstrosity. I had been right in feeling all things as odd, for I myself was at once worse and better than all things" (*Everlasting Man* 27; *Orthodoxy* 72–73). In regard to animals, humans are, as Ransom of Lewis's *That Hideous Strength* states, "More. But not less" (378). To prove his assertion, Chesterton creates an imaginative study where another animal takes the place of a human in occupation. In such a case, the extrapolation of human characteristics in an animal would be quite comedic. Chesterton imagines, in *The Everlasting Man,* a cow which creates a costume with four boots and two sets of pants; this cow is as illogical as a Superman or a Supermonkey—like a four-legged animal that can carve, paint, and cook like any human artist. But the illogical and imaginative end there for Chesterton, for he asserts that such imaginations are nothing like the real and immense distance between humanity and all other creatures (19). The inconceivability of this estate is Chesterton's point. He means that humanity can no more be imagined in a state like other animals than an animal can be imagined in a state like a human. MacDonald, according to Chesterton, did not see the beasts and fantastic creatures of his tales as fake or fictitious but saw them as, like Plato's ideals, "really existing in the eternal world, . . . dressed up here as men and movements. It is not the crown, the helmet, or the aureole that are to [MacDonald] the fancy dress; it is the top hat and the frock coat that are, as it were, the disguise of the terrestrial stage conspirators" ("George Macdonald [sic] and His Work" 4). MacDonald's perception of the Primary World occurred synchronously with his perception of the Secondary World. Hence, Chesterton further notes that *The Marquis of Lossie* and *The Princess and Curdie* are essentially the same story, with the former being a realistic novel version of the latter fairytale: "All the awkwardness, all the digression, all the abruptness or slowness of incident, merely mean that the hero longs to throw off the black hat and coat of Malcolm MacPhail and declare himself as Curdie, the champion of the faeries" (5). What this statement implies is that, while parts of the human are bestial, as one can observe by everyday life in the Primary World, other parts of the human long to be something more, something above all other creatures, as is observable by the wonder created in the elflandic Secondary World. Certain activities or characteristics are shared between beast and human such as the sexual instinct that Tolkien asserts is part of one's "animal nature," but as MacDonald claims, if humans "were an animal only, and not a man or a woman that did us hurt, we should not hate: we should only kill" (Tolkien, *Letters* 51; MacDonald, *Unspoken Sermons* 150).

Humanity, thus, has an ability unlike the lesser animals, or *beasts* as we shall call them, which act on impulse. The first characteristic of humanity which sets it apart from the beast is its ability to reason. Chesterton believes that, unlike the beasts, humans are "endowed with the power of thought"— a "human wisdom" which can even choose to deny hearing the voice of God (*Autobiography* 243; *The Man Who Was Thursday* 179). The power of thought among humans functions above the mental processes of beasts. Humans have a mind which unites two branches of thought: "one lobe of it dreaming" and the other completing calculations (*Everlasting Man* 248). Like Chesterton, Lewis posits for two lobes of the human mind: "I was assuming that the human mind is completely ruled by reasons. But that is not so. . . . It is not reason that is taking away my faith: on the contrary, my faith is based on reason. It is my imagination and emotions. The battle is between faith and reason on one side and emotion and imagination on the other" (*Mere Christianity* 115–16). While one part of the mind feels and communicates emotions, the other half of the mind completes calculations and reasons the surrounding world, what the narrator of *Perelandra* calls "a chattering part of the mind which continues, until it is corrected, to chatter on even in the holiest of places" (120). Thus, while Ransom stood in the presence of Maleldil—or, God—in prayer, his calculating side continued to "pour queries and objections into his brain" (120).

The ability to reason is the first defining characteristic of what makes, in Lewis's space trilogy, a creature a *hnau*, a reasoning creature capable of personal relationship with the divine. Lewis presents a clear dichotomy between the hnau and the beast with Mr. Bultitude the bear in *That Hideous Strength*. Although a "great snuffly, wheezy, beady-eyed, loose-skinned, gor-bellied brown bear," the bear is treated kindly and pronounced a safe animal (161). His "mind was as furry and as unhuman in shape as his body," having no ability to remember much of his history, to recognize himself as a bear and his caretakers as humans, or to know that he loved and trusted his caretakers: "The words *I* and *Me* and *Thou* [were] absent from his mind" (303). He is incapable of asking the question "why?" (304) Mr. Bultitude is, in fact, only a bear, able to feel his caretaker Ivy's love and care but unable to comprehend it, for he possessed a desire for human relationship and sadness when it was not present but "not one little raft of reason to float on" (305, 347). The bear's inability to reason, however, is what most separates him from humans and other hnau; thus, his part in the story consists of ruthless killings of many in the Belbury group. In the midst of his slaughtering of humans, the pride, glory, and carelessness of the beast's kills crush Mark's spirit until Mark falls unconscious; in contrast, Lewis provides Mr. Bultitude's awakening to his senses after the slaughter. Bultitude is neither troubled nor surprised by his unfamiliar surroundings, he is unable to understand mystery, and he only cares to find a female bear and food (347). The animal acts not on reason but bestial instinct, alone.

Glyer notes that Tolkien uses *hnau* in *The Notion Club Papers* and, in *The Treason of Isengard*, questioned the nature of Ents—as *hnau* who have become trees or trees that have become *hnau*, making use of Lewis's term (173).[2] The attribution of reason—of hnauness—to animals and fictional creatures is clearly anthropomorphic, a means of presenting human nature before the human eye in a new light. The Ents have their *Entmoot* to discuss whether or not to attack Isengard much the same as a reasoning group of humans might gather to discuss a battle plan, this moot lasting two days (Tolkien, *The Two Towers* 550). MacDonald, likewise, opens his fairytale *The Princess and the Goblin* with a history of the fall of goblins from humanity to the world below into the caverns of darkness. Called *gnomes* and *kobolds* by some and *cobs* by the miners, the goblins represent creatures who were once human but "for some reason or other" fled underground (6). Their reason has gone awry, and, as a result, they fled the kingdom, ultimately becoming less than human: bestial.

Consequentially, "they had greatly altered in the course of generations; and no wonder, seeing they lived away from the sun, in cold and wet and dark places" (6). All changes to the goblins were not physical, however, for the goblins were "not so far removed from the human" in appearance; rather, "As they grew misshapen in body they had grown in knowledge and cleverness, and now were able to do things no mortal could see the possibility of. But as they grew in cunning, they grew in mischief, and their great delight was in every way they could think of to annoy the people who lived in the open-air storey above them" (6). The goblins, thus, have advanced intellectually and, likewise, "had strength equal to their cunning" (7). Their "craftiness," as William Raeper terms it, has increased, while they have physically and morally degenerated (328). Despite their disfigurement into bestial appearance, then, the goblins are not lacking in the ability to think—but, perhaps, the ability to reason. MacDonald symbolizes this strength of mind but lack of reason by the hard head of the goblins. The goblin, Glump, divulges to his son, Helfer, "The goblin's glory is his head. To think how the fellows up above there have to put on helmets and things when they go fighting!" (40) The goblins' strength of mind is manifest in their hard-headedness, a clear metaphor for stubborn and sometimes unreasonable thought and action; additionally, they are weak at the foundation, one of many metaphors MacDonald utilizes in his fairytales. They are strong in mental ability but have soft feet: "it is a goblin-weakness" (40).[3] In his metaphor, MacDonald comments on intellectual prowess: while one's mind may be strong, such strength is powerless without a solid foundation and ability to reason. Thus, they claim that humans only wear shoes because humans cannot stand to look at their own feet, indicative of very poor deductive reasoning (41). The goblins, therefore, because of their transformation, lack something fundamentally human.

The king of the goblins elaborates on this concept when he states that the "sun-people," or humans, are "not at all like us, nine-tenths of whose bulk is solid flesh and bone . . . they must be quite hollow inside" (100). The goblins feel themselves superior to humans because of the goblins' immense mass in flesh, yet the humans possess a hollowness to be filled. To continue MacDonald's symbolism of the metaphysical in the physical: the goblins are nine-tenths of the way beast while the humans possess a hollowness to be filled by spirit. The goblins' spiritual capacity has been diminished by "things of the flesh," a biblical metaphor which would have been known to MacDonald as a minister: "For those who live according to the flesh set their minds on the things of the flesh, but those who live according to the Spirit set their minds on the things of the Spirit. To set the mind on the flesh is death, but to set the mind on the Spirit is life and peace. For this reason the mind that is set on the flesh is hostile to God; it does not submit to God's law—indeed it cannot, and those who are in the flesh cannot please God" (Romans 8.5–8, NRSV).[4] The goblins cannot establish a relationship with the God-character of the story—in this case, the Grandmother, or Queen Irene—who is the source of reason in the text.[5]

In "On Fairy-Stories," Tolkien hits on another distinct characteristic of the human: the human is amphibiously physical and metaphysical. Upset with the charge that historical fantasies failed to separate human from beast (what Lewis would undoubtedly deem an act of "chronological snobbery" or others may call an *anachronistic fallacy*), Tolkien turns the tables, asserting that the "sense of separation" between human and beast has been attacked not by fantasy but by scientific theory: "Not by stories of centaurs or werewolves or enchanted bears, but by the hypotheses (or dogmatic guesses) of scientific writers who classed Man not only as 'an animal'—that correct classification is ancient—but as 'only an animal'" (160). Thus, according to Chesterton, humans are not beasts, but something more due to a supernatural component: "He seems rather more supernatural as a natural product than as a supernatural one" (*Everlasting Man* 34). Unlike the *beasts*, humans have an eternal part to them which makes humans naturally supernatural: a part called the "soul," which Chesterton regards as "the shrine of all mysticism" (212). That eternal aspect—the soul—essentially, is what makes the natural human supernatural, like God.

Lewis reiterates this view of the human construct through the words of Screwtape to his advisee demon: "Humans are amphibians—half spirit and half animal. (The Enemy's determination to produce such a revolting hybrid was one of the things that determined Our Father to withdraw his support from Him.) As spirits they belong to the eternal world, but as animals they inhabit time" (*The Screwtape Letters* 206). Humans, therefore, are hybrids of animal and spirit, time and eternity. *Bios* is the term

Lewis gives to the natural, animal side of humans which is subject to decay, maintained only by supplies from the biological world in forms such as air, food, and water (*Mere Christianity* 131). In regard to the spiritual side, however, Lewis uses the term *Zoe* to refer to the spiritual energy and knowledge that is of God (131). Because of the *Bios* and *Zoe*, paradoxically present in one creature, humans are at the top of the animal chain, for humans are the closest representation of God in nature (131).[6] MacDonald refers to *"the old Adam," "the flesh," "his lower nature,"* and *"his evil self"* as the parts of a human where God and His truth are not (*Unspoken Sermons* 475). The soul is the highest part of the human, with the mind and body following after. As Lewis writes in *Miracles*, "Man is a tower in which the different floors can hardly be reached from one another but all can be reached from the top floor" (455).

Obedience to the *Bios* rather than the *Zoe*, for these authors, means that the person is becoming less metaphysical and more physical, less supernatural and more natural, less Godlike and, accordingly, more evil.[7] In *The Princess and Curdie*, Curdie is given the ability to see the human soul by touching someone's hands. Queen Irene posits, "Since it is always what [humans] do, whether in their minds or their bodies, that makes men go down to be less than men, that is, beasts, the change always comes first in their hands" (220). For MacDonald, then, being beast-like is in accordance with the heart; the appearance of the beast occurs "first of all in the inside hands, to which the outside ones are but as the gloves" (220). The Queen explains, however, that people cannot see when a person is becoming beast-like because most people can only see the outer, physical hands.

For this reason, the Queen gives Curdie the gift to perceive the spiritual hands of people by touching their physical hands. Thus, when he touches the hand of an evil doctor, he observes "the belly of a creeping thing," concluding that "this man is a snake" (271, 276). Not all beast-like people are snakes, for different varieties of beasts appear within people as Curdie touches hands. The Lord Chamberlain, for instance, is "a bird of prey—vulture or eagle, he could not tell which" (293). Each internal beast encapsulates the evil of the human's soul and according bodily action: the doctor is a deceiver like the snake in the Garden of Eden; likewise, the Lord Chamberlain is a bird of prey, having formed a coup d'état in order to usurp the king. For MacDonald—as well as Chesterton, Lewis, and Tolkien—the soul is a part of the human which reflects one's spiritual state and, therefore, signifies of one's humanness.

No human is perfect due to the inability to balance one's amphibious nature; however, the absence of one's perfection helps to give him purpose to acquire it—another quality which separates humans from beasts. Accordingly, since prehistoric times, humans have resorted to religion to discover the purposes for their lives, for humanity has a tendency to act from either religious or irreligious causes (Chesterton, *Everlasting Man* 66). Chesterton refers to the human drive for purpose as sought through religion or the rebellion against it. As MacDonald comments, "Man is man only in the doing of the truth, perfect man only in the doing of the highest truth, which is the fulfilling of his relations to his origin" (*Unspoken Sermons* 471). Furthermore, in his *Autobiography*, Chesterton posits that humans may have an appreciation of colors in a rock or pool, but, when purpose or presence in the scene is of no importance, then, for the perceiver, the colors and imagery may as well be in a wastebasket (331). Purpose, therefore, defines how humans perceive the world—as the measurement of all creation. The irreligious person who has lost purpose loses value in how she perceives the world and, accordingly, becomes pessimistic. GKC believes that the pessimism and the loss of purpose are evident even in the rising poets who do not respond to religion: "Their philosophy of the dandelion is not that all weeds are flowers, but rather that all flowers are weeds" (331).

Thus, as humans philosophically evaluate the world around them searching for purpose, they naturally ask existential questions; Chesterton goes as far as to claim that existence is the most common thought a human has; the human being questions his place in the world each day (*Everlasting Man* 139). MacDonald, Chesterton, Lewis, and Tolkien are all of the opinion that life is storial. Thus, in their fiction, a character's purpose is of the utmost importance. It is what makes the hnau's events significant. Curdie, in *The Princess and Curdie*, recognizes his purpose as the savior of Princess Irene and her father, and, in *That Hideous Strength*, Lewis's Ransom recognizes his role as the Pendragon (271). Sam of *The Lord of the Rings* realizes his purpose is to support Frodo and not to bear the ring—which is Frodo's purpose. When it appears that Frodo has been killed by Shelob's work, Sam places the chain and Ring of Power around his neck, says farewell to his master, and continues his journey to Mt. Doom—this time, alone. He asks himself, "Have I got it wrong?" while trying to make up his mind, feeling like carrying the Ring is not his purpose (Tolkien, *The Two Towers* 716). When he returns to find the orcs taking Frodo away, he contemplates attacking to save Frodo, realizing it would mean his purposeless death. No, Sam discovers, "My place is by Mr. Frodo. . . . I can't be their Ring-bearer" (718). Sam wants to complete the journey—which seems like the larger purpose; however, he knows his purpose is to bear not the Ring but the Ring-bearer.

The power of reason is combined with purpose in the final distinctive characteristic of all that is human: creating. The unity of the two seemingly opposing parts of the mind allows humans to create both purposefully and creatively: "This [human] creature was truly different from all creatures; because he was a creator as well as a creature" (*Everlasting Man* 35). Chesterton cites art as the highest mode of human creativity. Integrating the evolutionary argument, Chesterton evaluates the creative difference between humans and monkeys. He believes that a monkey and a human's artistic abilities are incomparable because a monkey does not have a capacity for art even in representation. Where a study might posit that a monkey begins to represent the world in a drawing—like a human, though more evolved, can represent the world—Chesterton argues that the monkey and the human are on two entirely different levels; the monkey cannot begin to represent the world in the way a human artistically represents the world (45); rather, Chesterton asserts that, whether contemplating the prehistoric cave drawings or the art of his current day, "art is the signature of man" (34). It is the ultimate mode of humanity's creative mental capacity. Art, says D. Williams, is not the signature of man because it is a development beyond animal behavior but because it is something entirely different from what an animal can do (21). The limitation of bestial creativity is, in fact, one of the shining signs of its inability to be compared to humanity. Chesterton deconstructs the creativity of animals when he compares a bird's capacity for creativity to a human's ability. Although a bird can build a nest, the limitation of a bird to create nothing more than a nest is testament to the mental and creative ability of humanity, for a human can build much more than a nest (37). Animals are limited in their capacity to excel as humans have—to advance in technology, thought, and capability. Humanity, in contrast, is unique in creating clothes and furniture (36). It is not surprising, then, that the goblins in MacDonald's *The Princess and the Goblin* are troubled by Curdie's singing. As he creates his simple songs, the goblins shy away; it is art that scares the bestial—perhaps because they do not understand it.

Lewis also notes the ability to create art as a point of separation from beasts. To do so, he defines the words *creating* and *begetting*. *To beget* is to become the parent of something—something or someone in the likeness of oneself in the way that a human begets children. *To create* is to make something different in kind from oneself (*Mere Christianity* 130). Lewis may have adopted the create/beget dichotomy from MacDonald in "The Imagination": "It is better to keep the word *creation* for that calling out of nothing which is the imagination of God; except it be as an occasional symbolic expression, whose daring is fully recognized, of the likeness of man's work to the work of his maker" (3). Similar to Chesterton's claims that art is the highest form of human creativity, Lewis and MacDonald argue that by establishing a difference between creativity and reproduction, any animal can reproduce, but humans are the only animals who can create. They believe that originality only comes from God in the same way that Christ copies the operation of the Father (Green and Hooper 137; MacDonald, "The Imagination" 3). The soul, where the *Zoe* resides, thus, provides the means by which one can create differently from beasts. Human creativity is sub-creative, or in the likeness of the way God created. In one of his topic headings for what appears to be either notes on a text or an outline for a text, Chesterton writes, "God makes out of nothing; men out of something" ("Misc. Notes and Sketches" 10).

According to Garth, Tolkien may have had the words of fellow TCBSite, Christopher Wiseman, on his mind when creating his Middle-earth mythology, since Wiseman said, "The completed work is vanity, the process of the working is everlasting. . . . The 'conquests' vanish when they are made; they are only vital in the making . . . the fugue is nothing on the page; it is only vital as it works its way out" (qtd. in Garth 254). In light of this comment, Tolkien deals with his literary creation as a form of sub-creation—a mode of magic, or art—which reveals elements of a greater truth on "its way out." Tolkien's mode of mythopoeic literature is art and contains art. Tolkien uses art in many ways within his canon—including the hobbits' art of escape and the smoking of pipe-weed (*The Fellowship* 1, 8). Treebeard creates poems and songs, like Bilbo, the elves, and the humans, whereas Shadowfax and the eagles—those greatest of the bestial realm—are not able to create, only to beget. Creation is everywhere in Tolkien's Middle-earth. Tolkien, thus, presented Middle-earth as a place in constant creation in light of "The Music of the Ainur," which sang the world into being. The prehistoric song in the heavens is the song which was made real by the copula, *Eä*—by being. So the song creates not only a planetary existence but also a fate through time.[8] MacDonald, likewise, asserts that creation in the image of God is a kind of fatherhood, and to disregard one's role in God's creation will cause someone to be more beast-like, traveling "down the scale of creation" (*Unspoken Sermons* 64, 278).

HIERARCHY AND ITS CENTER

"The scale of creation," as MacDonald terms it, alludes to a significant characteristic of all that is human: hierarchy. While the role humanity plays in it is distinctive from other animals, this characteristic extends beyond the beast-versus-human dichotomy to other species. The Great Chain of Being is somewhat resurrected in the worldview of MacDonald, Chesterton, Tolkien, and Lewis, clearly in contrast to other nineteenth- and twentieth-century minds that argue to the extreme for animal rights, that see no difference between human and beast, and that discard the presence of divinity. The hierarchy here differs from the Great Chain of Being in that these authors do not believe in a class or occupational hierarchy within humanity that places one person closer to or farther from the divine. Additionally, the Medieval and Renaissance-era devaluation of non-white, non-male individuals disappears in this hierarchy; all people have souls, and all hold the same potential for relationship with the divine.

In Lewis's sci-fi universe, the hierarchy of the angelic realm—with its planetary Oyéresu and lower eldila that look constantly to the supreme being, Maleldil—clearly echoes the seraphim, cherubim, and thrones of the Middle Ages that Lewis outlines in "Imagination and Thought in the Middle Ages" (53–54).[9] The hierarchy goes further, however, in that humanity, as hnau, falls somewhere below the eldila but above other animals—or beasts. Gilbert Meilander claims that Lewis's prizing of hierarchy is for the following four reasons: "(1) sheer delight in diversity over against 'flat equality'; (2) the belief that equality concerns interchangeable units rather than persons; (3) the statement that love knows nothing of quantitative assessments; and (4) the belief that our most important pleasures require hierarchy" (79). That is, each person, though differently created, is equal on a hierarchical scale of bestial to divine, is loved equally by the divine, and is only able to fully enjoy important pleasures due to differences in the hierarchy. Humans can enjoy divine goodness because they are not wholly divine, and humans can enjoy bestial pleasures because they are not wholly bestial. D. Williams astutely observes the reason for Lewis's concern that hierarchy is forgotten and why he seeks to rehabilitate it. The universe is to be in harmony when matter, soul, and reason are in harmony, reflective in the mind of God as well as the tripartite structure of state, church, and family: "The problem of course is that by rebelling against God, we have corrupted not only ourselves but also the order which he designed for the world" (74).

Hence, the Lord Chancellor in MacDonald's *The Princess and Curdie* is not meant to be king, despite his aspirations. When he attempts to reach that position, he has to disrupt the hierarchy by trying to kill the king and usurp the throne. The deity Queen Irene is at the top of the hierarchy, followed by humanity, then the beasts—both animals and the goblins of the prequel. Each human is given gifts, talents, and abilities, which give them certain roles, though loved equally by the deity, for, while she appears a queen to royalty, she appears also to the miners in form of Old Mother Wotherwop (198). Like the Lord Chancellor, whose talents are best played as a servant to the king, Curdie, likewise, needs to decide whether he wants to be a killer or a saver, "the Curdie he had been meant to be" (182). He finds himself in discord and savagery, experiencing sadness rather than joy and pleasure, because he is not fulfilling his place in the hierarchy.

Tolkien's hierarchy begins with the Godlike character Eru Ilúvatar, who creates the angelic beings, the Ainur (later, except for Melkor, becoming the Valar). One Vala creates the dwarves while Ilúvatar creates the elves and the humans, first and second comers of the Children of Ilúvatar. Next in line are the beasts, whose abilities cannot reach the level of reason or creativity of the hnau—the dwarves, elves, and humans. Finally, because Melkor fell from his high place as an Ainur, not unlike Lucifer's fall from heaven, he is all the more below the neutral humans and beasts; accordingly, Melkor and his followers—Sauron, Ungoliant (the spider ancestor of Shelob), and the fallen Maiar (lesser Valar) known as Balrogs—maintain the lowest place on the hierarchy, followed by the orc varieties. Hobbits may appear to be missing from the hierarchy here, but as Tolkien writes in his *Letters*, they are a branch of the human race, which is the reason why hobbits and humans dwell together in places like Bree and are called Little Folk and Big Folk. Hobbits simply lack some of the capacity for greed and ambition as well as adventure and imagination, though their heroism can be called upon "in a pinch" (158). The hierarchical constraints are clear for the hobbits, since Frodo was only able to travel into the West at the end of *The Lord of the Rings* due to the pleading of Arwen to the Valar; however, she was unable to go directly to the Valar. She needed to speak to Gandalf or Galadriel who were next in line to the Valar in the hierarchy (327).

The hierarchy of God, angel, human, beast, and evil incarnate is clear in Lewis's space trilogy with Maleldil, eldila, hnau, beast, and the Bent One with his evil eldila; it is clear with MacDonald's array of Queen Irene, human, beast and goblin, and evil, beast-like characters (though no angelic representatives are present, except, perhaps, the Queen's doves); and it is clear in Tolkien's Eru Ilúvatar, Valar and Maiar, hnau (e.g., elves, dwarves, and humans), beasts, and Melkor's league.[10] Chesterton, however, is not as demonstrable in his concern for hierarchy. Rather, in the typical Chestertonian way, he approaches the issue directly: "In so far as I am Man I am the chief of creatures. . . . Man was a statue of God walking about the garden. Man had pre-eminence over all the brutes; man was only sad because he was not a beast, but a broken god" (*Orthodoxy* 87). The soul sets humanity apart from beasts in the hierarchy, for the moment that God's image was reflected in nature—as a human—humanity, in its godlikeness, took dominion over nature (*Everlasting Man* 138). Chesterton is undoubtedly referring to the Creation story of Genesis 1.26–28 where God placed humans in control of the animals, and as a result of humanity's mimetic image of God and command over nature, "man is the measure of all things" (35). Humanity is central to the hierarchy as the amphibious creature. It is "the roof and crown of things" (MacDonald, "The Imagination" 33). As Lewis writes in *The Problem of Pain*, humans are only to be understood in their relationship with God; animals are only to be understood in their relationship to humans and, via humans as the image of God, to God (634). Humanity is the lowest of the divine but the highest of animals. The more humanlike an animal is, the higher its status as an animal in the hierarchy.

An animal's status in the hierarchy is dependent on its likeness to humans, and the status of a human is reliant upon her likeness to the divine. This subscale on the hierarchy relies on a key concept of the hierarchy: discipleship. Discipleship takes the form of the divine helping a human and a human helping another human to rise in the hierarchy. In the relationship between God and humans, then, God says, "Let us pretend that this is not a mere creature, but our Son. It is like Christ in so far as it is a Man, for He became Man. Let us pretend that it is also like Him in Spirit. Let us treat it as if it were what in fact it is not. Let us pretend in order to make the pretence into a reality" (*Mere Christianity* 155). When discipleship happens by humans discipling animals, the more appropriate term, in light of these author's texts, is *beast-mastering*. Lewis uses the metaphor of a human's relationship with a dog, concluding that dogs become nearly human because they are treated as if they were nearly human (155). A dog's knowledge does not result from growing older; rather, the knowledge to be more humanlike is a result of being treated in a humanlike way. Hence, Lewis believes that the higher animals are drawn to humans out of the love a human shows to them, making them more human than they were created to be (159). Lewis effectively summarizes the principles of discipleship and beast-mastering in *Miracles:* "We can understand that if God so descends into a human spirit, and human spirit so descends into Nature, and our thoughts into our senses and passions, and if adult minds (but only the best of them) can descend into sympathy with children, and men into sympathy with beasts, then everything hangs together and the total reality, both Natural and Supernatural, in which we are living is more multifariously and subtly harmonious than we had suspected" (401).

Paradoxical to the separation of hierarchy, discipleship promotes a necessary unity and harmony throughout the hierarchy. The separation between divine and human is healed by discipleship, and the separation between human and beast is not degrading or domineering to the beasts because it is meant to raise them up in community.

In MacDonald's work, the best example of the master-beast relationship is portrayed by Curdie and Lina. When Curdie meets Lina, she is "an animal whose gruesome oddity even he, who knew so many of the strange creatures, two of which were never the same, that used to live inside the mountain with their masters the goblins, had never seen equaled," yet when he touches the paw of Lina, "instead of the paw of a dog, such as it seemed to his eyes, he clasped in his great mining fist the soft, neat little hand of a child" (215, 223). Accordingly, when Curdie introduces her to the Princess, he explains, "I believe . . . from what your grandmother [Queen Irene] told me, that Lina is a woman, and that she was naughty, but is now growing good" (277–78). Lina is serving the Queen and establishing a relationship with not only the Queen but also Curdie and the Princess. As protector and aide in Curdie's mission, Lina is relieved of her beast form when the quest is complete, although nothing more is said of her after being cleansed by the Queen's roses.

Hnau, therefore, are supposed to act as beastmasters like Curdie does for Lina by training the beast to be more hnau-like. Ransom, likewise, observes, to the Lady of Perelandra, that the beasts on Perelandra seem rational. The Green Lady responds that she makes them "older," or more mature, each day, which is what makes them bestial; they are discipled

(56). Accordingly, the King of Perelandra claims that they will make the highest of the beasts wise enough that they are able to speak and live a life aware of Maleldil, the God character; in short, they will become hnau, like humans (181). Lewis, therefore, posits that hnau, including humans, must take care of the world around them; Maleldil must rule over the eldila (angels), angels over hnau, and hnau over beasts (*Out of the Silent Planet* 102). In *That Hideous Strength,* Ransom follows the command to master beasts with the bear, Mr. Bultitude. Merlin prophesizes the significance of the bear's role in the story of the world (279–80). Ransom's beast-mastering effectively leads to Bultitude's wandering to the Belbury Group, killing many of them, and helping to save the world from disaster. A cultivated beast under the hnau responsibility of Ransom and his house, Mr. Bultitude represents one of the higher beasts like the elephants who go away to make love: "private as human lovers . . . not common beasts" (376). One does not have to search far in Lewis's canon to find examples of the beast-mastering principle: from Shasta and Bree in *The Horse and His Boy* to the cabby's horse-turned-unicorn in *The Magician's Nephew* to Ransom and Mr. Bultitude in *That Hideous Strength.*

Like the hnau of Lewis's space trilogy, each of the rational beings of Tolkien's world has a responsibility to master a beast. In *The Hobbit,* the thrushes and ravens are tamed birds that are friendly to the dwarves and the folk of the Dale (205, 231). This beast-mastering, ultimately, leads to Bard's slaying of the dragon Smaug (224). Likewise, the Rohirrim are the praised horse-masters: "in the Riddermark of Rohan the Rohirrim, the Horse-lords, dwell, and there are no horses like those that are bred in that great vale between the Misty Mountains and the White" (*The Fellowship* 255). Legolas exemplifies a similar relationship with horses and other beasts as they follow his verbal commands—a speech and mastery common to the elves (*The Two Towers* 429). A chain of mastering occurs when the master-beast relationship is done appropriately. After the elves wake up the Ents, the Ents, in turn, train and teach others (457); as Treebeard claims, "Long we have tended our beasts and our fields" (536).

Perhaps the best example of the hnau who trains a beast is that of Sam and his pony, Bill. After observing the mean treatment of Bill's former master in Bree, Aragorn cannot imagine an animal such as Bill returning to the abusive master if it managed to escape (*The Fellowship* 175). The pony is near death from the treatment of his former master, Bill Ferny; however, after Sam rescues and nurtures him, the pony grows full and strong, showing affection for its new "masters." The pony's ill-treatment in Bree must have been terrible in order for the trek across Middle-earth to be better than his former home life (194). After Sam's continued mastering, the pony is soon able to pick out a path for his master and avoiding discomfort for his rider (199).[11] As Lewis asserts in *Perelandra* with the teaching of animals how to speak, Sam, having named the pony Bill, states, "That animal can nearly talk . . . and would talk, if he stayed here much longer. He gave me a look as plain as Mr. Pippin could speak it: if you don't let me go with you, Sam, I'll follow on my own" (273). Gandalf, thus, tells the pony, "you are a wise beast" (296). Bill is, in fact, wise enough to know his former master when Sam returns with the pony to the Shire, for Bill gives Mr. Ferny a kick as he runs away (*The Return* 976).

Such kind treatment of beasts, like on Perelandra, are traits of a royal character. Faramir, the steward who acts like the kings of old, does not kill animals without purpose, and, even when he does kill them, it is not a joyous experience (*The Two Towers* 650). Faramir's soldiers know his character, for they refuse to shoot Gollum despite his trespassing in the forbidden pool: "You will not have us slay wild beasts for no purpose, and it seemed no more, so I tried no arrow" (660). Accordingly, Beregond of the city guard claims, "That will be the Captain: he can master both beasts and men," a statement repeated by a set of guards watching Faramir's troups march instead of flee during the siege of Gondor: "Faramir must be there. . . . He can govern man and beast. He will make it yet" (*The Return* 791, 801). The hnau—the New Human—like Faramir, therefore, must master others in a way that facilitates a divineward growth rather than a beastward devolution.[12]

Beast-mastering and discipleship do have their limitations. D. Williams writes, "To make slaves of human beings—or talking beasts—*is* to mistreat them because it is to deny their God-given nature and force them to live a lie" (99). Discipleship goes awry when the master proceeds to dominate other wills. It only makes sense that the mad world of *The Napoleon of Notting Hill*, Chesterton's first novel, has a king who thinks everything is a joke and a neighborhood ruler who is domineering of others' wills because he takes everything too seriously. The ruler, Adam Wayne, has caused war in the streets due to his extreme patriotism, forbidding a road to be built through Notting Hill. He is accused of making the rest of the country "slaves" to his patriotism, and his neighborhood's "Council and its crowds have been so intoxicated by the spreading over the whole city of Wayne's old ways and visions, that they try to meddle with every one, and rule every one and civilize every one, and tell every one what is good for him" (360–61). Truly, as the king, Auberon Quin, who makes everything a joke, and Wayne meet at the end of the text, they recognize that they are the two lobes of the mind: one humorous without gravity and the other with gravity but without humor, among other opposites (378). Without the two lobes of the mind together, their work is oppressive, even enslaving, to those around them. Discipleship and control need an element of restraint and certainly an element of gravity. Perhaps the young writer, Eric Blair, to whom Chesterton gave a break to write his first published piece in *G. K.'s Weekly,* found this sentiment all too powerful when, forty-eight years later in 1948, he would write a novel set in the same year, *1984,* with a similar theme under the pen-name George Orwell (Ahlquist, "Lecture 6: *The Napoleon of Notting Hill*").

Tolkien considers the same problems with discipleship when he writes in his *Letters* that *The Lord of the Rings* is, essentially, about the evil motive of dominating others' wills (200). Sauron, for example, "puts beasts to evil use," and when the control ends upon Sauron's defeat, Sauron's orcs, trolls, and other beasts either commit suicide or run mindlessly away from battle (*The Two Towers* 426; *The Return* 928). Most of the humans, similarly, either flee or fight to the death, leaving only a few who beg for mercy. After the Downfall of Númenor, it took Sauron a long time to rebuild because his will, or energy, had been spent; he was not in a position to be able to dominate other wills because his was weak (*Letters* 260). Similarly, Frodo's will developed since his experience at Weathertop with the Ring and the Ringwraiths. Tolkien admits that Frodo's will had so increased that he may have been able to command the Wraiths to an extent, though their ultimate master—the stronger will—was still Sauron, and his will would win the Ringwraiths over Frodo's (*Letters* 331).[13]

Likewise, Saruman's beast-mastering is injurious to his beasts. His human servant and protégé, Wormtongue, travels beastward in his becoming like Saruman, and therefore, becomes less human. While in the company of Théoden, for example, Wormtongue's eyes appear like a beast looking for a means of escape from his enemies, his lips like a snake (*The Two Towers* 508). His name, likewise, implies a beast-like quality to his character; accordingly, he is further commanded by Gandalf the White to get down on his belly, calling him a snake as if addressing Lucifer in the biblical story of Adam and Eve (509). Gandalf explains, however, that Grima Wormtongue used to be more human before he went beastward: "Here is a snake!

With safety you cannot take it with you, nor can you leave it behind. To slay it would be just. But it was not always as it is now is. Once it was a man, and did you service in its fashion" (509). Wormtongue, under the flag of his master, Saruman, has chosen the beastward path away from humanity.

Sauron and Saruman's pursuits match the antagonists Weston and Devine in Lewis's *Out of the Silent Planet,* whose interplanetary pursuits are to oppress other races and commandeer resources. They believe it is their right to overcome all other races as "the right of the higher over the lower," says Weston to the Oyarsa of Malacandra (Mars) (134). Malacandra responds to Weston, noting that he fails to recognize the moral laws known to all hnau (137). Hnau have a code to abide by, which beasts do not. In *Mere Christianity,* Lewis argues that a human must follow certain biological laws in the way that an animal must follow them, but humans have a certain law in addition to animals that they can disobey if they choose—what Lewis calls the Law of Nature, the Law of Decent Behaviour, or the Moral Law, which every human knows and does not need to be taught (16). The Moral Law is a certain tune or rhythm that all humans feel they must follow; it is the tune of good conduct which directs human instincts (21). This Moral Law is the guide by which one must use to treat and disciple other hnau and, accordingly, by which hnau must appropriate to beast-mastering. Thus, Malacandra says of Weston that bent, or evil, hnau can do more damage than a broken one, and Divine, broken, is naught more than "a talking animal" (*Out of the Silent Planet* 138). Domination of others leads to being bent and broken—to being nothing more than a talking beast.

Such is Lilith: a pale, cold vampire, living on the blood, lives, and souls of humans (MacDonald, *Lilith* 148). "She loves no one," and admits, "I will do as my Self pleases—as my Self desires" (196, 199). She is the opposite of her daughter, Lona, who cares for the Little Ones selflessly, and in complete disregard for any hnau moral law, Lilith preys on any children such as them. It is only after she is caught, purified, cleared of her selfishness, and laid to sleep (death) that she begins to look younger—a metaphor for innocence (229). Despite her ignorance of a moral law and discipleship to others, the antagonist, Lilith, is discipled; as a result, she begins to look human again. Additionally, unlike the city of the old Lilith, Bulika, which is dark and terrifying, the new city at the end of the tale is bright and welcoming: "serpents grow birds here" and animals are to be tended to at the royal stables (248–49). There, as through the tale, Mr. Vane and Lona journey together, climb together, and pass homeward (250).

In an unpublished poem, "Man," Chesterton writes, "Goodness is more to him / Baseness is less . . . / He, be he strong, / Someway a story is, / Someway a song . . . / This thing is good for him / Still, to do well." Part of doing well is fulfilling the hnau's moral law and preserving the hierarchy. As D. Williams observes of Narnia, dehumanization is the result of sin, and redemption is the restoration of humanity at its fullest (103). "There is utter joy," writes Terry Lindvall, "in finding and filling one's proper place in the divine dance of the cosmos" (83). But, for all this talk of humanity and hnauness, a significant moment has yet to be discussed which defines humanity not by its characteristics but by its broken nature.

THE FALL

The bentness and the brokenness of humanity source from disruption in the hierarchy. Ultimately, each hnau story is affected by a significant break. The amphibious nature of the human is, as we have seen, fragile, and free will only encourages the hnau to yield to either their *Bios* or their *Zoe.* Chesterton asserts that "the whole human race has a tradition of the Fall" (*Orthodoxy* 138). The Fall upset the hierarchy and corrupted humans as they were built to be. Shippey, in *The Road,* observes that Lewis's doctrines of the Fall of Man, drawn from Milton's *Paradise Lost,* are nearly unchanged in Tolkien's *Silmarillion:* "It seems very likely that Lewis and Tolkien co-operated in their analysis of Christian essentials" (235–36). Shippey likely refers to the Augustinean principles of the Fall, which, according to Lewis, appear in Milton:

1. God created all things good, without exception.
2. Evil is perverted goodness.
3. Good can exist without evil, but evil cannot exist without good.
4. God foreknows that some creatures will turn toward evil.
5. Without a Fall, humans would have eventually risen to angelic status.
6. Eve was the target of Satan because she was less intelligent.
7. Adam was aware of his actions but acted in accordance to his bond with Eve.
8. The Fall is about disobedience, not an object.
9. The Fall resulted from Pride.

10. Humanity was punished by the loss of authority over his inferiors—over passions and the body.
11. The human body's disobedience to her owner is evident in the function of reproductive organs' involuntary responses—the reason for an unrestrained sexual scene after the Fall in *Paradise Lost* (Lewis, *A Preface* 66–70).

In summary, the Fall's presentation and acceptance of evil—of corrupted good—by humanity hindered its chances of rising in the hierarchy. The refusal of humans to accept God as sovereign Father of the human race is "the one central wrong in the whole human affair" (MacDonald, *Unspoken Sermons* 276). Humanity's pride and disobedience led, ultimately, to humanity's inability to beast-master and disciple in the way they should—even sexually among themselves.

Lewis's *A Preface to Paradise Lost* does more than hint at his fascination with the Fall, a trend that would reappear in *Perelandra* where Ransom must try to prevent the Fall on Venus by guarding the Green Lady from Lucifer's incarnation in Weston[14] and again in *The Magician's Nephew* in the new world of Narnia. Tolkien, likewise, explains the Fall as it takes place in Middle-earth. Sauron exploits humanity's weakness in obedience, which occurs in three phases: acquiescence, unwilling obedience, and finally rebellion (*Letters* 155). The parallels from Middle-earth to biblical record are simple: acquiescence to the authority of God, unwilling obedience of Adam and Eve to not eat the forbidden fruit, and their rebellion to God's authority and their obedience to it. With Adam and Eve's rebellion, humanity becomes "a horror" to God, writes Lewis, not because of how God created humans but because of humanity's abuse of free will (*Problem of Pain* 588). Humanity had broken a law, which, Chesterton claims, was able to be broken, but humanity was unable to escape the "cosmic prison" of the world in which we were created, "for we ourselves were only a part of its machinery" (*Orthodoxy* 54).

Yet, the Fall had begun sooner than Adam and Eve's disobedience, for they were not the first to acquiesce, unwillingly obey, and ultimately rebel. Chesterton defines *insanity* as "reason used without root, reason in the void. The man who begins to think without the proper first principles goes mad; he begins to think at the wrong end" (19). Lucifer is the first to go insane in the Christian story of the Fall. He reasons that he can be as

God, but his reason is without root. As MacDonald writes, the focus on oneself leads to madness (*Unspoken Sermons* 271). Ironically, Chesterton's claim that mad reasoning is "reason in the void" is dramatized in Tolkien's Middle-earth through Melkor, or Morgoth, the Lucifer-like character of his mythology. As the Ainur sing, with Ilúvatar, the song of creation, "it came into the heart of Melkor to interweave matters of his own imagining that were not in accord with the theme of Ilúvatar; for he sought therein to increase the power and glory of the part assigned to himself" (*Silmarillion* 16). Melkor's discord begins when he journeys into the void in search of something for himself. His song is filled with a selfish desire to fill the Void and elevate himself. His power and knowledge, gifts greater than that of the other Ainur, had become corrupt. He rebels, challenging Ilúvatar in song, of course, failing in his attempt to overpower his creator. When the song is over, Ilúvatar took them to the Void and showed them a world created by their song, now imperfect by Melkor's rebellion (16–18). It is only right that, after repeated rebellion and corruption of the realm of Eä, the Valar cast Morgoth through "the Door of Night beyond the Walls of the World, into the Timeless Void" (255). Like Lucifer's banishment to Hell, he is, in a sense, sealed away from the physical world; "Yet the lies that Melkor . . . sowed in the hearts of Elves and Men are a seed that does not die and cannot be destroyed; and ever and anon it sprouts anew, and will bear dark fruit even unto the latest days" (255). As MacDonald says, it matters little whether Adam's Fall is the reason for his own Fall because he Falls repeatedly in his own life: "there is a shadow on my soul which I or another may call a curse; I cannot get rid of a something that always intrudes between my heart and the blue of every sky" (*Unspoken Sermons* 277).

The individual Fall of Adam and Eve, as the father and mother of humanity, caused a genetic problem, a viral disease in their spirits and all of their descendants. The disruption in the hierarchy had occurred in two places, leaving the machinery of the cosmos infected. The world becomes a venue where good, sourced from God, is affected by the evil of other creatures; therefore, Lewis, claims, life is a dance which balances these conflicts and the suffering that results from evil's effects (*Problem of Pain* 598). The result, says Tolkien: the world continues "going to the bad" through history, each step presenting a new set of problems (*Letters* 48). Chesterton believes that, even if one does not recognize the Christian belief of the Fall, they are conscious of a Fall, even if they are unaware of the height, for they recognize that something has gone and continues to go awry in humanity (*Everlasting Man* 94). Lewis concludes that humanity, at the center of the hierarchy, is corrupt, and corruption breeds further corruption, for each time a new civilization or institution is built, selfishness and cruelty eventually bring pain and destruction upon it (*Mere Christianity* 49).[15]

Thus, humanity begins as the measure of all creation but ends as the corrupted center of the hierarchy. Humanity is higher than other animals—than the beasts—because humans have the ability to reason, are amphibiously *Bios* and *Zoe*, are purposeful, and have the ability to create. Because of their amphibious characteristic, they are the highest of animals but the lowest of the divine, able to lean in either direction according to their free will. Yet, the Fall brought ruin to the human heart, a dissension of the spirit from its source, which makes the human journey—both individual and historical—a far more difficult task than it was intended to be in Eden. His purpose has become confused, and his ability to create is no longer necessarily in the sub-creative likeness of God's creation. His reason may follow the tune of the Father or find its selfish desires in the void. To that journey we now turn.

The Journey

As discussed in the previous chapter, the hnau's existence is distanced from the beasts in part due to its purposeful journey. After all, the journey is a uniquely human attribute apart from the beast, so to ignore the human journey is to be beast-like. While the beast clings to survival and id functions, the human weighs and balances options for the benefit of others or self. While the beast grows only chronologically, the human who seeks to be more fully human progresses on a purposeful journey of, paradoxically, selflessness and self-discovery through his or her chronological lifetime. Purpose is the guiding principle of these decisions through the human journey—as each individual has their own purpose in their story and the story of the universe. All humanity, in these authors' view, is purposed to embrace the *Zoe* rather than the *Bios,* to choose to become more Godlike and less bestial.

When words like *purpose* and *choice* enter the discussion of the journey, however, others like *free will* and *fate* are bound to follow. In fact, when universals are taken into consideration, individual decisions seem complicated and less individual. Words like *determinism* and *fate* in terms of a cause-and-effect universe seem to contradict *free will* and *decision,* implicit in whatever benefits individual cognition, emotion, and soul. The individual journey, with its fate and free will, impact the greater fate and free will of the universe and vice versa. As Lewis writes in *Miracles,* all aspects of the universe are interconnected, even if the connections may not be apparent (354). When the individual connects with the universal, such connections may take the form of a very complex road map in which individual choices intersect with the fates of others; hence, these authors utilize the motif of paths and roads to symbolize the human journey through free will decisions and accompanying fate. Rosebury claims that, in *The Lord of the Rings*, the Road represents possibilities and probabilities of "adventure, commitment, and danger; for the fear of losing oneself, and the hope of homecoming. At the same time, it is markedly true of Middle-earth, as a narrative locale, that it is a world of Roads" (30). Paths and roads, indeed, are a common literary motif for the journey or the quest—whether the protagonist takes the common path or, as Robert Frost calls it, "the one less traveled" (line 19). Tolkien, Lewis, Chesterton, and MacDonald each utilize the motif in their literature. Even for one like Anodos in *Phantastes*, whose name means "pathless,"[1] he eventually finds his way—his path—for, believes Chesterton, "I had always felt life first as a story: and if there is a story there is a story-teller," one who knows all the best paths to take and sometimes sends the characters down a fated road (Knoepflmacher xi; Chesterton, *Orthodoxy* 53).

Both the fairy-story and the human story require a storyteller, perhaps, a force of nature, as ancient mythologies deemed fate to be. Norse and Old English texts use *wyrd* to describe an insurmountable fate, like the hand of God that cannot be dissuaded from shaping the individual's path. These elements of the story have already been written by the storyteller—fated, regardless of any person's free will. Norse and Mediterranean myths alike deal with universal human challenges like love, fate, and death (Noel 5). Aeneas's lost love and journey around the Mediterranean were the results of toying gods who shaped his story; Odin's clan in Valhalla will offer a fight, but the doom of Ragnarok and their deaths is inevitable. Free will is actively engaged by characters of these myths, but some fates seem insurmountable. The struggle with fate that permeates myths like these fascinated MacDonald, Chesterton, Lewis, and Tolkien. Though Tolkien claimed that Chesterton knew nothing of Norse or Old English literary tradition, as Milbank has shown, key narrative elements of Chesterton's epic *The Ballad of the White Horse* reappear in Tolkien's literature (Tolkien, *Letters* 92; Milbank x–xiv). Some of those same elements of pagan versus Christian and of fate versus free will are evidenced in MacDonald, whom Lewis compared to mythopoeists like Spencer, William Morris, and Chesterton's treasured W. B. Yeats (*Surprised by Joy* 173). The Northernness, "a vision of huge, clear spaces hanging above the Atlantic in the endless twilight of Northern summer, remoteness, severity" (69), of Norse mythology reappears in Lewis's space trilogy and Tolkien's Middle-earth. It is in those spaces that the paths and roads appear—that one decides which route to take. What follows is a discussion of whether it is free will that provides the decision or if it was fated for them to take a certain trail.

Free Will and Fates

FREE WILL

If birth is a beginning and death is a destination, then one may only surmise that each person chooses a unique route for the journey. *Choice,* here, is the key word. In *The Great Divorce,* Lewis describes the road map of the individual journey in terms of choice. Not all roads in life meet neatly at the center of life; rather, some roads divide into others, splitting again, and still again after each decision is made. Even for those who choose a wrong road, Lewis does not believe that they will necessarily perish for it, but "their rescue consists in being put back on the right road" (465). We will discuss what this "right road" is in a moment. For now, we are interested in the choice of road that leads the individual away from the center—from the origin—to their destination, death. The walk along the road of life is influenced by personality, past experience, and belief. In "Three Kinds of Men," Lewis posits three personality types: those who live entirely for self-fulfillment; those who live according to a higher claim like "the good of society" and go no further; and those who surrender the self entirely to a higher purpose (21). Each of these personality types suggest one's ability to choose who they want to be and what they want to do. They make their experiences, and they choose what they want to believe about the world. Predestination, or predetermined life and fate (as it is commonly understood), arrests any chance of freedom, according to the MacDonald of Lewis's *The Great Divorce.* Time and the actions that fill time are important, even to someone standing outside of time, because, without each person's unique freedom, time and individual lose their purposes—and the soul, its individuality (539).

If the lost souls who still refuse heaven in *The Great Divorce* are not convincing enough, then Ransom in *Perelandra* demonstrates what it means to choose a path. When Weston seems to be winning the mental and spiritual battle with the Green Lady, Ransom begins to wonder why Maleldil did not send a miracle to combat the miracle of Hell, Weston (the Un-Man). Ransom failed to understand why the God of his world did not act when evil had such a strong representative in the Un-Man (119). Suddenly, in his loathing, Ransom realizes that, in doing all he could do, he had been and would become the miracle Maleldil sent. Although the scenario sounds predetermined, it is not entirely, for "No definite task was before him. All that was being demanded of him was a general and preliminary resolution to oppose the Enemy in any mode which circumstances might show to be desirable" (121)—what he eventually discovers means physical violence. It sounds fateful, but as Lewis demonstrates by the "voluble self," which wants to rationalize each step in the reasoning process here, Ransom was not forced to do his best or commit any violence. Yet, because the Un-Man resorted to wearing down the Green Lady and Ransom physically to overcome them, Ransom chose to respond to that front of the battle (123–24).

Together, Tolkien and Charles Williams even discussed the difficulties of establishing common factors associated with cultural perceptions of freedom, concluding that the word, *freedom,* had been so abused by propaganda that it no longer held any value. *Freedom,* he believed, had turned into nothing more than a source of heated arguments (Tolkien, *Letters* 93). Tolkien articulated a belief in free will to his son, Christopher, in the way that any person has the chance to throw away Christian salvation (76). Each person seems to arrive at their destination in different ways, by different choices, in the same way that Frodo arrived at Rivendell from Hobbiton, despite his aimless wandering, for he maintained his purpose toward the elven sanctuary (*The Fellowship* 225). Noel notes that Middle-earth's fate, likewise, was "not entirely predestined" because the choices of individuals could change the result of any given event (19). As Gandalf says to Frodo, "All we have to decide is what to do with the time that is given us" (*The Fellowship* 50). One is left to wonder whether Gollum, perhaps, may yet have been saved in some way if Frodo had been able to destroy the Ring on his own instead of *deciding* to keep it,[2] if Middle-earth may have had a slower speed of degradation through history had Isildur cast the Ring into the fire when he had the *choice.* As early as his escape from Boromir, Frodo experiences the clash of will in him when he must decide whether or not to take off the Ring. The choices worked at odds within him: one moment poised between the two decisions, the next, pained with the unavoidable choice before him: "free to choose, and with one remaining instant in which to do so" (392). He chooses to take the Ring off, now all the more aware that he must exercise his will to avoid submitting to the will of the Dark Lord.

Chesterton paradoxically comments apologetically to "freethinkers," who see human thought as solely the result of conditioned response, that he intends to allow himself the freedom to think freely, for the idea that one's thoughts are solely conditioned responses means that no thinking ever occurs (*Autobiography* 42). Free thinking, of course, relies on thought, so, for Chesterton, the idea of conditioned response as the cause of all decision is ludicrous, for one could not be aware of thinking freely. Hence, Chesterton continues his banter against conditioned response, remarking that argument would be useless if it is the result of one's conditions, for no person would have an opinion to correct if all opinions were preconditioned (42). That is, no one could convince another that free thinking does not exist, if the person's thoughts are only the effects of causation. One must have the ability to think freely in order to change one's thinking by accepting or rejecting another's view.

Chesterton's comments are perceptively illuminated by MacDonald's Wise Woman, who does all she can to shape the stubborn Princess Rosamond's view. No matter how hard the Wise Woman tries to direct Rosamond on the right path, an embittered Rosamond goes the other way. At one point, the Wise Woman tells her, "You are taking the wrong turn, child," only to receive the response that the Wise Woman knows "nothing about where I want to go." "I know that road will take you where you don't want to go," but Rosamond goes that way, anyway, as the Wise Woman goes the other (*The Wise Woman, or the Lost Princess* 280). When the Wise Woman rescues her from the black pool in which she is trapped on the path she chose, the Wise Woman invites her to her home, promising no beasts will attack her as long as Rosamond continues to journey to her house. Rosamond's childishness is rekindled, however, when the Wise Woman disappears. At once, Rosamond begins an inner dialogue with what Freud calls the *superego* and the *id:* one concerned with others and social constructs and the other only with self-satisfaction. "Why didn't she take me with her?" and "nothing to be done," says the id, but the superego battles back that Rosamond did not speak when spoken to about the journey, and, "Cannot you rise, and walk down the hill, and through the wood?" (282–83). Repeatedly, Rosamond is given the opportunity to follow the right path, and it is her free will to choose what direction to go—at this point, whether to continue her own stubborn way or to submit to the path to the Wise Woman's home.

FATE AND WYRD

Free will, however, is not a sufficient explanation for the seemingly fated occurrences in life. The Wise Woman's repeated interventions to put Rosamond on a certain path appeal to words like *purpose,* that uniquely human storial quality, and *fate.* Free will fails to explain the origination of the purpose or of the fated destination. Frodo reiterates Bilbo's view of fate, free will, and the journey:

> He used often to say there was only one Road; that it was like a great river: its springs were at every doorstep, and every path was its tributary. "It's a dangerous business, Frodo, going out of your door," he used to say. "You step into the Road, and if you don't keep your feet, there is no knowing where you might be swept off to. Do you realize that this is the very path that goes through Mirkwood, and that if you let it, it might take you to the Lonely Mountain or even further to worse places?" (Tolkien, *The Fellowship* 72)

The Road, then, is the central connection between beginning and end but encompasses all paths along the way. Shippey believes that the Road is a symbol of Providence in Tolkien's texts, in agreement with Lewis's belief in "the right road" mentioned earlier (Shippey, *The Road* 188; Lewis, *The Great Divorce* 465). He further asserts, "Much of Tolkien's tonal intention for *The Silmarillion* can indeed be deduced by looking through its threads at his archaic alternatives for 'luck', the words 'fate' and 'doom'"; Shippey defines *fate* as something which was previously spoken and *doom* as having the additional meaning of a "judicial sentence, a law or a decision" (*The Road* 253). *Doom* implies an ending while *fate* implies something aforesaid; they are related in that fate will eventually lead to doom, but the words should not be confused. While *doom* is the end of the journey, *fate* is, for these authors, understood as the path that one chooses to follow, with its consequences, and the guides that direct one along the way. The larger, Providential Road, then, is simply the roadmap of fate—the central force which unites all roads and paths.

Tolkien writes, "You really do very little choosing: life and circumstances do most of it (though if there is a God these must be His instruments, or His appearances)" (*Letters* 51). For Tolkien, once someone is on a set path, the circumstances will guide the person along the way. God, the storyteller, has generated opportunities available to the individual, and free will decisions lead to further opportunities. Tolkien's texts hint at the differing fates of each individual, when, on the way to the city of Galadhrim, where Galadriel resides, the characters' "paths" lead to the same place (*The Fellowship* 344). The individual paths, each with its own fate, at this point intersect at Galadhrim. The storyteller has brought their potential fates together. There, Galadriel encourages them to rest, for "we will not speak of your further road for a while" (348). Sam and Frodo's paths are joined nearer at this point, for Galadriel takes the two of them away from the rest of the group to her mirror. As Noel comments on the Mirror of Galadriel, it shows a fate which is reliant upon "certain conditions" (19). Galadriel admits that it can dip into the past, the present, and "things that yet *may* be" (*The Fellowship* 352, italics mine). After Sam looks into the mirror, sees hints of the possible dangers that he and Frodo may experience followed by the dangers that will befall the Shire, he wants to turn back, but Galadriel warns him that some things never happen unless those who have seen the vision make them happen by turning from their present path to prevent a possible future—which they, in effect, create. She, thus, warns that the mirror is not a safe guide for deciding one's future (354). Of course, there is no need for a guide when everything is predetermined; thus, *fate* becomes something that is a result of free will decisions to follow a certain path. The storyteller has an outline for which individuals choose the branches of their fate. Even Galadriel, who, like the other ring-bearers, can see into the future, discourages the hobbits from worrying too much about the future because she does not know what will come to pass. She warns them not to worry about "the road" that night because "the paths" that each person may walk may already be in front of them, even if the paths are presently unclear (359). Frodo echoes this sentiment when he and Sam break from the Fellowship, recognizing that they were "meant to go together" and hopes the others will find "a safe road" of their own (397).[3]

In Chesterton's *The Man Who Was Thursday*, Gabriel Syme joins the police force with the purpose to go undercover in an anarchic terrorist organization. Through the terrorist organization, he meets the man called Sunday, who he later finds out is actually the chief of police who hired him to infiltrate the terrorist organization. Ironically, the members of the anarchic organization were also assigned as undercover police officers. In the end, all members reconvene at Sunday's home, recognizing that they each played a part in a story that had been planned—fated, if you will—from the start. Certainly, any one of the officers had the ability to choose whether or not to become an officer or to take the assignment to go undercover—even to go so far as to pursue the mysterious Sunday. We might say that the men were *fated* to pursue this journey, but here the storyteller is at work. Sunday, like a storyteller, has devised the story and how it should play out in a very ordered sequence. The characters have merely to decide to work for the police or the anarchists, and the consequences will guide them.

Similarly, MacDonald writes, "What a man likes best *may* be God's will, may be the voice of the Spirit striving *with* his spirit, not against it; and if, as I have said, it be not so—if the thing he asks is not according to his will—there is that consuming fire" (*Unspoken Sermons* 39). Anodos of *Phantastes* thinks the "Faint traces of a footpath . . . must surely be the path into Fairy Land, which the lady of last night promised I should so soon find" (10). He comes upon a little girl in his journey through Fairy Land, who claims she will show him "another path, which will join the first beyond it" (54). At times, he meets people who intersect his path, but his path is unchanged in its fate—for some of them turn out to be quite "hideous" when they are at opposite directions than his own (61–63). Several times, "waves repeatedly all but swept me off my path; but I kept on my way . . . ," but he finally reaches the end of his path—his death (126, 180). The path taken will eventually lead to one's doom, as fate and doom are irrevocably intertwined.

Doom is certainly met in *The Chronicles of Narnia,* for as Ward observes, Lewis does the unexpected, killing off every character with whom the story began (198). When *infortuna major,* or Saturn, is awakened as Father Time in *The Last Battle,* the doom of Narnia appears to be underway (200). Some ask for the justice of Aslan to be brought upon them, like King Tirian, who accepts the fate to which he is doomed regardless of the result (Lewis, *The Last Battle* 682). Others, like the dwarves in the stable, have the opportunity to hear the voice of Aslan but, out of predisposition, fail to hear him (747). Shasta's experience in *The Horse and His Boy* is a particularly strong case for Lewis's belief that fate is a certain path chosen by the individual. In his journey to Narnia, he experiences several obstacles—none of which he really understands at the time. Aslan, however, explains the significance of some of these obstacles and how he survived them. He was the lion who directed Shasta to Aravis, who scared the jackals away, who strengthened the horses, through fear, to reach King Lune before it was too late, and who pushed the boat along the water to safety, as a young Shasta lay near death. He was even the cat, which helped him in the houses of the dead (281). His path is his story, and, as Aslan makes clear, he will not share a person's story with anyone except that person (281). Fate appeared in several forms to Shasta to put him on the right path. The same sort of fate may be comparable to Odin's placement of the sword in the tree trunk (*The Saga of the Volsungs* 38). Sigmund did not need to draw it, but that path was placed before him, and he took it.

In contrast to this roadmap of decisions, Norse mythology recognizes another kind of fate—one apart from paths and signposts. This fate is one designed by the storyteller to happen regardless of individual free will or providential fate. Doom is one of these *wyrds;* it is a fate that is already written to happen, though the time and place may change depending on the *wyrd* the storyteller designed. At times, inalterable events occur—sometimes at a particular time. It is not Sigmund's fate that the same one-eyed god who presented the sword, Gram, to him is the one who breaks the sword, killing Sigmund in battle (53). Norse belief would, however, assert that it was *wyrd.* While *fate* works in terms of what Classical Greeks call *chronos,* or the continual passing of time, *wyrd* refers to events, to what the Greeks call *kairos,* or particular moments in time. Fate is the chronological passing of decision and consequence. In returning to Lewis's example of roads branching outward from the center, if Road A is chosen, Path 1, 2, or 3 will be the following options; if Road B is chosen, Path 4, 5, or 6 will be available. *Wyrd* says that, no matter whether one chooses Road A or Road B and consequent Paths 1–6, every option will lead to the same immanent event; they will be forced to cross the river. The passing may occur for one person between Road A and Path 1 while it occurs for another after Road B and Path 6—or further yet for the person on Road B, Path 5, and Walkway Z. Some instances of a river may force all paths to cross at the same time. Nonetheless, each person must cross the river, the *wyrd,* at some point to continue their journey, but fate—their particular trail—will lead them to cross, perhaps, at different times. It is the will of the storyteller.

Shippey also disagrees with the general translation of *wyrd* as fate. The *Beowulf*-poet seems to suggest that *wyrd* is a supernatural force, and King Alfred claims Providence is what is meant by the current thoughts of God, only to become *wyrd* once the thoughts have become history. Shippey views *wyrd* along these lines in that, while the person still has free will, fate works as a natural force outside of the individual's actions—what Shippey believes Tolkien means by *luck* in his tales (*The Road* 153–54). Shippey offers Shakespeare's Macbeth as one who exemplifies a naivety of the paradox of free will and luck (184). Common to both *fate* and *doom* is "the idea of a Power sitting above mortals and ruling their lives by its sentence or by its speech alone. This sense is completely absent from 'luck' or 'chance,'" what Shippey equates to *wyrd*. Tolkien notes, in "Beowulf: The Monsters and the Critics," that the *Beowulf* author appears to have little differentiation between God (our storyteller) and *wyrd* (40). Insofar as the storyteller holds all power, the storyteller may "intrude the finger of God into the story," what one might call a *miracle*, he writes in his *Letters* (235). As an example, Tolkien explains that, due to Manwë's appeal, Sauron was conquered the first time by the direct, miraculous action of Ilúvatar (279–80).

Not coincidentally, it is Aslan, the God-character of the Narnia series, who takes on the Saturnine role of Father Time in Lewis's *The Last Battle* (749; Ward 201). An unalterable fate, or *wyrd*, awaits the characters at the end of *The Last Battle*, for no matter their choices in delaying this kind of fate, they will eventually have to face the *wyrd* death before them. The patriotic dwarves have the opportunity to leave, but by free will, they alter their fate. When Lucy pleads with Aslan to do something to help them, he responds that he will show her what he can and cannot do (Lewis, *The Last Battle* 747). He growls to get their attention and gives them food, but they did not hear or taste what Aslan offered: "They will not let us help them. They have chosen cunning instead of belief. Their prison is only in their own minds, yet they are in that prison; and so afraid of being taken in that they cannot be taken out" (748). In other words, the dwarves value their safety and security so highly that they fail to notice what can make them entirely secure. It is intentional that Aslan, in the following paragraph, cries, "Now it is time!" They watch as a different fate takes over. Father Time begins to bring down the sky and Narnia to an end. As the Narnians flee, running past Aslan, each creature looks into Aslan's face for judgment: "I don't think they had any choice about that" (751). Some passed to the left of Aslan into the shadow and were never heard from again; others went through the door to his right—to Aslan's country. *Wyrd* had occurred—an inalterable point of fate in which death and judgment were bound to take place, even for the dwarves who refused the opportunity for that fate to come sooner.[4]

MacDonald writes of a "divine fate" which no human can withstand, a fate operant upon God's will (*Unspoken Sermons* 29). In the same way that the Wise Woman knows what Rosamond is eventually going to be, some points of fate are unavoidable (*The Wise Woman* 294). Similarly, the young boy, Mossy, and the old lady of "The Golden Key" engage in a conversation about fate. Mossy asks what she should do, to which Tangle responds, "You must look for the key-hole. That is your work. I cannot help you. I can only tell you that if you look for it you will find it" (130). Leaving her home, they find a winding path to follow, which leads them into a dark valley. Here, MacDonald extrapolates Psalm 23 into the description of the valley. The green pastures and still waters of David's psalm start the paragraph: "Looking down, they could not tell whether the valley below was a grassy plain or a great still lake. They had never seen any space look like it. The way to it was difficult and dangerous, but down the narrow path they went, and reached the bottom in safety" (132). Safety is relative, of course, when Psalm 23.4's "valley of the shadow of death" is the valley in which one walks (NRSV). When they reach the sea, accordingly, the Old Man of the Sea admits, "You have tasted of death now" (142). MacDonald's tale is universal since it is a tale of the transition from death to life. Death, for MacDonald, is the greatest *wyrd*—the fate which each person is bound to experience, regardless of time and place.

BOTH FATE AND FREE WILL

MacDonald's pathless one, Anodos, contemplates some of the books he has studied. He considers the contradicting truths of philosophical texts and tries to discern the truth—"the root of the manifestation . . . and to find the point in which their invisibly converging lines would unite in one, revealing a truth higher than either and differing from both; though so far from being opposed to either, that it was that whence each derived its life and power" (*Phantastes* 76). So the problem of fate, in both forms, and free will appears irreconcilable; however, each of these authors sees the unity of the two opposing truths. In *Orthodoxy*, Chesterton explains what keeps a person sane despite these surreal contradictions: "Thus he has always believed that there was such a thing as fate, but such a thing as free will also. . . . The determinist makes the theory of causation quite clear, and then finds that he cannot say 'if you please' to the housemaid. The Christian permits free will to remain a sacred mystery; but because of this his relations with the housemaid become of a sparkling and crystal clearness" (20). That is, fate and free will are not contradictory but paradoxical; they are two opposing but valid truths, neither of which negates the other. The sane person, according to Chesterton, "has permitted the twilight," allowing day and night to converge in the same moment; "he has always cared more for truth than for consistency. If he saw two truths that seemed to contradict each other, he would take the two truths and the contradiction along with them" (20). In other words, the proposition that fate and free will coexist is truth, whereas the proposition that life is based on fate or free will is false.

Such coexistence is represented in Lewis's *Perelandra.* Ransom discovers that his presence on the planet has, in fact, been a *wyrd* moment, a eucatastrophe[5] of sorts. Certainly, he had the option to ignore his responsibility, for the prevention of a Fall on Perelandra was going to happen regardless of his actions. But, the paths that he had chosen were the right ones, and as a result, Maleldil had prepared him for the encounter with the Un-Man on Perelandra. The narrator, Lewis, observes that "the power of choice" had been negated by an "inflexible destiny"; on the contrary, says Lewis, one could quite as easily claim that Ransom had overcome his struggles within and had found true freedom: "Ransom could not, for the life of him, see any difference between these two statements. Predestination and freedom were apparently identical. He could no longer see any meaning in the many arguments he had heard on this subject" (127). Some events, like these, are *wyrd.* They are immovable moments set in place that can and will happen regardless of anyone's will in the story. As Lewis claims in *Mere Christianity,* God cannot force someone along the best path because freedom would no longer be freedom, but some events are bound to happen, regardless of choice (167).

Some events are not clearly the result of free will or of fate—in either form. One could look at Ransom's situation and call it a result of the choices of his own free will; another could call it the result of conditioned responses or of following a certain path to that point, and still another could call his place there as a point of divine intervention in the world of Perelandra. As Ransom realizes, perhaps it is all the same. Gollum's fall into the fires of Mt. Doom is an eucatastrophic event. Though the fate of the Ring had already been immanently decided, the means and time of that event are not static; rather, the means to the end are dynamic. Isildur, Bilbo, Gollum, Frodo, or Sam: any of these ring-bearers could have conceivably succeeded in destroying the Ring. One could argue that Frodo's exposure to the Ring conditioned his response to hold onto the Ring in the same way it conditioned him to fight the already-conditioned Gollum for the Ring, leading to the struggle and resulting plunge from the ledge. Likewise, one could argue for the free will of Frodo to keep the Ring and Gollum's decision to take the Ring as a contest that would lead to his doom when Frodo decided he wanted the Ring back. Or, as Tolkien explains, Gollum had the choice to repent but did not, leading to his death; Frodo's salvation is achieved by his pity offered earlier to Gollum; and the quest to destroy the Ring would unavoidably fail as a plan from within the world but not necessarily as a plan from beyond the world—a *wyrd* fate like the eucatastrophe, or sudden turn of events, that promised a happy ending and, therefore, the destruction of the Ring (*Letters* 100–101, 234). As Chesterton remarks, "The morbid logician seeks to make everything lucid, and succeeds in making everything mysterious. The mystic allows one thing to be mysterious, and everything else becomes lucid" (*Orthodoxy* 20). To take the unity of an event apart and say that it is only fate, only free will, or only *wyrd* may only serve to make the scenario mysterious. By allowing the event to be mysteriously any or all of the three, suddenly the wonder of the event and all of the contributions to it become clear, not isolated contributions to a singular argument of occurrence. Perhaps, it would be best to simply understand that the Road is there, and it is the way we all must go, via one set of paths or another.

A Story Beyond the Self

As we have discussed, the journey of life is composed of paths and roads; this journey, however, is also a story. Lewis said that he disagreed with theories like Aristotle's theory of catharsis and I. A. Richards's similar theory of calmness resultant from the conclusion of a tragedy, but Lewis did agree that literature has a transformative value to it (*An Experiment* 134). As change happens in the story, change happens in the reader. The difference with real life, of course, is that the viewer and the protagonist are very much the same person, and MacDonald, Chesterton, Lewis, and Tolkien demonstrated this merging in their tales. They showed how, like Aristotle's catharsis, the protagonist engages with fear and pity (sometimes for oneself), or other emotions, on their journey, and they must work through those feelings to achieve victory. Unlike Aristotle's catharsis, however, the aim is not to achieve a state of relief where emotions are purged; in fact, at times, the pity and fear, or other such emotions, are embraced by the protagonist as healthy virtues. The goal of such emotional states in the works of these authors is not to purge emotion so much as it is to purge the self and, as a result, discover one's true self.

Hein argues the meaning of *Anodos,* in addition to "pathless," means "rising" (56). Unlike Aristotle's view of fear, MacDonald finds fear as a healthy means of rising. In his *Unspoken Sermons,* he claims, "Fear is nobler than sensuality," because sensuality is self-pleasing while fear allows for a god (7). Self-pleasures, thus, present a greater danger than the emotions of fear and pity with which Aristotle found such problem. As Hein asserts, Anodos's search for the marble lady, the Maid of the Alder, is self-pleasing and must be purged, which is symbolic of his journey of self-denial and self-discovery. Eventually, when in the presence of the Maid of the Alder, Anodos is able to deny himself and allow another suitor to the Maid. He has moved from lust to love (70–72). Anodos's initial fascination with the Maid of the Alder is clearly detrimental to himself and his journey. MacDonald writes that to convince people that fear is a "vile thing" is to encourage them to fall "in love with their own will" and become slaves to their own impulses (*Unspoken Sermons* 317). To place his statements in a Freudian context, fear can be a healthy part of the superego, the guard of self-preservation and morality, and the id is the part which operates on impulse and self-satisfaction. MacDonald is simply arguing that the superego should take higher consideration than the id. Failing to embrace healthy fear and, instead, feeding the id will result in evil (317).

This perspective is a discovery of the self as much as it is a purging. Chesterton posits that original sin is an unattractive idea, but it forces humanity to recognize our faults, "for only with original sin we can at once pity the beggar and distrust the king" (*Orthodoxy* 150). Pity is a concern for others instead of the self, and distrust of the king is embracing a healthy fear that the king is not to be trusted because of his flaws. Pity and fear come as a pair, as Aristotle suggests, but such virtues have been contorted to be something they are not. Chesterton claims, "Thus some scientists care for truth; and their truth is pitiless. Thus some humanitarians care for pity; and their pity (I am sorry to say) is often untruthful" (22). The will, like Tolkien's Ring of Power, is wrong when it is egoistic instead of altruistic. It places the self on the throne and others in lesser places. Instead, says Chesterton, "Let him say anything against himself short of blaspheming his original aim of his being; let him call himself a fool . . . but he must not say that fools are not worth saving. He must not say that a man . . . can be valueless" (88). Pity's goal is to look with "frantic intentness outwards" (124). Healthy fear, in a different way, helps one to let go of the self. Chesterton, thus, does not attribute pity to democracy but ascribes fear and reverence of the common human to true democracy (*Heretics* 186). Fear helps one to pay attention to that which is outside the self—sometimes good and sometimes evil. Fear can be a way for someone to submit, in a healthy way, to a good and greater thing,[6] or face a dangerous thing, as Professor De Worms tells Syme: "Who would stoop to be fearless—like a tree? Fight the thing that you fear" (*The Man Who Was Thursday* 85). Syme realizes, later, that fear is a means of feeling the "vivid value in all the earth around him . . . the love of life in all living things" (116). He begins to value all life—like pitying the beggar—but has a fear which forces him outside of himself, again, to value a love for his life—and, perhaps, distrust the king.

Tolkien had warranted cause for political distrust. Forged amidst the fear of dark powers brought on by the World War I, Tolkien's literature may be considered as a part of the trench writing genre, which Paul Fussell situates in Northrop Frye's ironic narrative mode, given the protagonist's frustrated lack of power (Garth 302). Like Wilfred Owen, a trench warfare poet who considered his primary focus to be pity rather than heroism, Tolkien's characters struggle largely with problems of fear and pity (302). For instance, when a character like Fëanor or Melkor considers either their own greatness or their own lack of power, often partnered with pride, a fall is soon to come because they act out of selfish reasons. As Tolkien writes to a bookshop owner, pity requires one to show restraint from acting on immediate desires and apparent advantages (*Letters* 191). He writes to another individual that Frodo is an example of one injured by fearful burdens (186). When Frodo makes his decision to keep the Ring, explains Tolkien, Frodo becomes simpleminded, negligent of the complexity of a single moment of time and, accordingly, the elements of pity and mercy, which allow him to fulfill his quest. It is only through his earlier practices of patience and mercy toward Gollum that saved Frodo, shining over his failure (326).[7] Arguably, it was his fear, no doubt misplaced, of losing the Ring that brought about his decision to keep it. He had forgotten the greater fear of Sauron's evil. He failed to look outside of himself and face his fears of loss and of Sauron. Compassionate for his protagonist, Tolkien claims that Frodo's failure to drop the Ring into the fires of Mt. Doom was not entirely his fault, having exhausted all of his strength, in both body and mind, for the task (251). Rather, the story's logic is how Tolkien clarifies that problematic destruction of the Ring via the bitten finger and Gollum's fall; that is, Gollum refused redemption through love, causing his fall into the fire and the completion of the quest. Tolkien admits to having the final parts of the Lord's Prayer in his mind: "Lead us not into temptation, but deliver us from evil" (252). Tolkien wrote to another correspondent, the cause of Frodo's quest triumphed but not the hero, for "the exercise of pity, mercy, and forgiveness of injury" were all that saved the quest (253). The mission succeeded, but as Tolkien writes, the story failed, were it about Frodo as a successful hero: "He 'apostatized'" (234). He failed to reach nobility.

In Lewis's *The Screwtape Letters,* fear goes awry when it turns into cowardice and yields hatred. Hatred is the reimbursement for one's sense of entitlement after experiencing the pain brought by fear, for as one is pained by fear, she begins to hate (270). Lewis, therefore, agrees with Tolkien and his forerunners that unhealthy fear must be combatted with courage; otherwise, the focus turns inward, and the person is corruptible by hate. Additionally, the hatred can lead to shame; the unhealthy fear, when not faced, can eventually even injure one's capacity for love and courage until it breaks the person down (270). Courage, or fortitude, is one of the four cardinal virtues Lewis writes about in *Mere Christianity* with two parts: one, which faces danger, and the other, which keeps going even under painful circumstances (72). In either case, the person presses on, not simply out of going through the motions or concern over public perception but out of sincere concern (73). Healthy fear, however, as Wormwood claims, may help one to learn more about himself (*The Screwtape Letters* 270). Too much fear may, as with Frodo, break someone down, but even in their brokenness, sometimes fear may yet have positive effects. In *The Problem of Pain,* Lewis asserts that pain is at the root of what is both feared and pitied, and each of these cathartic parts aids in one's ability to rediscover obedience and charity (by which Lewis means *love*) (612). In the same way that fear helps one to recognize the important things in life—because all else may be taken away—pity helps individuals to love others because they are part of humanity, even when they fail to appeal to one in any other way (612). It asks one to forget about oneself and care for another.

Summarily, healthy fear places individuals in obedience to a good master. Detrimental fears are those that must be faced with courage. In either case, the individual learns to let go of the self because either the master is of greater importance or the fearful matter awakens one to recognizing what is truly important. It, like pity, forces the individual to step outside of oneself. Sadness resulting from pity, as Lewis says, is pointless if it does not encourage one to find help (587). Tolkien agrees, in that pity can only be a virtue if it is effectively directed toward some goodness; pity is useless if only used out one's selfish desire to be pure of hatred and injustice, even if they are good goals (*Letters* 330). Fear and pity are helpful in moving one to action along the journey—in choosing the obedient, courageous, or assisting path, in all cases beyond the self. Indeed, the journey for these authors is not intended to be about oneself, even though it is that person's story. The person reaches the highest point when their story is not about them, which pity and fear help them to remember.

Signs along the Way: The Virtues and Vices Within

Laden with fear for their journey and pity for those affected by the Ring, Frodo and Sam, as they make their journey, are given certain guides and aids along the road. According to Gimli, the Fellowship of the Ring was only intended to help the ring-bearer on his journey, and no one made any commitment to proceed the entire way to Mt. Doom (Tolkien, *The Fellowship* 393). He admits that the Fellowship reached the end of their choice to remain committed—whether to stay with or depart from aid to Frodo—when the path was cut off from them by Frodo's decision to leave. Though they are not given the opportunity to continue to guide and protect Frodo, they have been virtuous companions, except for Boromir, whose heightened patriotic virtues turned vicious. Individuals along their journeys need guides to remain on the best path. Some of those guides take the form of people and others in the form of events or circumstances; however, there are guides within the individual, too—principles known as vices and virtues, which help to provide the steering of individual choice. To these vices and virtues we now turn.[8] MacDonald, Chesterton, Lewis, and Tolkien were concerned about the state of culture: the lack of emphasis on traditional, knightly virtues and the twisting of virtues into vices.[9] Virtues and vices are clear signs along the journey that one can see either at the moment or, at least, in hindsight as reasons why one path was taken and not another.

In *The Abolition of Man*, Lewis refers to Augustine's *De Civitate Dei*, where he defines *virtue* as the affectionate condition in which each object or person receives a certain amount of love appropriate to the object or person (700). Love, therefore, is at the center of all the virtues, so much so that none of the other virtues are virtues unless they include love. MacDonald calls it the "consuming fire . . . the active form of Purity,—that which makes pure, that which is indeed Love, the creative energy of God" (*Unspoken Sermons* 30). The problem with the purity of love is that it is no longer comprehended purely as it is. Screwtape tells Wormwood that evil's "Philological Arm" has succeeded in confusing the meaning behind *love* (Lewis, *The Screwtape Letters* 260). *Love*, as a result, can mean lust, the sexual act, unselfishness, fascination with something, or a feeling of satisfaction derived from something. Tolkien sources Western culture's idealization of love as physical pleasure rather than purity, fidelity, self-denial, courtesy, honor, and courage, to the courtly game observed historically in culture and literature (*Letters* 48–49). His assessment is in agreement with Lewis's *The Allegory of Love,*[10] which traces the rise of courtly love. Lewis posits that love appears in virtues such as humility and courtesy, but it also appears in such vices as adultery and the worship of love in and of itself.[11] In courtly love, the lover is appalling, and his acts of love are done out of mere obedience, without any deeper purpose; obedience, says Lewis, is the sole reason and only virtue of the lover in giving into his lover's requests and accepting her complaints (2). This love was considered dishonorable by the nineteenth century because of the adulterous nature of it. Adultery is an act which embraces the vice of selfishness instead of the virtue of love. The concern of courtly love is as much with the rival spouse as it is with the lover, and the only way to save the adulterers turns out to be the true, pure love: God's love, which is never unfaithful to his worshippers and which never gives into wrongful, evil attraction (3). The reason why this problematic form first escapes the reader is because it has, according to Lewis, become a part of the "erotic tradition of modern Europe" that is mistaken for what is "natural and universal" (3). This love was unknown to the Dark Ages, who treasured stories of salvation and journeys to heaven (9). This kind of love is turned inward; it has, in terms of our earlier discussion, forgotten the fear of God and the pity of fellow humanity. This love is self-serving and lustful. As MacDonald claims, "*Otherness* is the essential ground of affection" (*Unspoken Sermons* 136); self cannot be the foundation for love. Where selfishness is the vice, love is the virtue which requires one to surrender herself, to sacrifice herself for the sake of others, and to be grateful and accepting of the sacrifices of others (Lewis, *Miracles* 408). As Chesterton asserts, charity (the cardinal virtue term meaning *love*), means "pardoning unpardonable acts, or loving unlovable people," either of which case removes self from concern (*Orthodoxy* 88).

Indeed, the desire for things in a selfish way carries down the line of the virtues and vices to follow. The virtue of wisdom is often confused with knowledge. The former, as a virtue, is incorruptible in its purity, but the latter is only a tool for the virtue; knowledge is sometimes manipulated for selfish, vice ends. In "Fools and Facts," an unpublished essay, Chesterton is outraged in a defense of reason: "It seems to me that the whole modern world is \being/ weakened by information without intelligence. As men might stuff themselves with food, and then not take enough exercise for their digestion, so men now stuff themselves with statistics, and then not take enough exercise with their brains. But is it much good to have hard facts, if we are not hard-headed enough to handle them rationally?" (1).

Christopher Marlowe's *Doctor Faustus* is par exemplar to this view, for it is the desire for knowledge for the sake of knowledge that is the vice; like Faustus, says Chesterton, knowledge is no good without wisdom to use it virtuously. The Steward Lord Denethor is a representative of knowledge without wisdom in Tolkien's *Return of the King*. To Gandalf, Denethor remarks upon the wizard's obvious wisdom, intending to hurt Gandalf in saying he does not possess all wisdom. Gandalf, then, inquires about Denethor's wisdom, which the steward implies Gandalf does not possess. Denethor evades the question by simply saying, "Enough to perceive . . ." (795). Gandalf's question was about the source or kind of wisdom; Denethor responds with an answer of quantity. He hints at the Faustian desire for quantity of knowledge rather than Solomon's request for wisdom, or discernment. The text reveals, immediately before his demise, that Denethor's knowledge was drawn from a palantír by which he connected with Sauron's knowledge (835–36). The steward admits that he has seen more than Gandalf knows, and as a result of his sight, he knows Gandalf (835). Clearly, his trust is placed in knowledge, like Faust, and not the discernment of wisdom, which uses knowledge virtuously. In his *Letters*, Tolkien says that Elrond symbolizes "the ancient wisdom," and his home, Rivendell, is a place of reflection rather than action. Characters may visit there on their way to adventures or actions—sometimes necessarily, "on the direct road," as in *The Hobbit*—and other times, they must depart unexpectedly from a clear path to seek the reflection found in Rivendell (153). Reflection on knowledge promotes wisdom or discernment about how to use knowledge. The same dichotomy between wisdom and knowledge occurs between Weston and the Oyarsa of Mars in *Out of the Silent Planet*. Weston claims he is a "wise, new man," but he disregards all of the laws of a virtuous humanity (136–38). In *Perelandra*, he admits that the specialization of knowledge is the tragedy not only of his life but also of the entire modern world, for such knowledge is a proponent not of wisdom but of utility (77). Utility is, simply, knowledge put to use, not knowledge that is considered through wisdom. True discernment, for MacDonald, comes from God, for nothing that any human says should be taken simply as a given (*Unspoken Sermons* 228, 276). As Mr. Raven (the Edenic Adam), asserts, "That is one of the pet falsehoods of your world! Is man's greatest knowledge more than a little? or is it therefore dangerous? The fancy that knowledge is in itself a great thing, would make any degree of knowledge more dangerous than any amount of ignorance. To know all things would not be greatness" (*Lilith* 142). That is the root of the problem for the madman in Chesterton's view, for "The madman is the man who has lost everything except his reason. The madman's explanation of a thing is always complete, and often in a purely rational sense satisfactory" (*Orthodoxy* 11). The madman obtains knowledge, but he lacks wisdom to sort out the knowledge and apply it appropriately.

One of the applications of knowledge that takes wisdom is the virtue of justice. In *Mere Christianity,* Lewis defines *justice* as more than what goes on in politics and legal defense; as one of the cardinal virtues, it includes what has traditionally been called *fairness* as well as honesty and trustworthiness (72). Chesterton, in his *Autobiography,* claims that justice is about liberty and equality, the defense of the "rights of man as included in the rights of property . . . [and] Human Dignity" (335). Human dignity, unfortunately, is so often unrealized that MacDonald claims it is an "impossibility": "It does not exist between man and man, save relatively to human *law.* Justice to be justice must be much more than justice. Love is the law of our condition, without which we can no more render justice than a man can keep a straight line walking in the dark" (*Unspoken Sermons* 152).[12] Love, clearly, needs to be the foundation of justice, which MacDonald further claims is not "the punishing of sin" (504); rather, as Chesterton asserts, justice and mercy should be brought concomitantly among humanity (*Orthodoxy* 98–99). In "On Fairy-Stories," Tolkien cites Chesterton's essay, "On Household Gods and Goddessess," published originally in 1922 and reprinted in *The Coloured Lands* in 1938, owned by Tolkien. In that text, Chesterton observes that children have a strong sense of justice while adults have a strong sense of mercy (Milbank xii). Noel claims that Tolkien, similarly, brought justice to the table in Middle-earth from both pagan and Christian perspectives, as meeting fate honorably and rejecting evil, respectively. In pagan fatalism, Sam returns home, and in Christian idealism, Frodo goes to eternal life (11).[13] For their efforts, justice is realized.

It may appear that the next virtue, mercy, is in opposition of justice, but as MacDonald asserts in *Unspoken Sermons,* "Two rights cannot possibly be opposed to each other. If God punish sin, it must be merciful to punish sin; and if God forgive sin, it must be just to forgive sin" (508). The two function in paradox. God is just because His justice is merciful (528). Kreeft asserts, "'Pity' sometimes means a *feeling,* but when it is used in such a way as to be virtually identical with mercy (as it is in *The Lord of the Rings*), it is a *deed.* It is mercy, not justice or courage or even heroism, that alone can defeat evil" (217). Mercy is the enactment of love to those who do not deserve it but need it. Accordingly, mercy, pity, and forgiveness are ultimately what save Frodo and the quest to destroy the Ring (Tolkien, *Letters* 252). Lewis claims that mercy, above all the other virtues, is one that should be cultivated at the expense of any of the others (*Problem of Pain* 580). Mercy cannot be used for profit. Although TV shows and movies display a merciful verdict in court for one who has given people of the law something they want, true mercy cannot operate for the offeror's gain. Tolkien writes that such selfish action does not constitute mercy or even pity, for both of those occur in times when an action does not seem prudent (*Letters* 253). Lewis describes a man who rose to wealth and power by treacherousness, cruelty, and mercilessness to others; justice and mercy, in this case, seem as though they come from God as one contemplates what to do, for mercy, alone, seems as though it is not capable of hoping this man will perform this act for eternity (622–23). As Chesterton asserts in *Orthodoxy,* for someone to find a severe sentence that combines mercy is "a strange need of human nature" for all its faults (92). He argues that, without both, humanity would be quite miserable. It is realizing that the two function together, as part of the same concept, that is difficult for the human mind to comprehend. It is the unity of the two which allows the human to feel guilt and have the need for reconciliation; it is the justice that creates guilt and the need for reconciliation through mercy (MacDonald, *Unspoken Sermons* 535).

Chesterton writes, "You can praise an action by saying that it is calculated to bring pleasure or pain to discover truth or to save the soul" (*Orthodoxy* 31). Indeed, pleasure and pain are both signifiers of the right or best path when grounded in love. Lewis writes, in one of his most popular passages, that one's pleasures are God's whispers, one's conscience is His voice, and one's pain is His megaphone to awaken a world that cannot hear (*Problem of Pain* 604). In the same vein, MacDonald observes that Christ suffered to lead humanity to perfection (*Unspoken Sermons* 27).

Suffering, therefore, is a means of leading one to the best path, the perfect path, even after one has strayed. Lewis reiterates Thomas Aquinas's view of suffering, that suffering is a kind of knowledge of evil which leads to goodness; otherwise, people would be ignorant of evil (*Problem of Pain* 623). A tale, like that of Beren and Luthien, must extend beyond happiness and even sorrow (Tolkien, *The Two Towers* 696). The path is never entirely easy, for the story requires its ups and downs, happy and painful parts, but as Tolkien asserts, grace is always there to help when the burden of suffering is too much (*Letters* 326).

The demon Screwtape writes to his student to remember that normal, healthy pleasures come from God (Lewis, *The Screwtape Letters* 210). Pleasure, like any virtue (though not traditionally considered one), is something that these authors see as having been twisted for evil use. Hence, pleasures may be at the right hand of God, but Screwtape encourages Wormwood to turn the human from enjoying pleasures that he actually enjoys to pleasures that are only nominally pleasures: what society praises as the best or most significant things (223, 249). Evil wins when pleasures become something else, like achieving social approval or using pleasure to avoid dealing with truth. Even Screwtape admits that pleasures and pains are grounded in reality and, consequentially, can bring someone back to reality; their aim is to get the human's mind off the pleasure and onto something related, whether business, vanity, situational irony, or even boredom (222). It may seem odd that Merry and Pippin come across Saruman's stores of food, drink, and pipe-weed upon the defeat of Isengard, but Tolkien's purposes were twofold. On one hand, he needed to reveal some connection between the Shire and Saruman; on the other, he needed to show that pleasures can ground people in reality when they have been experiencing darkness and despair. Gimli, Legolas, and their party cannot believe that they have found the hobbits enjoying good food and smoking—two pleasures unfitting for a dark environment (*The Two Towers* 544). Gandalf explains that hobbits will talk about "the pleasures of the table" even as their worlds are about to end, and these pleasures, rightly so, make them feel less angry toward Saruman than they did before (545, 562). Their conversations "began and ended in smoke" while Gandalf's did not, and, admittedly, he does not feel less ill toward Saruman (562). Their use of pleasure as grounding them in reality is in stark contrast to Saruman's "private use" and the commerce made by these pleasures that eventually enslaves the Shire (548, 560). Saruman, like the leaders in the Shire, has become dependent on pleasures and no longer enjoys them as pleasures that bring him back to reality. As Chesterton claims, "The whole case for Christianity is that a man who is dependent upon the luxuries of life is a corrupt man, spiritually corrupt, politically corrupt, financially corrupt" (*Orthodoxy* 111). The problem, as MacDonald claims, is when these pleasures become possessions—objects that are held dearer than eternity (*Unspoken Sermons* 189). It is the trust in pleasures, alone, rather than the God who gives them, that is the problem for these authors (195, 199, 201): "To enjoy heartily and thankfully, and do cheerfully without, when God wills we should, is the way to live in regard to things of the lower nature" (366).

If pain and pleasure help to ground the self in reality and be attentive to the Creator, then hope is what moves the person through a world that sometimes seems filled more with pain than with pleasure. Kreeft discusses two kinds of hope: surface-level hope, or optimism, and deep hope, which is hope or trust that is outside of the self—in others or something beyond the known world. Frodo and Sam, for instance, lost hope in the success of their mission but maintained hope in one another, which de-centers the self (199–204). In Tolkien's *The Return of the King*, hope seemed to fade in Sam, but it found renewed strength; his face transformed to a grim, hard look, and his limbs felt a thrill. He felt as though he were transforming into a new creature, strong and impervious to despair, weariness, or dread (Tolkien, *The Return* 913). His hope is not for himself but for something outside of himself, what Gandalf calls "a fool's hope" (797). Gandalf asserts that the despair and hopelessness of Denethor will ensure the victory of Sauron, to which the steward mockingly, laughingly responds, "Hope on then!" (835) Believing Gandalf intends to overthrow him, the steward calls such hope "ignorance," but as we know by the conclusion, Gandalf's hopes were not misplaced. He trusted in the will of Ilúvatar to see the task through—and he does. Lewis describes it well when he commands his reader to pursue Heaven because one's life on Earth will be a part of that pursuit; conversely, if one pursues only what one can obtain on Earth, he will obtain neither. On a larger scale, says Lewis, to improve the world, humanity must aim higher than what it sees in the world before it (*Mere Christianity* 112). In this chapter on hope, Lewis's definitions of "The Fool's Way" and "The Way of the Disillusioned 'Sensible Man'"—as those who believe hope is found in other things or that there is no hope in the world, respectively—could not be more appropriate to the fool Saruman, who tried industrialism, political pursuit, commerce, knowledge, and shaking hands with the devil, and the disillusioned Denethor. They are both hopeless, and as Gandalf says of Saruman, pitiable (*The Two Towers* 569). MacDonald writes, "The true man trusts in a strength which is not his, and which he does not feel, does not even always desire; believes in a power that seems far from him, which is yet at the root of his fatigue itself and his need of rest—rest as far from death as is labour" (*Unspoken Sermons* 305). It is the animal side of the human which, when it is scared, responds without pity or hope (Chesterton, *The Ball and the Cross* 46). The atheistic Turnbull in *The Ball and the Cross*, thus, trusts the "industry of the intellect" rather than hope (206). The insane asylum's room is as hopeless as "the hopeless cosmos of his own creed" (222). It is not long before Turnbull realizes that those believers he always found to be hopeless cases because of their hope in greater things were the ones actually grounded in reality. The psychologist at the asylum calls one patient, Mr. Wilkinson, a "hopeless case" because he claims two men stole his boat and Turnbull a "hopeful case" because he "understands the scientific point of view" (243); however, Turnbull admits that Mr. Wilkinson is telling the truth, for Turnbull tells the psychologist that he stole the boat. Suddenly, the psychologist diagnoses Turnbull, the "Elentheromaniac," with "Rapinavititis—the delusion that one has stolen a ship" (244). Truth, Turnbull now realizes, is on the side of the hopeful—those people called the "hopeless cases" by the truly hopeless, Chesterton's madmen who need a complete explanation of a thing like Lewis's Sensible Man.

Reality is, as Lewis claims in *The Great Divorce*, connected to Heaven through joy (504). Joy is a virtue embraced more than any other by these authors because it has that direct relationship with Heaven. MacDonald writes that God made humans to be joyful in order to enter into His joy (*Unspoken Sermons* 378), and Chesterton concurs: "Joy, which is the small publicity of the pagan, is the gigantic secret of the Christian" (*Orthodoxy* 153). In Tolkien's "On Fairy-Stories," joy is an essential trait of a fairy-story because it allows the reader to see, if only for an instant, a deeper reality or truth. Joy, in the fairy-story, is not only a reward for the sadness of the world but also a pleasure in itself. Eucatastrophe, as the ultimate joy of the fairytale, the joy which arises from the sudden turn of events, glimpses at something greater than the tale of which it is a part—even of the divine, of *evangelium*, claims Tolkien (155). Meaning, joy, as seen through eucatastrophe in elfland, reveals truth in the Primary World of reality. This joy, as experienced in reality, is often mistaken for pleasure in life itself (MacDonald, *Unspoken Sermons* 303).

If their belief about joy seems simplistic, then it is because their view of joy is significantly different than the common understanding of *joy* as "A vivid emotion of pleasure arising from a sense of well-being or satisfaction; the feeling or state of being highly pleased or delighted; exultation of spirit; gladness, delight" (*OED*). Joy is not to be confused with general pleasures, which are substitutes or references for joy (Lewis, *Surprised by Joy* 68, 164); joy does not exist for humans, but humans exist for the sake of joy (*Problem of Pain* 644). Chesterton writes of MacDonald that he knew that melancholy has to do with death while joy is part of "the renewal and perpetuation of being" ("George Macdonald [sic] and His Work" 6). Joy is the essence of what one may call living life to the fullest. It is what helps someone to press on purposefully. The fairy-story, which embraces joy as its chief sentiment, is concerned with desire and satisfaction rather than mere possibility (Tolkien, "On Fairy-Stories" 134). *Joy* is a desire or longing which is only partly satisfied in a moment: an unquenchable thirst for more joy once it is tasted. The momentary experience with joy is a sign for "an indescribable longing for something, they know not what" (MacDonald, *Phantastes* 81).[14] In *Surprised by Joy*, Lewis first experienced this kind of joy in Northernness, with its sense of joint desire and loss (69). In MacDonald's sense of the word, *joy*, as defined by Lewis, reminds the reader of itself, never as something final or entirely satisfactory, but a longing for something more that could happen soon (74, 169). It was this kind of joy that he found in the works of MacDonald and Chesterton, ultimately leading him, with Tolkien's use of joy in eucatastrophe, to believe there was something more to the universe than what Pragmatism or Materialism could offer (161, 169, 172–75, 182–85). Ultimately, he concludes, like his fellow authors, that all joy is a yearning for unity with "the Absolute," God (Lewis, *Surprised by Joy* 214; MacDonald, *Unspoken Sermons* 588; Chesterton, *Orthodoxy* 153–54; Tolkien, "On Fairy-Stories" 156).

All of the previous virtues encourage selflessness and recognition of what is outside of the self; joy, along with love, is an element which brings unity to the virtues. Each of the vices, or twisted virtues to the point of opposition, of course, work the other way—toward self-centeredness and egoism. At the heart of the vices, then, is what Lewis calls "Self-Conceit" and "The Great Sin," pride (*Mere Christianity* 103). The other vices, says Lewis, work through the animal nature—the *Bios*—whereas pride works directly from Hell to the dark parts of one's spirit, the Diabolical Self (89, 105). Pride is different from confidence, which is simple belief in one's competence and capability. Pride acts in comparison to others, when a person believes she is better than someone else without concern for what the other person may think (106). Unlike confidence, which exists when one is in isolation, pride is always in relation to others, elevating the self by comparison. Sam, for instance, is the model of servitude and loyalty in *The Lord of the Rings;* unfortunately, Tolkien claims Sam developed a bit of pride and possessiveness about his service, a demonic tactic described in the text Lewis dedicated to Tolkien (Tolkien, *Letters* 329; Lewis, *The Screwtape Letters* 224).[15] That is, as Chesterton calls it, "humility in the wrong place" because nothing is truly enjoyable without humility (*Orthodoxy* 23). As he would say of Nietzsche's egoism, which turned to "imbecility," "Thinking in isolation and with pride ends in being an idiot. Every man who will not have softening of the heart must at last have softening of the brain" (34). No growth is possible, then, if one is only thinking of oneself: "The first thing in all progress," says MacDonald, "is to leave something behind; to follow him is to leave oneself behind," for, in the end, "There is no joy" in embracing one's animal nature when giving up oneself will result in joy "direct from their source" (*Unspoken Sermons* 364, 377).

In the same way that one needs to know traffic lights and signs for the journey, these signs need to be known for the journey through the human story of life. Only when all the virtues are used together and "in their best proportion or relation" will progress really happen (Chesterton, *Orthodoxy* 107). When one stays the path of virtue, the evil challenges they face are met with the virtues of fortitude, patience, pity, and forgiveness, yielding, still, complex goods regardless of the evil done on the other side (Lewis, *Problem of Pain* 616). As Gandalf says to Pippin after meeting with the stubborn Denethor, even treachery may cause a traitor to unintentionally betray himself to cause some good (*The Return* 797). No matter the path chosen, some good may come out of it.[16] Even Hell, offers MacDonald, will provide a "just mercy" of God (*Unspoken Sermons* 535).[17] These guides to the path help one in their free-will decisions, the fate those decisions lead to, and may prepare them for those *wyrd* moments that are inevitable. Progress, however, is not achieved entirely alone. While the individual may be infinitely more important than the masses to these authors, journeys are not made alone, nor do those paths fail to cross others at a bridge or, largely, in civilization. Beyond the chronology of a single lifetime, history and civilization provide considerable contexts for the journey, and as the sum is made of its parts, history and civilizations have stories of their own.

Civilization and Origination

The last two chapters examined the human nature of the individual and the individual journey. This chapter does the reverse by considering how humanity is comprised of individuals. The sociological term for a collective body of humans who have some advanced form of "cultural, social, and intellectual" development which aids in the "progressive" nature of humanity is *civilization* (*OED*). In other words, humanity journeys on a path like the individual, from a beginning to an end, with the same principles of free will, fate, and *wyrd,* although humanity is not steered as much by a single individual (albeit, at times, it can be) but by many individuals. For a variety of reasons, MacDonald, Chesterton, Lewis, and Tolkien each resisted the concept which has been called *civilization.* Chesterton, for instance, disliked how the individual becomes increasingly represented by materials in civilization—from clothing to housing: "I had perhaps got no further than the feeling that those imprisoned in these inhuman outlines were human beings" (*Autobiography* 137). Chesterton's statement captures the overall philosophy of the group's opinion regarding civilization. Their overarching argument would be that all too easily, humanity mistakes the buildings, fences, and bridges on the road as civilization. Technology, whether the birth of literacy, the plow, or the microchip, is confused as signs of human civilization. The group sees this mistaken identification as only encouraging the downward spiral of civilization. Such mindsets that see the wooden bridge for the trees bring about philosophical and moral challenges so that the Moral Law is not as clear as it may have once been. Humanity regarded the raw materials that were to be signs for the human journey as becoming more important than the human on the journey, and, hence, the products of these materials become symbols of civilization. The problem is not the advancement of technology but civilization's decentering of humanity for the sake of technology or, in Marxian terms, the product the base can produce for its superstructure. Furthermore, materials, then, supplant belief. A civilization which values the materials over the individual is inevitably going to lose value in the immaterial. Empiricism, because of its supposedly hard data, trumps faith in the unseen. Suddenly, even beliefs in the history of humanity and civilization are brought into question by pressure of scientific observation. The Modernist view of the world becomes, as Barfield thought, a "materialist paradigm," what Lewis called "the Age of the Machine" (qtd. in Duriez, *The Oxford Inklings* 215). Oral and written traditions no longer matter to the amorphous mob once known as humanity or older civilizations because those beliefs cannot always be proven accurate by organized, modern civilization. This opinion is declaimed by the group because the stones, clay, and dirt on the road cannot tell us entirely where we came from, when we arrived, where exactly we are, or especially why we are here, even if modern civilization has placed its faith in these materials. For these answers, argue MacDonald, Chesterton, Lewis, and Tolkien, one must look beyond what is measurable and material and turn our attention to story, faith, and the numinous. Human purpose cannot be found in the empirical and bleak existentialism of Sartre and Camus; it can only be uncovered in the human quest for the numinous. Each of these authors agree; throughout the long journey of humanity, humanity has torn itself apart at the seams into pieces of what we call *civilization.*

The Civilized and the Barbaric

Chesterton, in *The Everlasting Man*, claims that civilization existed before any human record, for "the curtain rises upon the play already in progress"; all else—history and the universe—is left to assumption (43, 61). Like Chesterton, others in the group regard this observation as important because it can help us deconstruct the binary terms of *civilized* and *barbaric* that assume a superior and inferior relationship. Duriez recalls that Lewis and Tolkien were some of the last of what Lewis called "Old

Western Culture," for they believed the new machinistic culture was not unlike Mordor, Saruman's Orthanc, or the NICE in *That Hideous Strength* (*The Oxford Inklings* 18–19). Labeling people according to their technological or scientific advancement is, according to MacDonald, "the backward undoing of the tapestry-web" (*Unspoken Sermons* 464). Untangling the web, first, ignores that the web is made of the same stuff, and, second, that each piece of the web is essential to its overall construction. At no point is the web any better than any other part of the web. In "On Fairy-Stories," Tolkien asserts that so-called "'primitive' people" and their beliefs are misunderstood by a hasty glance at those, "who are not, as we say, civilised" (124). This inattentive approach produces poor labeling and assumes that newer is better, what Lewis calls *chronological snobbery:* "the uncritical acceptance of the intellectual climate upon our own age and the assumption that whatever has gone out of date is on that account discredited" (*Surprised by Joy* 201).[1] Lewis essentializes the opinion of him and his fellow authors well in *The Problem of Pain,* where he says that *brute* and *savage* are words used rhetorically, offensively, and scientifically as descriptors, but the problem of their meaning rests upon a disbelief in humanity's Fall. For one to assert that humans evolved from *brutality*— from animals—is acceptable; however, for one to assert that earlier human history is one of *brutality,* meaning evil or wicked, the word is misattributed—confused for *wretchedness,* of which animals are incapable. Likewise, *savagery* means not a cruel, ferocious personality but a crude, undeveloped technology (590).[2] The words *savage, brute,* and *barbaric,* then, may be applied when describing the technology of a certain people or to characterize their bestial qualities prior to becoming human (if one believed in physical evolution, which these authors do not); however, the terms may not be applied to describe their historical period, behavior, or humanity because such activities assume that humans now are better than humans then. As Chesterton exemplifies in *The Everlasting Man,* writing may not have been a prehistoric art, but arts clearly did exist, even though they are seen as symptomatic of civilized culture (43). After all, says Chesterton, poetry did not arise from preexisting forms of poetry; arts existed before they were recognized as arts (49). Although technology may have advanced over history, humans have not advanced in their nature. Humanity has simply performed its potential with the means available to them. This "false notion of the whole history of humanity" establishes that "a barbarian evolved into a civilised man," and modern humanity, accordingly, views its nature as always evolving into something more than it already is, better in its moral and technological senses (71).

MacDonald's goblins demonstrate this kind of confusion of civilized and barbaric: "As they grew misshapen in body, they had grown in knowledge and cleverness, and now were able to do things no mortal could see the possibility of" (*The Princess and the Goblin* 6). Goblin Glump tells his son, Helfer, that he has not quite reached universal knowledge, but being a goblin, his defining characteristic is his head (40–42). One of the more educated miners makes it clear that the goblins are "the primordial condition of humanity, and that education and handicraft had developed both toes and fingers," a supposition that Curdie's dad laughed at (43). McGillis endnotes this passage, claiming that MacDonald was poking fun at modern education and Darwinian evolutionary theory, which he would target further in *David Elginbrod* and *Gutta Percha Willie* (350). These pillars of knowledge MacDonald mocks when he furthers the conversation. Glump claims "no wild beasts" exist in their underground realm and chastises his son for saying he felt something lick his foot (which Curdie stealthily touched): "Will you malign your native realms and reduce them to a level with the country upstairs? That is swarming with wild beasts of every description" (44–45). The knowledgeable goblins find the humans above ground to be uncivilized and bestial; some of the humans above theorize that the goblins are Cro-Magnon men.

Granted, MacDonald is using the goblin/human dichotomy to illustrate how humans can become either more bestial or more human, but in this juxtaposition lay his view that civilized humanity is a fable. What is primitive or what is civilized change only in their appearance (Lewis, *Miracles* 348). Chesterton affirms this sentiment when he asserts that the barbaric and the civilized have always been alongside one another, absorbing and transforming into one another repeatedly, as he demonstrates with ancient Egyptian and Babylonian civilizations (*Everlasting Man* 63). Hence, it is the royal garden that is "civilized" in *The Princess and the Goblin,* not the "wild mountain" in which the goblins live (57).[3] Tolkien's universe of Eä demonstrates the same contrast between barbarism and civilization. Early civilization in Eä has great magical power, like that which is used to create the Silmarils, magical swords, and rings of power. Fëanor, for instance, utilized all of the lore, power, and skill he could muster to make the Silmarils (*Silmarillion* 67). Later civilizations have greater technology than early Eä: catapults, gears, industrial facilities. Yet, they lack great magical power—what was in Eä at the beginning. Saruman's banner is for "the high and ultimate purpose: Knowledge, Rule, Order," all elements that oppose not only the magic of the world but also all that is hnau (*The Fellowship* 253). Radagast, the wizard whose lore is of herbs and beasts, is the greatest example of a beast-master, and Saruman has nothing more to say of him than to call him a bird-tamer, simpleton, and fool (251–52). The tower of the wizards, Orthanc, which is managed by Saruman, is plagued with forges, pits, and dark smoke (254). What was once a home to magic has become an industrial complex where the wizard's staff is broken. The irony, of course, is that Radagast's beasts are what magically free Gandalf from being trapped on the tower, and the Ents are the primitive creatures who destroy Saruman's technologically innovative civilization. Tolkien makes the situation quite clear. The ability to create magically (artistically in the Primary World) is an attribute of a true hnau.[4] When one's ability to create is for the sake of power or superiority in civilization, then the innocence of creation is lost; art is corrupted. True civility seems to be in the embrace of art rather than in the barbarity of technological development for power or superiority. As Tolkien demonstrates effectively with the Silmarils, Fëanor's creation of them was artistic and good, but when the Silmarils become technology to be possessed, bloodshed occurs and civilizations disburse.

Perhaps no clearer nor more comical an example of the barbaric/civilized dichotomy appears in the works of these authors than in Lewis's *Out of the Silent Planet.* Weston and Divine have journeyed to Mars in hopes of colonizing the seemingly primitive planet. Weston's evaluation of his situation and the hnau in it at the end of the text utilizes scientific language, such as *hypothesis, theory, behavior,* and *yield* (126). Because he cannot empirically observe the angelic eldila but hears the high angel of Mars, Oyarsa's voice, he says they are using ventriloquism, which is common for savages to do (125). Weston says that he may appear a robber to these savages whose tribal, Stone Age, bug-like, and even primitive social structure cannot compare with his more innovative and developed civilization, by which he means advanced science, medicine, law, military, architecture, commerce, and transportation. These characteristics show his and humanity's right to dominate Malacandra, for it is "the right of the higher over the lower" (134). With Weston as civilization's representative, all the Oyarsa can really think in response to Weston's civilized, colonialist claims is that the poor fool is mentally retarded or that something went wrong in his brain (128–29,

135). It is the civilized who play the fool, shouting the onomatopoeic "pouf! bang!" to signify their guns, which they use as a threat (130).

CHRONOLOGICAL SNOBBERY: THE POLITICAL POSITION

Civilization, as Weston exemplifies, looks down on those who are less technologically advanced as if those civilizations (or barbarians) are less intelligent or less human. Yet, at the age of fifteen, an astute Chesterton observed that people are people regardless of technological advancement or empirically based knowledge, for "the prehistoric nurses were telling their shaggy-haired little barbarians stories substantially the same as those which are told to more decorously attired children of the present day" ("GKC on Fairy Tales"). That is, humanity seems to have the same needs regardless of the advancement of a civilization, and some of the same stories are told to modern civilizations that were told to the supposed barbarians. Lewis argues that, while classical learning valued tradition and ancient books for the truths that could be found within, modern culture and industrial civilization have brought about the rejection of ideals and the embrace of Provincialism, or the belief in facts presented from a narrow point of view. Because, for example, Paul wrote his epistles nearly two thousand years ago, modern civilization assumes that his texts are useless (Lewis, "Modern Man and His Categories of Thought" 62). The prehistoric discoveries of language, family, clothing, fire, animal domestication, agriculture, the wheel, the ship, and poetry are undervalued and considered primitive or uncivilized because they were not invented in the observable present (*Problem of Pain* 591). To modern civilization, ancient and prehistoric civilizations— if they are so generous as to call them such—have little to offer the new, and, therefore, it is assumed that we have nothing to learn from that past about how presently to guide the individual path or the collective journey. Meaningful signs for the journey no longer hold meaning. What is meant by the term *Christian morality*, for instance, is understood to be the same as *civilized, modern, democratic*, or *enlightened* in a political speech because the loss of meaning in these words has happened without any recognition ("The Death of Words" 107; "Is English Doomed?" 27); none of these words truly signify Christian morality, but over the course of history, these terms quietly became associated with it during the early to mid-twentieth century. These signifiers, then, are used to create propagandistic sweeping generalizations intended to satisfy audiences of political speeches. Modern civilization, in an attempt to rectify or change what has happened in the past, engages in chronological snobbery on not only social but also political levels. Hence, these authors resisted, overall, the dominant political movements of their era. Alternatively, they advocated for rights of the individual to private property and self-governance and for a government which regulates rather than dominates a nation.

MacDonald, Chesterton, Lewis, and Tolkien did not side with the rising socialist fad or the trust of the mob, which they called *democracy*, at least not as it is commonly understood today. While these authors' lifetimes, when combined, span about one century and a half (1824–1973), their political worldviews are strikingly similar. MacDonald, for his entire life, and Chesterton, for half of his, experienced Victorian England, contrary to Western Modernity endured by Lewis and Tolkien for the entirety of their lives. Yet, the two eras are clearly related. Modernity is sometimes understood to be the evolution of or response to the Victorian period. In the Introduction to "The Victorian Age" in *The Norton Anthology of English Literature,* the editors write about this evolution and reaction of Modernism to Victorianism: "The Georgian reaction against the Victorians is now only a matter of the history of taste, but its aftereffects still sometimes crop up when the term *Victorian* is employed in an exclusively pejorative sense, as prudish or old-fashioned. Contemporary historians and critics now find the Victorian period a richly complex example of a society struggling with the issues and problems we identify with modernism" (1046). While the Victorian perspective, apart from its countercultures, not only valued superficialities and mannerisms but also valued what was hidden beneath the surface of those superficialities, Modernity called for realism and a plainspoken, brusque attitude, charting solely what was empirically known.[5] Victorian England valued morality over introspection, domestic propriety over human purpose, social and national enterprise over the individual, and early Moderns would look back on the Victorians as "prudish" or "old-fashioned," though "It was then the fashion for most literary critics to treat their Victorian predecessors as somewhat absurd creatures, stuffily complacent prigs with whose way of life they had little in common" ("The Victorian Age" 1044–46). The formal religion and agnosticism of the Victorian period, which struggled with its honest belief in Christianity, became Spiritualism in the Modern period to describe, simply, all of the metaphysical that was unknown.[6] Jane Austen, Charles Dickens, the Brownings, and

Alfred, Lord Tennyson, whose Victorian literature demonstrated the culture's mannerisms and hinted at the human nature and spiritual state signified beneath, were replaced by Thomas Hardy, James Joyce, W. B. Yeats, and Philip Larkin, whose plainspoken literature is explicit in its description of human nature and Spiritualism. As Chesterton remembers, "by the time I passed from boyhood to manhood, the pessimistic doubt [of the Victorian period's Christianity] had considerably clouded the optimistic dogma" when Modernity arrived (*Autobiography* 170). Roger L. Green and Walter Hooper note Lewis's reaction against Modernism as early as 1919, leading to some ideas like those of the Inklings (64–65).[7] Chesterton, living transitionally from the Victorian to Modern periods, writes that, although he did not like everything of the Victorian period, what is now understood as *Victorian* is not what the Victorian period was:

> [I]t was almost a complete contrast to all that is now connoted by that word. It had all the vices that are now called virtues; religious doubt, intellectual unrest, a hungry credulity about new things, a complete lack of equilibrium. It also had all the virtues that are now called vices; a rich sense of romance, a passionate desire to make the love of man and woman once more what it was in Eden, a strong sense of the absolute necessity of some significance of human life. But everything that everybody tells me now about the Victorian atmosphere I feel instantly to be false, like a fog, which merely shuts out a vista. (*Autobiography* 142–44)

Even the term, *Victorian,* becomes pejorative for the Moderns as something barbaric to the new civilization ("The Victorian Age" 1046). The political position of these authors, then, becomes first a response to the moralistic and superficial Victorian episteme with secret religious doubt, intellectual unrest, sexual desire, and purpose in life, and second, for those living after the Victorian period, a response to Modernist chronological snobbery that finds its civilization above others. Hence, Chesterton found himself on the side of Yeats in battling against the materialistic culture of Victorian England, which began to value empirical study over belief in the unseen, but in an "odd double attitude towards the poet," Chesterton disagreed with Yeats's Spiritualist beliefs about which "most people agree with him" in the Modern era (*Autobiography* 147–49). Chesterton was brought up amidst Universalism (i.e., all religion leads to the same God) but aware that many others were turning agnostic and atheist. Half of those transitioning in his life believed in a God who would see that all was right in the world because He was above it; the other half argued that no God existed and that all was wrong with the world: "One of these movements of progress led into the glorious fairyland of George MacDonald, the other led into the stark and hollowed hills of Thomas Hardy" (169). MacDonald's world led to an optimistic belief in the unseen, and Hardy's pessimistic outlook led to atheistic empiricism.

MacDonald turns out to embrace all that Chesterton, Lewis, and Tolkien loved of the Victorian era. As Reis notes, MacDonald's symbolism was out of place in the Victorian period (9). Even Tolkien found MacDonald to be an exception to the Victorian era, for Tolkien cited *The Hobbit* as sourced from epic, myth, and fairy-stories that were entirely not Victorian, except for the tales of MacDonald (*Letters* 31). Lewis goes so far as to admit to having never composed a text without quoting from MacDonald (Preface to *George MacDonald* xxxvii). MacDonald was more of a poet than a novelist, according to Lewis and Chesterton, for he saw humanity from a singular standpoint whereas the novelist must see it from many (Lewis, Preface to *George MacDonald* xxxvii; Chesterton, "George Macdonald [sic] and His Work" 5). In fact, the humanism which MacDonald clung so dearly to in the Victorian era is what D. Williams believes vanished in the Modernist era. Modernism became posthumanist, even subhuman, in its tendencies, rejecting the *Tao*—what Lewis refers to as the Law of Decent Behavior in *Mere Christianity* (25)—in a way that would become more radical in Postmodernity (Williams 91). The ideals, optimism, sentimentalism, and even the hypocrisy that appeared in the magic and elves of the Victorian Age died when the "black clothes and black shirt" of the "funereal" Modern tossed away all of the remaining Victorian conventions and convictions (Chesterton, *Autobiography* 150–51, 195).

When the little humanism that remained in the Victorian era disappeared, Modernism reared a grim perspective of humanity. These cultural clashes set the stage for their political opinions. According to Oser, the clash between a relativist Modernism and Christian humanism is at the core of twentieth-century literature when "a cadre of specialists, usurping cultural authority . . . ruled over the dialectic between religion and literature" (x). While Chesterton, for instance, entrusted the individual as the "custodian of democracy," Tolkien was "an empiricist aware that empiricism has its limits" (Oser 22, 60). As D. Williams asserts, "If we reduce man to an animal or to a machine, thus ignoring our spiritual accountability to the *Tao*, then we must not expect ideals like democracy, equality, or justice to be more than words, arbitrary sounds floating in the air" (37).

Thus, the term, *democracy*, in its modern sense, becomes an enemy of these authors. Burns claims that Tolkien believes in hierarchical fellowship—one that is not entirely democratic but that embraces shared human need (3). Chesterton, likewise, finds modern industrial civilization grounded in injustice, and he believes that the things humans hold in common should be the first principles of democracy, not what is held separately, unlike the contemporary "political instinct" (*Autobiography* 335; *Orthodoxy* 39). Greville MacDonald calls his father a "theocratic individualist" as opposed to a Christian Socialist (401). Like the circumstances in MacDonald's fairytales, a monarch presides over the land as a figure and organizer, but the people are left to their individual duties with the deity who appears to them to be the high ruler. The individuality and right to private property situates MacDonald in the same position as the distributism in which Kreeft claims Tolkien fits: distributism being the political view of Chesterton and Hilaire Belloc, which aims to "maximize the distribution of private property" (164–65). This initial distribution, then, is handed down to one's children, no longer needing to be regulated by government. Burns asserts that Tolkien "is strongly attached to the concept of inherited rule" (3), but such an attachment is evident not only on the royal level but also on the common level. Bilbo's Bag End, for example, is to be passed down as an inheritance like Chesterton and Belloc's distributism. He does not want it to go into the hands of the Sapho-Baggins relatives, so he embraces his other close relative, Frodo, whom he trusts with the estate. Upon their return from Mt. Doom, Frodo, then, makes Sam a part of his family by living in Bag End together with Sam's new family, which allows Frodo to pass the estate to Sam, a brother of sorts.

The apparent problem with my argument for a unified political perspective is, no doubt, that Lewis claims outright, "I am a democrat . . . ," and Tolkien abrogates, "I am *not* a 'democrat' . . ." (Lewis, "Equality" 17; Tolkien, *Letters* 246). If we go no further than these words, then, certainly, they are at a disagreement, and my argument is false; however, as we have already discussed, words such as *democrat* have lost or changed meaning. We must go further than the label and onward to the purpose. Tolkien writes that he is not a democrat because the politics attempt to standardize humility and equality, corrupting them from their spiritual origins; as a result, the nation sees pride instead of humility, superiority instead of equality "till some Orc gets hold of a ring of power—and then we get and are getting slavery" (*Letters* 246). He felt that humanity, without any superior being, would corrupt everything: from individual to culture to environment (Zaleski and Zaleski 213). The problem, for Tolkien, is the loss of meaning in the words by transferring them from their spiritual origin to political theory and application. The problem is that, instead of humility and equality, corruptions such as pride, power, and slavery reign. Lewis, likewise, sees a problem with political implementation of these concepts because of the Fall. The commercialization of democracy, grounded in Rousseau, explains that each person deserves a voice in government; Lewis's support of democracy is for the opposite reason, for humanity is so far fallen that all of humanity cannot be trusted without having power checked by others ("Equality" 17). His argument begins to sound strikingly like MacDonald, Chesterton, and Tolkien the further he goes, claiming that legal and economic equality should be understood as medicine to help remedy the Fall but should not be something "which hates all superiority," a mindset which he calls "the special disease of democracy, as cruelty and servility are the special diseases of privileged societies. It will kill us all if it grows unchecked" ("Equality" 17–18; "Democratic Education" 33). As Meilaender observes, Lewis appears to disagree with flat equality (individuals have equal worth) because he does not want individuals to be compared to one another, and he does not agree with equity (individuals should be treated as if everyone has equal merit and ability—as identicals) (77–78). Lewis claims that flat equality is only a concept of society and is not absolute unless used in mathematics. As a social concept, equality is for politics and economics, not for description of mental capability ("Democratic Education" 34). Political equality, however, is necessary because humans cannot be trusted to have power over one another, but we should realize that it is only a social and political function (Meilaender 83–84). As Chesterton claimed, this function of democracy is to realize what is fair in "the essential things" of humanity held in common, not in difference (*Orthodoxy* 39).

One might quickly jump to the assumption that these authors, in asserting equality in what is common to humanity, favored socialism as a political orientation; on the contrary, each of them spoke against socialism. Chesterton viewed socialism the same as imperialism, "and I was strengthened and deepened in my detestation of both of them" (*Autobiog-*

raphy 286). Chesterton summarizes his view of socialism via the thesis of Hillaire Belloc's *The Servile State:* that socialism leads not to socialism but to slavery (*Autobiography* 289). While Lewis may have been against an economy dependent on buying and selling, luxury and the desire for luxury, and large factories, as Meilaender recognizes, each individual needs to accept a certain level of joyous, noble, and loyal obedience to government, along with an embrace of individual inequalities ("Equality" 18–19). Hence, he argues for a legal democracy but favors the ceremonial monarchy, the former safeguarding against power plays and the latter satisfying human nature's need for inequality (20). In agreement with Lewis and Chesterton, Tolkien was as much an anarchist as a monarchist, for the "abolition of control not whiskered men with bombs" appealed as much to him as an "'unconstitutional' monarchy" (Kreeft 164; Tolkien, *Letters* 63). He argued that rarely is one fit to lead a country constitutionally via monarchy, nor should the government have a capital *G* because it is "an abstract noun meaning the art and process of governing," not a "Theyocracy" of what they—whoever "they" is—wants (Tolkien, *Letters* 63–64). We return, cyclically, to what MacDonald models in his fairytales: a king, a country, and a people who go about their lives with obedience to royalty but higher obedience to the divine.

Lewis would argue that someone sits on the throne to satisfy the need for inequality, for without a crown, culture will idolize the wrong forms of inequality. People will, instead, honor the wealthy, athletic and film stars, or even criminals: "For spiritual nature, like bodily nature, will be served; deny it food and it will gobble poison" (Lewis, "Equality" 20). Active government, however, to these authors, means the facilitation of rights for all people to be who they are. The focus of government comes back to the qualities of human nature. When an understanding of the qualities of human nature is lost, so is the focus of government. But, that is the problem of what happened in the transition from the Romantic to the Victorian to the Modern era: humanism was traded for empiricism. Chesterton summarizes the movement in terms of the change in the word *liberal,* which should mean "freethinking"; unfortunately, *liberal* no longer means "a man who thinks for himself" (*Orthodoxy* 118). Not even a decade into the twentieth century, Chesterton observed what was happening to liberal thought: a liberal thinker "means a man who, having thought for himself, has come to one particular class of conclusions, the material origin of phenomena, the impossibility of miracles, the improbability of personal immortality and so on. And none of these ideas are particularly liberal. Nay, indeed almost all these ideas are definitely illiberal" (118).

THE LOSS OF HUMANITY

The dialectic between liberal and illiberal thinking comes to its bottleneck with materialist and mystic perspectives. The materialist view embraces science as the basis for all knowledge because modern science is supposed to rely upon empirical data. Duriez clarifies: "[Lewis and Tolkien] were not against science or scientists, but the cult of science, found in modernism, and its tendency to monopolize knowledge, denying alternative approaches to knowledge through the arts, religion, and ordinary human wisdom" (*Tolkien and C. S. Lewis* 107). To these authors, a solely scientific perspective is the illiberal view of thinking because of its narrowness in allowing, supposedly, only the empirical. Mysticism, on the other hand, allows for both empirical and metaphysical dimensions: "A mystical mind is one which, having perceived that the highest expression of which the truth admits, lies in the symbolism of nature and the human customs that result from human necessities, prosecutes thought about truth so embodied by dealing with the symbols themselves after logical forms. This is the highest mode of conveying the deepest truth . . ." (MacDonald, *Unspoken Sermons* 67). The mystic not only accepts the physical but also examines the physical as symbolic of the metaphysical, much like these authors' evaluation of language and literature—something lay beyond the initial presentation. Where science has presented fact about the physical, the imagination allows one to take those laws and move beyond them ("The Imagination" 2). The scientific mind establishes boundaries under the label *law*, a term which is avoided in the mystic's mind (Chesterton, *Orthodoxy* 44). The mystic must be allowed to think freely without human-made boundaries created by the observation of repetitions or, inversely, scarce occurrence. Appearances in the physical world may reveal knowledge, but wisdom is in the thought process, which, to the mystic, should not be limited to data alone. Denethor, for instance, appears more like a wizard than Gandalf due to his beauty, stateliness, power, and age, but Pippin recognized by a sixth sense that Gandalf's power, majesty, and wisdom were deeper than those of Denethor (*The Return* 741). Denethor recognizes Gandalf's wisdom but declares that Gandalf does not have it all (795). Denethor prefers to "sit here in my tower and think"—Tolkien's mockery, no doubt, of the ivory tower of learning—but, although the knowledge "he obtained was, doubtless, often of service to him," it brought him to despair and "overthrew his mind" (800, 838). Gandalf asserts that, when Denethor was wise, the steward would not have thought to challenge Sauron, but his heightened knowledge and according despair occurred when "his wisdom failed" (838).

The palantír was the source of knowledge and knowledge alone, like scientific empiricism; wisdom, which allows one to think, like a mystic, outside of what is known, was lacking in his use of knowledge. From what he knew from the palantír, Denethor saw the rising darkness of Mordor and Sauron, the loss of Osgiliath, and the attack on Gondor: the sum of the equation, in his mind, being death. This trend of knowledge versus wisdom reappears often in Eä, from the repeated separation of elves and humans in *The Silmarillion* to the Númenorians who "in high cold towers asked questions of the stars" until they fall to Saruman's belief that knowledge is power (*The Fellowship* 252–53; *The Two Towers* 565, 663). Tolkien posits that knowledge is insufficient on its own; wisdom is required to interpret and apply knowledge effectively and justly. In the same way, empiricism, which sees facts without wisdom, will misapply knowledge. The human conquest over nature, according to Lewis in *The Abolition of Man,* is an expression used to describe applied science (718). The irony, however, is that the final part of the conquest can only result in the conquest of humanity by eugenics, genetic design of babies, education and propaganda of applied psychology; human nature will be human no more because it will have been conquered by an idea of what human nature should be—not what it naturally is (720). By neglecting the wisdom to consider and apply knowledge ethically—for knowledge alone ignores ethics—humanity acts self-destructively. Like Denethor, we step into the fires of our doom. Levi-Strauss is a theorist in favor of human conquest over nature: "We are able, through scientific thinking, to achieve mastery over nature . . . while, of course, myth is unsuccessful in giving man more material power over the environment. However, it gives man, very importantly, the illusion that he can understand the universe and that he *does* understand the universe. It is, of course, only an illusion" (17). The mystic's belief and use of myth—whether religious or storial—is both "primitive" and "inferior," according to Levi-Strauss, for they attempt to explain the world without complete understanding (17). Chesterton declares that such a desire to have a complete explanation is characteristic of a madman:

The madman is not the man who has lost his reason.

    The madman is the man who has lost everything except his reason. The madman's explanation of a thing is always complete, and often in a purely rational sense satisfactory. Or, to speak more strictly, the insane explanation, if not conclusive, is at least unanswerable; If a man says (for instance) that men have a conspiracy against him, you cannot dispute it except by saying that all the men deny that they are conspirators; which is exactly what conspirators would do. (*Orthodoxy* 11)

The madman cannot be reasoned with because his reason is based on knowledge alone. Even for someone to declare that he is Jesus Christ cannot be refuted by saying "that the world denies his divinity; for the world denied Christ's" (12).[8] In the same vein, with Jesus's miracles, like the feeding of the five thousand, MacDonald recognizes that such events appear as "pure nonsense" to the scientific mind—belonging, fittingly, to the "region of fancy"—but MacDonald believes a time will come when "a higher reason, a loftier science" will be realized in the miracles of Christ (*Unspoken Sermons* 93). MacDonald believes that, although humanity cannot now understand the miracles, at some point, it will. For now, they need only to be mystical—revelatory of God's work in the world. The former chemistry and natural philosophy student's claim is based on his reading of factual events, for it was not the philosophers or the scientists who first posited the existence of things out of the dimension of time but the theologians (Lewis, *Mere Christianity* 138).[9] The complete explanation is what the empiricist pursues, but, at a singular juncture in time, not all explanations can be complete. The mystery, for these authors, therefore, is what is revelatory of the metaphysical.

    The term *liminality*, used by Philip Ellis Wheelwright, effectively characterizes the juxtaposition of knowledge and wisdom, empiricism and mysticism. The existence of humanity is liminal in that science can describe the "thinglike," physical characteristics of humanity; however, the whole human character cannot be reduced to empirical understanding, which is why a true science of humanity is impossible (18–19).[10] Lewis suggests that, in order to declare exactly how the human mind works, reason is necessary; without admitting that human reason is beyond biology, no knowledge, then, is possibly true (*Miracles* 313). To support his claim, Lewis cites an antagonist of his, Prof. J. B. S. Haldane, from his text *Possible Worlds,* in support of Lewis's argument: "If my mental processes are determined wholly by the motions of atoms in my brain, I have no reason to suppose that my beliefs are true . . . and hence I have no reason for supposing my brain to be composed of atoms" (qtd. in *Miracles* 314). Hence, the theories of science—no more founded on fact than mystical belief—turn out to be nothing more than fiction of the fairytale sort. It is no surprise, then, that Chesterton claims in his *Autobiography,* "It was the same scientific uncle who told me various fairy-tales of science, which I regret to say that I believed much less than the fairy-tales of fairy-land" (109).

Consequentially, though, each of the authors had intellectual antagonists with their theories—MacDonald versus organized, orthodox Christianity; Chesterton versus H. G. Wells and George Bernard Shaw; Lewis versus Haldane (among many others); and Tolkien versus those who were less purist in myth and philology. One particular theory, evolutionary theory, stands out as the most disputatious. The biological theory of adaptation has some foundation, which Lewis admits no Christian need quarrel with, but what he refers to as *Developmentalism*[11] is a view of reality which views all life as a progression. For modern humanity, illogical developments are easily accepted: an ordered universe which spawned from nothing, an ability to reason which arose from natural instinct, a life which came from inanimate matter, a civilization which developed from savagery, and a system of virtue which evolved from bestiality[12] ("Modern Man and His Categories of Thought" 63); however, analogies like the oak from the acorn or the human from the spermatozoon to human from beast are false and refute the Christian understanding of Creation and Fall (64)—two important characteristics of humanity aforementioned in Chapter 2. Additionally, evolutionary theory lacks the factual basis which empiricism claims to have over mysticisms like Christianity. Chesterton, accordingly, wrote *The Everlasting Man* in part to combat the "vague notion" of evolution (71). Because science devalues the Creation story for the absence of empirical evidence, Chesterton argues that the evolutionary theorists are guilty of the same problem in their theory. The scientific myth lacks evidence that humanity ever evolved—slowly, naturally, or otherwise (38). Humanity does not demonstrate its likeness to other creatures. The premise of evolution, rather, seems to rely more upon a human desire to have order, sequence, process, or development in a wondrous world around humanity. Chesterton proposes, however, that humanity can only be accepted on grounds that it is a mystery and that it is an animal only if it is an extraordinary animal. Albeit once process, sequence, and development enter into the discussion, the wonder, mystery, and extraordinary disappear, as humanity becomes another ordinary object (39). Humans, on the contrary, are superior from whatever perspective the race is viewed—as fact or as animal; if one establishes a process of evolution from animals to humans, then the uniqueness of humans is entirely lost by devising a miraculous and unbelievable process of beginning and development, for humans are only another link in the chain of evolution and, therefore, nothing special. The problem is the theory of progress (developmentalism), not the idea that humans are animals. The theory devalues humanity, denying "any particular sanctity about this particular two-legged being. . . . In other words, Science attacks that thing which I have called the 'corner stone of Christianity'—the sacredness of the ordinary man, that the ordinary man is a person to be reverenced" ("Preachers from the Pew—'Vox Populi, Vox Dei'"). In the Platonic cave, the evolutionist is attempting to discover the universe by examining the shadows "because he cannot see the primary significance of the whole" (*Everlasting Man* 34). Science attempts to find certainty by escaping belief as well as disbelief through the accumulation of knowledge via evidence—ironically, with evidence less certifying than the evidence which leads a person to have an opinion about her friends (Lewis, "On Obstinacy in Belief" 526, 528).

Tolkien, in his usual way, rarely tackled ideas directly. In fact, one of the few places where he forcefully refutes developmentalism is in his poem to Lewis, "Mythopoeia": "I will not walk with your progressive apes, / erect and sapient. Before them gapes the dark abyss to which their progress tends—/ if by God's mercy progress ever ends, and does not ceaselessly revolve the same / unfruitful course with changing of a name" (89). Tolkien refuses to submit to the scientific acts of categorizing and labeling—including humans as "progressive apes"—and of calling a theory of evolution "fact," for this scientific process leads to the "dark abyss" of fruitless, neverending naming of ceaseless "progress." Rather, for Tolkien, the wonder of the world is in its creation, not in its classification, which is why he chose trees; they are easy to classify but innumerable (C. Tolkien, Preface to *Tree and Leaf* viii). To unpack this point, it is necessary to cite a scriptural passage critical to Tolkien's view of humanity. In Genesis 1.26–30, God creates humanity in His image, giving them dominion over nature, not as an evolved form of nature. In particular, Genesis 1.27 states, "So God created humankind in his image, / in the image of God he created them; / male and female he created them" (NRSV). Creation, not categorization nor progress nor development nor evolution, is a key part of what makes a human, a human; insofar as a human is created, she is also created in God's image—a God who creates—so she must also create.[13] This progress from creator to created, who is also a creator, is the only progress that Tolkien sees in human creation.

He also wrote his ideas into Middle-earth where he advocates for creationism and rejects evolutionary theory. If Tolkien's belief in a true language where signifier and signified match completely or if Eru Ilúvatar's creation of Middle-earth in *The Silmarillion* by the word *Eä* are not mimetic enough of Genesis or John 1.1–5,[14] then Tolkien hints elsewhere, though not as effectively, of his embrace of the Christian story of Creation rather than evolution. Tom Bombadil is, like Adam, fatherless and the giver of names (Shippey, *The Road* 107). Similarly, Tolkien's meticulousness with dates alludes to another creationist point. Sauron is defeated on 25 March, which, in Anglo-Saxon belief, is the date of the Crucifixion, Annunciation, and the final day of God's Creation of the world—all hints by Tolkien of his embrace of the total Christian myth (200–201).

As MacDonald asserts, "For things as they are, not as science deals with them, are the revelation of God to his children" (*Unspoken Sermons* 464). All that is understood as developmentalism or progress are theoretical approaches to what *was* when humanity cannot recognize entirely what *is.* Humanity's attempts at science, says MacDonald, discover only small parts of the infinite science of God (464). *Evolution* simply means "automatic unrolling"; *progress,* "merely walking along a road—very likely the wrong road"; and *reform,* that something appears out of shape and needs to be shaped. Chesterton argues, however, "Progress should mean that we are always changing the world to suit the vision. Progress does mean (just now) that we are always changing the vision" (*Orthodoxy* 98). The vision has been lost because empiricism functions on knowledge without wisdom—without the mystical tendency to look beyond the facts. As Lewis posits in *English Literature in the Sixteenth Century Excluding Drama,* each new kind of learning seems to create a new kind of ignorance. Modern culture observes the decline of the humanities in favor of the sciences in the same way that humanism once overcame metaphysics. Humanity seems only to have a large enough attention span for one focus at a time (31).

CIVILIZATION AND MORALITY

One focus which seems to be driven out as a result of developmentalism is the focus of morality. Mysticisms such as Christianity draw clear lines between good and evil, human and bestial, but developmentalism sees good on a sliding scale because it is always changing, always evolving (Lewis, "Modern Man" 64). Lewis notes three common strands across all developed religions: the experience of the numinous, or awe; the acknowledgment of a morality; and, third, that the morality is under the control of the numinous power (*Problem of Pain* 553–57). These common strands elucidate a set of key principles of morality, which MacDonald, Chesterton, Tolkien, and Lewis hold in common. Christianity, furthermore, includes a fourth key strand: a historical moment in which the numinous power became human (558). Empiricist thought has sought to remove the unexplained, that which is unobservable via material means: the numinous. One can see, quite simply, that if the numinous power is not believed to exist, then all strands of morality break, for if morality is no longer in the control of the numinous, no morality need then be acknowledged because it does not originate from a source higher than humanity (therefore, made by an equally perfect or flawed human whose moral code could not be any better than another person's code), and Christianity's belief in a numinous being that became human could not have happened. As Tolkien asserts, good and evil, right and wrong depend not upon a particular situation but upon principles, values, and beliefs assigned by a judge; otherwise, the principles, values, and beliefs would not have meaning (*Letters* 242).[15] The true purpose of law and morality is to lead one to the numinous (MacDonald, *Unspoken Sermons* 130). Otherwise, Lewis asserts, no one would have any reason to prefer a morality of Christianity or civilization over the morality of Nazism or savagery (*Mere Christianity* 22). The one who says that no right or wrong exists, Lewis claims, will be the first to complain of the unfairness when a promise is broken to them (17).

True relativist morality, to these authors, is impossible. The Moral Law on a societal scale, what Lewis calls the *Tao* in *The Abolition of Man,* is sometimes disputed on grounds that each culture and time period has its own moral codes, but these civilizations never had a completely different morality (17). Hence, a Pacific island girl in the nineteenth century wearing little clothing may be as modest as a Victorian lady dressed and covered to the hilt because modesty is determined according to their societies;[16]

the words spoken by a woman in Shakespeare's time may, likewise, make a nineteenth-century woman sound devilish, but each culture has its set of standards of what is modest (83). The moral principles are unchanged even though the standards by which they are measured may be different. The *Tao* is always present, especially in that they have always agreed on a singular concept: selfishness is not an admirable quality (*Mere Christianity* 17). Individually, morals should guide human purpose in life so that talents are not misused nor others injured in the development of talents, but beyond the individual, posits Tolkien, is sacrificial love (*Letters* 399–400). While some use biological and rational values to attack the *Tao's* traditional values, ironically, the values used to attack it are drawn from the *Tao* (Lewis, *The Abolition* 712). Kreeft explains in literary terms, that civilization once believed in gods like Zeus, Jupiter, YHWH, and Christ and understood history as a part of a great story, pitying "damned souls like Macbeth and wrote cautionary tales about them, like Marlowe's *Dr. Faustus*"; insofar as civilizations valued the *Tao*, regardless of their religious orientation, modern Western civilization has turned to the inverse, "no longer on the outside of Macbeth, looking at him with pity and terror, but inside Macbeth's mind, looking out at a world as objectively meaningless as his, full of sound and fury, signifying nothing" (131).[17] Modern civilization has forgotten that, to be true to the *Tao*, one must recognize a value higher than human law and principle (MacDonald, *Unspoken Sermons* 130). Civilization has simply fragmented the *Tao* as it has done with virtues that reflect the *Tao*. New ideologies contain the *Tao*, even if in fragments removed from their contexts to be made moral principles; still, these fragments, whether isolated or placed out of context, represent traces of the *Tao* they are drawn from (Lewis, *The Abolition* 714). Lewis is arriving at the Structuralist/Deconstructionist understanding of binary oppositions—that all ideologies are defined in reference to the transcendental signified, the *Tao*. Hence, Lewis continues his argument in an a priori response to Derrida's arche-writing. In the poem "Re-adjustment," Lewis presents a concern that civilization has lost "the ability to connect words with meaning," according to Don W. King, who further writes, "Although Lewis never lived to encounter deconstruction as a literary theory, his poem anticipates its approach to language and the possibility (or impossibility) of meaning" (270). A linguistic theorist might believe he sees his own language objectively from the outside, dictating certain changes that need to be made to his native language; on the contrary, a poet who

understands his language well from the inside might advocate for altera-
tions in the language that are in the spirit of the language. The linguist
fails to recognize that his objectivity is compromised by his subjective
experience—his forestructure, to use a Reader-Oriented Criticism term.
The poet, on the other hand, admits his subjectivity and recognizes his
suggested changes as part of the same organism (714). Like the poet who
attempts to alter or create new language, the moralist must work from
within the already-existing moral language. Tolkien demonstrated this
concept effectively, in that his created languages of Eä are sourced from
various other languages, dead and living. Morality operates on the same
principle. One who acts against the *Tao* is still functioning in relation to
the *Tao*, similar to the one who acts in accordance with the *Tao*.

Chesterton asserts that society has torn Christ "into silly strips, la-
belled egoism and altruism" (*Orthodoxy* 37). If, as MacDonald asserts,
"The whole secret of progress is the doing of the thing we know," society
has not done what it has known: "The first thing in all progress is to leave
something behind; to follow him is to leave one's self behind. 'If any man
would come after me, let him deny himself'" (*Unspoken Sermons* 364, 403).
The egoist, Weston, says to the Oyarsa of Malacandra, that no morality
is as important as life, itself, for life has developed from its smallest form
to humanity and onward to civilization. Through Ransom's translation of
Weston's statements, evolutionary theory gave way to the loss of morality, of respect to elders, and, ultimately, of people feeling pity (Lewis, *Out
of the Silent Planet* 135). Something happened on Earth (Thulcandra) that
did not happen on Mars (Malacandra): the Fall was not entirely rectified
on Earth. The world of Mars had a Fall, but the planet's geography has,
since, been changed to create harmony among its people and service to the
God-character, Maleldil. On Earth, however, the Fall occurred; salvation
has been made possible through the death of Christ, but it is not built into
the planet's geography because the Lucifer Oyarsa, the Bent One, controls
Thulcandra. Human nature is different from the hnau of Mars, in that humanity has not chosen to correct itself as a whole. In *The Problem of Pain*,
Lewis writes that God could certainly have miraculously removed the first
sin in the Garden of Eden to negate the Fall, but the act would have been
pointless unless God intended to remove forever the sin of every situation
that would follow the first (589). Humanity, since its awareness of God and
self, has been given the opportunity to choose between the two: between
egoism and altruism in God. Since the Fall, each person experiences an

individual fall every day. Even when someone attempts, at the start of the day, to offer his day to God, he already makes it a shared day between him and God by the end of his first task; God is given only the parts of his day that he feels so inclined to share—for it really always was his own day (592). The Fall has created a ripple effect, in that morality has been fragmented through the process of history, and humanity has seen history as one of its own making—not of God's world. The progress MacDonald and Chesterton speak of has been not a progress of the life and growth in civilization but a progress of death. A cultural groupthink which no longer recognizes an absolute morality, the *Tao*, no longer has a *normal*; rather, society has placed, as its baseline for morality, minimal, practical, and Quixotic decency (Lewis, *The Problem* 583–84). Kindness has replaced the virtues that were grounded in selfless love (585). In "The Psychological Man," Chesterton argues that "Medieval men" took things and people for what they were really worth to avoid paying too little or too much; next came the Economic Man, whose selfish aims sought what would gain him the most profit, regardless of innate value, and profited on supply and demand; finally, the Psychological Man arose in the late nineteenth century, who realized he could make the supply make its own demands to the demand by studying the weaknesses of humanity: "The Economic Man was replaced by the Psychological Man; and the only thing against the latter is that he is very much less of a man" (2–3).

Egoism has increasingly stepped in to replace altruism, and even altruism is seen as a kindness rather than something grounded in the *Tao* with truly selfless motives. D. Williams notes the resistance that Chesterton, Lewis, and Tolkien held to reductionist philosophies such as Freud's psychoanalysis (sex), Marxism (economics), Behaviorism (conditioned response), and Nietzschean ethic (power) (19). The last of these philosophies was repeatedly targeted in their texts in how it disrupted morality not only of an individual but also of a culture. MacDonald asserts, "The whole system of the universe works upon this law—the driving of things upward towards the centre" (*Unspoken Sermons* 132); since the center, the numinous God and His *Tao*, have been removed from civilized morality, civilized morality has worked in the opposite direction—toward self as the source of morality. If "In God alone can man meet man" (133), Chesterton is right in noting the opposite direction of progress: "along the opposite or Nietzschean line of development—superman crushing superman in one tower of tyrants until the universe is smashed up for fun" (*Orthodoxy*

106). The Melkors, Saurons, and Sarumans, then, compete to dominate the wills of others. As Saruman pleads to Gandalf, "A new Power is rising. Against it the old allies and policies will not avail us at all. . . . As the Power grows, its proved friends will also grow; and the Wise, such as you and I, may with patience come at last to direct its courses, to control it" (Tolkien, *The Fellowship* 253). But these Nietzschean ethics can only be accepted if humanity discards traditional morality and throws away the idea of any value judgments (Lewis, *The Abolition* 715).

Chesterton criticizes Nietzsche for using metaphors to escape giving real answers: "He said, 'beyond good and evil,' because he had not the courage to say, 'more good than good and evil,' or, 'more evil than good and evil'" (*Orthodoxy* 97). Chesterton is getting at the assumption that whoever decides what is good must embody good; therefore, evil must be the opposite of the good being's goodness. Inversely, one could decide what is evil because the being embodies evil—though, that evil, then, would be that person's good. Either way, one cannot actually go beyond good and evil; they are inescapable binaries. Hence, "when he describes his hero," argues Chesterton, "he does not dare to say, 'the purer man,' or 'the happier man,' or 'the sadder man,' for all these are ideas; and ideas are alarming. He says 'the upper man,' or 'over man,' a physical metaphor from acrobats or alpine climbers" (97). In other words, Nietzsche avoids more concrete descriptions in favor of abstract, theoretical descriptions. For this reason, Chesterton faults him for not knowing what kind of a person he wants evolution to produce as the *übermensch*: "And if he does not know, certainly the ordinary evolutionists, who talk about things being 'higher,' do not know either" (97).[18] As a result, people like Nietzsche who attempt to shape humanity by controlling values—people whom Lewis terms *Conditioners*—try to replace the *Tao* with their values by inventing ideologies. Humanism is suddenly gone because humanity no longer has value. The invention of ideologies, the view of humans as lab specimens to experiment the ideologies, or the treatment of humanity as a means to obtain ideologies transforms even the language in which one discusses morality. Modern virtues are wrongly determined by how one integrates into the cultural ideology and how their work is not diligent but dynamic (*The Abolition* 727). As Théoden says to Saruman, the wizard is a liar who has no license to have power over another, to corrupt them, or to profit from them as he so desired (Tolkien, *The Two Towers* 566). Instead of self-control via the *Tao*, Conditioners seek laboratory-like control of the human specimen:

civilization (Lewis, *The Abolition* 727). Civilization ceases to be a group of people but becomes a matter of numbers, of objects and artifacts: "Man's final conquest has proved to be the abolition of man" (723).[19]

LOSS OF COMMUNITY: THE THEME OF SEPARATION

Although humanity may be on track to self-destruction by rejection of the *Tao* and the numinous that is behind it, human morality did not begin there. The *Tao* provides the moral music by which humanity should play by its instincts; that is, this Moral Law is the code which guides human actions in good conduct (Lewis, *Mere Christianity* 20–21). God's laws were established to create harmony, and anything which breaks the harmony becomes a damning act because it breaks the tune; a person's "will and desires [should] keep time and harmony with [God's] music" (MacDonald, *Unspoken Sermons* 17, 619). The problem with pride, says Lewis in a letter to his friend, Arthur Greeves, is that the instrument—the person—plays itself "because it thinks it knows the tune better than the musician" (qtd. in Green and Hooper 106),[20] not unlike Melkor who corrupted his music by his own thoughts, which created discord, disruption, despair, and faltering in the song (Tolkien, *Silmarillion* 16).

Such discord will often spread or ripple farther into the music, so that others lose focus on the music they were intended to perform (16). As Ilúvatar and the Ainur create music and simultaneously create the world, Melkor creates discord in both. What was once unified in its creation becomes separated. This theme of separation characterizes MacDonald, Chesterton, Lewis, and Tolkien's view of history and civilization. As Chesterton writes in *Orthodoxy*, "This principle that all creation and procreation is a breaking off is at least consistent through the cosmos as the evolutionary principle that all growth is a branching out. . . . All creation is separation" (70). Lewis believes that no evidence supports the belief that more than one civilization has ever existed in history because each civilization is arguably derived from the same source (*The Abolition* 731). Lewis likely adopted this view from Chesterton's *The Everlasting Man* in which he notes that the antiquated civilizations of China, Mexico, and South America seem to find their roots around the Mediterranean and disburse (76–81). As the original civilization disbursed, so did the *Tao*, its according fragmentation spreading into what each civilization recognizes as moral codes, mores, and taboos. In his ironic humor, Chesterton asserts that the modern world is not evil but far too good because "It is full of wild and wasted virtues" due to the shattering of what began as absolute morality (*Orthodoxy* 22). Both vices and virtues do damage as they wander alone, isolated from one another: truth without pity, pity without truth (22).

Lewis begins *The Great Divorce* by joking that, if Blake wrote *The Marriage of Heaven and Hell*, Lewis may have written of their divorce (465). Lewis extrapolates the blending of Heaven and Hell in the earthly realm. Among other characteristics—from the mundane to the violent to the disturbing—one general problem in Hell is the loss of community. People do not have any needs because they get what they want by imagining it; they constantly move because it does not cost them anything. Without an economic foundation to the culture, no one need live in community. Without the need for shops, no one need remain within close vicinity. Without a need for a house, no one need live where a builder lives. The simple lack of need and loss of scarcity inhibit any existence of a society in Lewis's Hell (473). Dependence on one another and altruistic action because of the *Tao* keeps civilization civil, but when people no longer need to work with one another, independence reaches an extreme; separation becomes the norm. As the unpublished poem, "The Sea-bell," describes, it was separation from others, a lack of communication that haunts Frodo during his last three years before going to Valinor (Flieger, *Splintered Light* 147–58).

Separation is, in fact, a constant theme in Tolkien's work. In the beginning is Eru, whom the elves name *Ilúvatar;* he first created the angelic beings known as the Ainur, who spawned from his thoughts (*Silmarillion* 15). Of the Valar come the Maiar, servants and helpers of the Valar (30). Of the Maiar, Sauron follows the evil service of Melkor to become a dark sorcerer—referred to as the Necromancer in *The Hobbit* (126). Aulë, the Vala of elemental earth, with the desire to create, raises the dwarves secretly (43); he is, however, forgiven for his actions like the biblical story of Abraham who, eager for a child, conceives with his wife's servant. Ilúvatar admits to Aulë that the offering of the dwarves will be accepted, though tension and strife will arise between the Children of Aulë adopted by Ilúvatar, the dwarves, and the Children of Ilúvatar, humans and elves (*Silmarillion* 44).[21] The dwarves are, then, put into sleep until after the Firstborn, the elves, are born. After the elves are created, seizing an opportunity, Melkor tricks the elves into fearing the good Valar, and as a result, they become divided: some (the Eldar) desiring and going to the protection of the Valar in Valinor while others ignore the summons and remain throughout Middle-earth (*Silmarillion* 52)—the Avari who became the Moriquendi, or elves of darkness (309). Later, the treason of Feänor and the creation of the Silmarils further separates the Eldar elves, and division occurs again with the first murder—that of Finwë, King of the Noldor Elves (79). The Fall, thus, leads to elves killing other elves (*Letters* 148) and disharmony amidst the Firstborn.

When humans are born, then, they grow and expand as the number of elves diminish (151), for while the elves are the Firstborn of Ilúvatar, the humans are the Followers (*Silmarillion* 18); eventually, time brings about the Dominion of Humans and the fading of the elves (20)—the time of *The Lord of the Rings*. Indeed, after victory over Sauron, Gandalf explains to Aragorn, Middle-earth is entrusted to the Dominion of Humans, for the elves are departing into the West. The Third Age ended with the destruction of Sauron and his ring. Gandalf, accordingly, must depart, for his purpose was to oppose Sauron (*The Return* 950). Tolkien, like MacDonald, Lewis, and Chesterton, highlights the significance of humans over all other creatures: they are the focus of the entire Middle-earth saga as the Followers. The story of Middle-earth to the point of humanity's dominion has been the preparation, and the stories to follow are the crescendo to Ilúvatar's creation chorus. The humans have simply to decide whether or not to sing and play along.

A civilization rises which may temporarily improve living conditions, but all civilizations pass away, despite the wounds inflicted upon humanity during their existence that likely outweigh any aid they provided to help humanity's natural strife (Lewis, *The Problem* 552). It is not civilization but community that is important. Meilaender notes that community is one of the magical aspects of Narnia because of the various creatures who work and live together (45–46). Living conditions are bound to improve when community is doing what community—i.e., living in communion—is supposed to do. It is no wonder that these authors, with their emphasis on community, embraced the Christian faith. If the Fall is something that is accepted around the world, then Chesterton is right in claiming that religion turns on "the question of whether a man who was born upside down can tell when he comes right way up" (*Orthodoxy* 151). Christianity is not about making do with the human condition but about recognizing that "the normal itself is an abnormality. That is the inmost philosophy of the Fall" (151). Christianity sets its standards beyond what is to what should be; not to a metaphor about being beyond good and evil but about being good and not evil; and, instead of infinite separation, focusing on a return to unity. If the *Weltanschauung* relies on a singular principle which clarifies one's entire worldview, then Christianity is the overarching principle which originates and unites their worldviews, practiced in their mythopoeia.

5

The Overarching Hypothesis

Four men stand atop the Great Tower of Elfland. The Great Tower happens to be the tallest tower in all the land, and one can see all of Elfland from this single place. These four men are very different—for it is a human quality to be individual, made up of different tastes and opinions—but their view of the world is the same because they have the same foundation, the same structure, on which to stand. The four men, MacDonald, Chesterton, Lewis, and Tolkien, each has his own elements of individuality, but as we have shown in the previous chapters, their views are largely alike. Since we have clarified their unified *Weltanschauung* on literature, criticism, humanity, the journey, and civilization, it is now time to expound on the Great Tower on which they all stand: their Christian mythopoeia. Some scholars, no doubt, will contest Christianity as the unifying principle of their worldview. Each author had baggage, of sorts, that he carried with him in regard to his opinions about the Great Tower of Christian Mythopoeia. No one can dispute that their views on purgatory, sacraments, and other such doctrinal points differed to at least some degree;[1] however, what can agreeably be called *mere Christianity*—as Lewis describes like others before him—and their mythopoeic stance on it are what unify these authors' *Weltanschauung*. As Lewis declared in *Mere Christianity*, Christianity was itself ages before he was born, and it does not matter whether he likes what it is or not (6).[2]

In MacDonald, Chesterton found the mystical Tower of Christian Mythopoeia he needed. In Yeats, he found only "of the mixed and vague thing," which was unsatisfactory because "True Mysticism will have nothing to do with vagueness. . . . True Mysticism is entirely concerned with absolute things; not with twilight, but with the sacred black darkness and the sacred white sun" ("George Macdonald [sic]" 10). Chesterton would partly reform this view in *Orthodoxy,* where he found the need for paradox, which "permitted the twilight" in spite of contradictions like light and dark (20). It is in this twilight of paradox that Tolkien's mythopoeia provides "splintered fragments of the true light" and that Lewis borrows in *Miracles* when he references the Sun, which helps one "to see everything else" (Carpenter, *J. R. R. Tolkien: A Biography* 151; Lewis, *Miracles* 400). The foundation of their worldview begins with the greatest of myths because it contains "the Grand Miracle" of God's Incarnation and "the Great Eucatastrophe" of his death (Lewis, *Miracles* 398; Tolkien, "On Fairy-Stories" 156). As Peter Shakel remarks of *Till We Have Faces,* even the tale of Cupid and Psyche can be used to show how the pagan myth anticipates the sacrifice of Christ (84). Myth must grasp at something greater—something beyond the tale itself to some truth or purpose beyond the leaves of the text. Perhaps for this reason, in *The Everlasting Man,* Chesterton perceives the birth of Christ as an event comprised of three parts: myth, philosophical position, and purpose (182–83). Structured according to these parts, this chapter will present the stories[3] of the Great Tower of Elfland by dissecting MacDonald, Chesterton, Lewis, and Tolkien's overarching hypothesis: Christian mythopoeia.

Christian mythopoeia, first, demands myth: stories that ask and answer the why and the how of the universe. Myth uses knowledge to create theories and symbols, in the same vein of creativity as the imagination. Because these authors ground their mythopoeia in the same myth of Christianity, certain symbols are shared such as light and dark, joyful laughter and mockery, and humanity's liminal place in the universe's hierarchy, their presence in Primary and Secondary Worlds, and an individual's own journey. The shared myth colors the *Weltanschauung* of these authors in such a way that it identifies these symbols of their philosophical position, the second general category. The myth and symbols are, here, rooted in some of the essential characteristics of God, including His mysteriousness, goodness, transcendence, and lovingness—and such characteristics affect the authors' views of language, literature, and humanity. Ultimately, the philosophical position leads to the third and final section: purpose. Based upon their Christian beliefs, these authors find their purpose in being like God, and insofar as they must imitate, they must create. Part of their purpose, then, is to sub-create to reveal God in their work and to lead others to the myth they believe to be true. Hence, their views come to light about the nature of good literature and criticism, about a fallen world that is ever falling through history, and about the way in which one journeys to be nearer to or farther from God. But, to get to the purpose through their philosophical position, we must begin where they did, at the foundation of the tower, with myth.

MYTH

According to Chesterton, the belief in something beyond the known physical world in any faith begins with an instinct for myth, of both creator and perceiver. He notes the places of worship, the lands of the gods, the land of Elfland, and even the resurrection of the dead as symptoms of this instinct (*Everlasting Man* 182–83). Mythopoeic, or myth-making, writers engage in stories that inquire about something beyond the physical world. As MacDonald writes, the Norman word *Trouvére*, or *Finder*, is the more appropriate term for the imagining poet, for she pursues things that are of God ("The Imagination" 19–20). Without interest in truth from God, the stories become plain fantasy. Frye claims that "learned and recondite writers whose work requires patient study are explicitly mythopoeic writers," and identifies writers such as Dante, Spencer, Hawthorne, Henry James, Joyce, Charles Williams, and Lewis (117). But these authors are not all in pursuit of the divine, as GMD, GKC, CSL, and JRRT believe is essential to true mythopoeia, for even paganism "is an attempt to reach the divine reality through the imagination alone" (Chesterton, *Everlasting Man* 110). Chesterton, in tracing the Christian myth, asserts that the naturalistic, evolutionary mindset ignores the fact that "every seed comes from a tree, or from something larger than itself"; that is, "mythology grows more and more complicated, and the very complication suggests that at the beginning it was more simple" (87, 92). Tolkien rightly defines the realm of this world, of a Fallen world, as the world under the Sun, where God is lost in symbols and partial reflections (*Letters* 148). Jupiter, Pan, and Apollo, thus, contain elements of God, but the Christian God's elements fractured into these myths "meant that ancient light of simplicity, that had a single source like the sun, finally fades away in a dazzle of conflicting lights and colours. God is really sacrificed to the Gods; in a very literal sense of the flippant phrase, they have been too many for him" (Chesterton, *Everlasting Man* 94). That is, the truth of God is fractured into myths around the world, and His morality is disbursed as virtues wandering alone—mercy without justice, fortitude without healthy fear, love without temperance. Purtill explains three types of myth: original, or religious;[4] literary myth, using mythic characters and heroes solely for literary purpose; and philosophical myth, conveying philosophical ideas via allegory and metaphor (2–3). Purtill notes the similarity in Chesterton and Tolkien's view of myth—that original myths would be difficult to create today and that pre-Christian original myths appear to be only for aesthetic purposes (6–7), though it is clear that Chesterton and Tolkien also felt most, if not all myths, also point to fragments of divine truth. The original mythmakers—Homer and Socrates, for instance—aimed not only to tell a story but also to honor the gods and heroes and to inspire their listeners (1). Tolkien's work, according to Purtill, was an attempt to create literary myth which reaches toward original myth—a pursuit which I believe MacDonald, Chesterton, and Lewis also shared (3).[5] They have tried to bring myth and imagination back to a search for divine truth and, in the tradition of original myth-makers, to inspire their listeners to do the same.

Literary and philosophical myth that reaches toward original myth to reveal divine truth is the understanding of *mythopoeia*, which will henceforth be applied to the word. It has a rich tradition, from the ancients (many of whom created original as well as philosophical myths) to *Beowulf,* Dante to Milton, Blake to Hawthorne. The recent tradition finds roots in Coleridge, Sir Philip Sydney, John Dryden, and Percy Bysshe Shelley, in their defenses of poetry and the poetic imagination. Coleridge writes in *Biographia Literaria* that the Primary Imagination, which is the "prime agent of all human perception," is creation in the same way as "the infinite I AM" (190). Literary theorists seem to ignore the latter part of the Primary Imagination, but it is essential to what Coleridge is claiming about mythopoeia because the Secondary Imagination is humanity's attempt to imagine and create like God: "in the *kind* of its agency, and differing only in *degree*, and in the *mode* of its operation" (190). It "struggles to idealize and unify" because it is not perfect in the way that God's Creation, observed in the Primary Imagination, is perfect (190). "To inquire into what God has made is the main function of the imagination," MacDonald concurs, for "It is, therefore, that faculty in man which is likest to the prime operation of the power of God, and has, therefore, been called the *creative* faculty, and its exercise *creation*" ("The

Imagination" 2). Literary myth, as seen by MacDonald, Chesterton, Lewis, and Tolkien, combines Coleridge's Fancy and the Secondary Imagination in order to be original like God's Primary Imagination.[6] "The imagination of man," writes MacDonald, "is made in the image of the imagination of God" ("The Imagination" 3). As Coleridge asserts, the Secondary Imagination "dissolves, diffuses, dissipates, in order to recreate: or where this process is rendered impossible, yet still at all events it struggles to idealize and to unify" (190). Mythopoeia attempts to reach truth, which is a "verb active" (169); by applying this knowledge, one's self-consciousness is able to be aware of a "higher form of being" (169, 174). Dryden claims that the "original rule" of poetry was to study nature and imitate it, but by describing "things which really exist not," such as fairies, "we have notions of things above us, by describing them like other beings more within our knowledge" (111, 115). Shelley, in turn, claims that the Secondary, poetic world, then, influences the reader's understanding of the Primary World: "A poet participates in the eternal, the infinite, and the one" (xviii, 6). Sydney recalls that the vate, or Roman poet, was a "diviner, foreseer, or prophet," as shown by combination words *vaticinium* and *vaticinari* (5). Perhaps this is the reason why Sydney claims that the poet excels above others because he does not simply use or categorize nature, but he creates "another nature" (7). A Secondary World is created in mythopoeia, which is intended to help the author and the reader to enter into a higher truth, what Milbank calls "theurgic theology": "practical in taking the reader into an intuition of being through the enchanted experience of art" (166).

Tolkien's arguments on myth epitomize his, Lewis, Chesterton, and MacDonald's literary practices. For Tolkien, the relation of art and reality includes three key parts: "Fall, Mortality, and the Machine" (*Letters* 145). The Fall occurs in several different ways, for every human story must not only include a Fall but also be about a Fall (145, 147). Such a cosmogony includes the angelic Fall of Lucifer in the Primary World and the Falls of Melkor, elves, and humans (though offstage) in Middle-earth (147). The Fall, while traceable to a moment, is continuous throughout human history. As Lewis points out in *The Problem of Pain*, humanity is always drawing away from God at the center of the universe, as if humans resist gravity toward God in effort to have a world centered on themselves—like some sort of Socratic myth (593).[7] Myth, then, must have a Fall in which the divine and the un-divine separate. It is the first of the historical separations, when such a thing as *goodness* in association with the divinity comes into contact with an opposition—a falling away from it. Mortality, then, is the living of that Fall. Tolkien asserts that Mortality affects the sub-creative part of the person—included in what Lewis calls the *Zoe*—which is in strife with humanity's biological makeup, or the *Bios* (*Letters* 145). In I Corinthians 15.22, Paul writes that humanity dies in Adam—human *Bios*—but lives in Christ—the *Zoe*. Death, however, is not a punishment for the Fall but an innate part of the *Bios* that cannot be escaped—nor should such escape be pursued, since death is natural and a gift to humans from God (Tolkien, *Letters* 205). Hence, MacDonald's evil Lilith preys on others to maintain life. In her story as well as Vane and others', *Lilith* is, as Attebery asserts, "a story of fall and redemption" (16), a story of Mortality. Lewis believes, like Paul, that this dichotomy between Adam's death-in-humanity/life-in-Christ signifies the two poles of the spectrum of mortality—the two directions in which a person moves with every decision made (*The Problem* 599). Mortality, then, is the journey from the Fall to death in the *Bios* or life via God's *Zoe*. From their view, human Mortality should include sub-creation, an attempt to create as the divine created. Within the sub-creative text, then, is what Tolkien refers to as the *Machine*. By *Machine*, Tolkien means any device other than one's internal ability, whether something as elvish as art or as corruptive and dominating as the One Ring (*Letters* 145–46). Art is good machinery for which Tolkien uses the word *magic*, but other kinds of machinery are used to dominate wills—for which Tolkien typically uses the word *Machine*. Contrary to art, which creates a Secondary World, machinery carries "tragedy and despair" in its attempt to further desire and power in the world (87). Neither Tolkien nor Lewis liked cars, and they disliked the industrialization going up around them in Oxford.[8] MacDonald and Chesterton both faulted civilized societies—with their machinery—for missing the adventure and spiritual discovery available in the world around them.

These values of mythopoeia are obviously applicable to the Primary World. As Chesterton said of the sane person, she has one foot on Earth and the other in fairyland (*Orthodoxy* 20). Collins uses the term *liminality* to describe the balancing act between the real and the fantastic in *Lilith*. *Liminality* is derived from the Latin *limen*, referring to a threshold or portal between contexts (8). Such liminality has been present in myth since the beginning when, as Chesterton asserts, mythopoeists sought God through stories and philosophy (*Everlasting Man* 111). Shippey asserts, "Tolkien would not let 'fantasy' mean either the one (rational) or the other (mystic) activity, but kept hinting it was both" (*The Road* 50). As Noel suggests, Tolkien painstakingly maintained a correct calendar of events, seasons, and astronomical arrangements throughout *The Lord of the Rings* (36), but the world was, certainly, a fantastic world. The fantastic and real liminality are joined even in chronology at points, for May Day, the first of the month, known as Celtic Cétsamain or Beltane, was a day of purification; in Middle-earth, Tolkien placed Aragorn's coronation and Samwise's marriage to Rose on this day. Tolkien's concern for chronological accuracy and special dates is reminiscent of the pagan Celtic focus on holidays (38–39). Insofar as Tolkien drew connections between the Primary and Secondary Worlds, Shippey cites the common characteristics of hobbits to the English—from ancestry to founding tribes and names to even the geographical locations (*The Road* 102–03). The seeming divide between the rational and the mystical may be characterized in the way that Lewis describes miracles, a clear example of this juxtaposition: that is, from their philosophical approach, people take only what they expect to see from experiences. Experience, thus, means only what one interprets it to mean (*Miracles* 303). Lewis proceeds to characterize those believing only in the rational and natural as *naturalists* and those believing in something beyond the natural as *supernaturalists* (305).[9] The problem, Lewis asserts, is that a naturalist narrows the meaning of the word *nature* to two possible meanings: "everything," so "nothing else exists"; or only that which is perceived via physical sensation. In the former meaning, *nature* demands the possibility of something beyond measurability; in the latter, the emotions are already in the realm of the immeasurable because they are beyond sensation (306). MacDonald concurs, for emotions reflect the "primary meaning of the outer world" and, hence, are not a part of the outer world but of something beyond it ("The Imagination" 9). Lewis concludes that *nature* should be understood as that which happens spontaneously and unintentionally "of its own accord" (*Miracles* 306). Hence, the naturalist is unable to believe in free will—limited by his belief in nature's process alone. The supernaturalist, however, is granted the ability to see nature as well as that which is beyond—the *meta* of the physical. The liminality of mythopoeic literature for Tolkien, Lewis, Chesterton, and MacDonald rests on this central premise of their theological worldview: that, as supernaturalists, they assert a dimension beyond the physical, which exists both apart from and a part of physical, natural reality.[10] When Lewis discusses this philosophical concept, he demonstrates its relation to literature by way of Dickens, claiming that no seeming relationship appears between Mr. Pickwick of the *Pickwick Papers* to Mrs. Gamp in *Martin Chuzzlewit* unless one knows they are of the same author (309). Alcuin asks, "What has Ingeld to do with Christ?" Lewis seems to respond, "Their creator," for, while the former is physical (Lewis's *Bios*), the latter is miraculous, both *Bios* and *Zoe*. The former only has life because of the latter. As MacDonald claims of this liminality between physical and spiritual, "God is life, and the will-source of life" (*Unspoken Sermons* 299). And, according to Lewis, this interlocking of natures—natural and supernatural—is what composes a miracle (*Miracles* 309–10). Humans must decide not between mind/matter and soul/body dichotomies but reason/nature. It is not important in understanding miracles, says Lewis, that one determines where body ends and mind and spirit begin; rather, one must decide whether to accept the event through reason or to view the event, even a psychological occurrence, as mere material nature (323). The liminality of the miracle is between these two explanations, inside of them, and, at the same time, outside of them.

Their literary endeavors embody this liminality not only in content but also in character. In most of their fantasies, at least one character serves as what I will call the *elf-friend,* or the person who bridges the gap between Primary and Secondary Worlds. Lewis's space trilogy protagonist Elwin Ransom's first name translates to "elf-friend" or "Aelfwine" (Duriez, *Tolkien and C. S. Lewis* 106). He is the character who connects Earth with Mars and Venus. As Downing notes, Ransom is the Pendragon and the Head of Logres (England in Arthurian myth)—the Arthur figure of Christian and Celtic ideals (*Planets in Peril* 76). He joins myth and legend to known history. Tolkien, who Ransom is modeled after, has his own Aelfwine. As Flieger cites in *Green Suns,* Ælfwine in Tolkien's mythology was originally named Eriol, among other names such as Angol and Wæfre, meaning "one who dreams alone" and "restless, wandering," respectively (77). These names are given to someone who bridges the gap between Primary and Secondary Worlds—"neither wholly outside nor completely inside by in between, and thus qualifies as a true mediator" (76). MacDonald's Mr. Raven in *Lilith,* likewise, holds a dual identity. He is the Adam of the Primary World and the Adam of the Secondary World. While he creates such liminality for the reader, he also creates liminality for Mr. Vane, who needs a bridge between his Primary World and Secondary World within the text. The library becomes the first gateway by which Mr. Raven transports Vane to Elfland.[11] As Raeper notes, Vane "occupies two places at once" at the end of the story—in the library and in the House of Death: "He is always arriving, always waiting, always learning—just as the reader must go on pondering the meaning of myth and absorb it into his psyche" (382). The elf-friend functions liminally in the text and simultaneously generates liminality for the reader of the text, helping the reader to move between their own Primary and Secondary Worlds.

Sunday, in *The Man Who Was Thursday,* is perhaps the most elf-friend-ish of any character, as he represents the day of the week, the leader of order via the police, and the leader of disorder via the anarchist group. He takes each character in the story from common reality to the under-world of the anarchist and the undercover world of the police officer. Yet, while he represents all of these things in the text, he is characteristic of the Christian God. In the same way that God shows his back in the Old Testament to show that He was there—and Moses sees His face—Syme explains his view of Sunday: "I was suddenly possessed with the idea that the blind, blank back of his head really was his face—an awful, eyeless face staring at me: And I fancied that the figure running in front of me was re-ally a figure running backwards, and dancing as he ran" (169–70). When his back is turned, Sunday shows the chief-of-police side, condemning one to death and chaos. Ten minutes after Syme's realization of who Sunday is in the text (leader of both order and disorder), Sunday "put his head out of the cab and made a grimace like a gargoyle, [and] I knew that he was only like a father playing hide-and-seek with his children" (170). The grimacing face of Sunday, on the other hand, is the Sunday of the Council of Days, or, the Central Anarchist Council, who is "the peace of God" (180). It is no surprise, then, that like Christ who takes up the cup of suffering on the eve of his death, Sunday asks the Council of Days, "Can ye drink of the cup that I drink of?" (183) Sunday is the ultimate elf-friend of liminality, who con-nects characters in the story with the liminalities of their Secondary World and demonstrates the liminalities of the Primary World: the real with the fantastic, the ordered with the disordered, and the *Zoe* with the *Bios.*

As Sunday elicits in his liminality, mythopoeia's highest characteristic is that it is revelatory of the divine metanarrative. MacDonald's symbolism and imagination were clearly shaped by his theology, for his literature took on the opportunity to preach that he no longer held (Hein xvi; Reis10). His, at times, preachy voice, no doubt, discouraged some readers but encour-aged him to share what he believed to be the result of divine inspiration

(Greville MacDonald 33, 375). As D. Williams asserts, having a creator of the universe means that creator is, ultimately, the progenitor of all stories—the constructor of a metanarrative so adamantly denied by postmodernity. As a result, Tolkien and Chesterton, says D. Williams, can posit that the *imago Dei* is critical not only to humanity's creation but also to humanity's salvation in a climactic eucatastrophe of the world's metanarrative: the life, death, and resurrection of Jesus Christ (49). The liminality of the text to real life is evident in the journey one makes from life to death to what comes after, and each life is a part of a divine metanarrative—a story about all stories. Tolkien writes that *The Lord of the Rings* is about God's right to divine honor. The Eldar and Númenóreans both embraced the real God of the world and found worship of other gods as sinful; on the contrary, Sauron pursued a role as a god, and his servants viewed him as such (*Letters* 243). Shippey can draw such a connection between Primary and Secondary Worlds, small story to great story, in Tolkien's literature. Shippey reiterates Alcuin's "What has Ingeld to do with Christ?" only to respond, "Nothing. But Fróda had something to do with both. He was a hinge, a mediation, like *The Lord of the Rings* in its suspension between pagan myth and Christian truth" (*The Road* 208). Fróda, mentioned only in passing in *Beowulf*, is Ingeld's father, for whom Ingeld seeks vengeance against the Danish king; however, the Norse form of the word, *Fróthi*, means "the wise one," and, in myth, is believed to be a contemporary of Christ, in whose reign there were no murders, wars, thefts, or competition for power; unfortunately, this king is forgotten, and instead, his son, Ingeld, is the legacy who lives on—much like Frodo, whose journey was for peace but who receives little honor in his Shire home (208). Carpenter records Tolkien's words to Lewis that even flawed human myths have the ability to reveal "the eternal truth that is with God. Indeed only by myth-making, only by becoming a 'sub-creator' and inventing stories, can Man aspire to the state of perfection that he knew before the Fall" (*J. R. R. Tolkien: A Biography* 151). In "On Fairy-Stories," Tolkien mentions *spell* and *evangelium*, two words that Shippey elaborates upon Tolkien's likely reason for use. Greek *evangelion* (good news) became Old English *gód spell* (good story) and, eventually, modern-day *gospel*. In relation, *spell* meant "a story" or "a formula of power" like "a magic spell" (*The Road* 51).

Lewis reiterates this sentiment in "God in the Dock," where he notes that *evangelium* was a promise of healing to the spiritually sick (464). *Evangelium*'s vehicle is story, and Lewis did not hesitate to claim, as Tolkien did, that mythopoeia is one of the means by which humanity connects with its Creator: "If God chooses to be mythopoeic—and is not the sky itself a myth—shall we refuse to be *mythopathic?* For this is the marriage of heaven and earth: Perfect Myth, and Perfect Fact: claiming not only our love and our obedience, but also our wonder and delight, addressed to the savage, the child, and the poet in each one of us no less than to the moralist, the scholar, and the philosopher" ("Myth Became Fact" 344).

On 5 September 1931, Lewis told Greeves that he valued literature more and more for "expressing the great *myths*" (Green and Hooper 115), like that of the resurrection, which would stew on his mind for the next fourteen days until he met Tolkien and Dyson for their famous walk, which led eventually to Lewis's conversion. Of Lewis's view, Meilaender writes, "The story of creation, fall, incarnation, redemption, and *eschaton* [end of days] shapes the contours of the entire Christian life" (38). It is no surprise that Lewis's view of the Christian life, as outlined by Meilaender, mimics Tolkien's structure of the fairy-story and his requirements of mythopoeic literature: creation (fantasy in the fairy-story), fall (in both real and fantastic realms), mortality (with the chance of recovery via incarnation and redemption), and the machine (the magic which encourages escape and allows for consolation with *eschaton*). If "mythology is a *search*" and "has at least an imaginative outline of truth," according to Chesterton, then it is only right that humanity's finite imagination pushes humans toward contemplating the infinite in myth, "For the imagination deals with an image. And an image is in its nature a thing that has an outline and therefore a limit" (*Everlasting Man* 30–31, 113; *Autobiography* 111).[12] Thus, the imagination, via myth, helps one to understand how his finite narrative fits into the infinite metanarrative of the divine.

Philosophical Position

Myth, as we have mentioned, is a means by which one may discuss philosophy, which brings us to the next element of these authors' Great Tower. Chesterton asserts, "The second element is a philosophy *larger* than other philosophies. . . . It looks at the world through a hundred windows where the ancient stoic or the modern agnostic only looks through one" (*Everlasting Man* 183). The larger philosophy is, in their view, Christianity. The word *Christian*, as Lewis notes in *Mere Christianity*, should be used for those who accept the common doctrines of Christianity—the mere essentials Lewis outlines in the text. Unfortunately, asserts Lewis, the term has lost its concrete value like the word *gentleman,* which used to mean a man of privilege and property but currently is useless, holding only as much value as the speaker intends the word to have (9). In the roughly seventy years since Lewis first composed these words, the word *Christian* has changed little in its social understanding, except, perhaps, that it is more out of favor presently than in his time, but it has not changed in its meaning over the course of its existence. As Lewis admits, it is what it is whether he likes it or not (6). Essentially, *Christian* may be defined as one who accepts the common doctrines of believing in the triune God, birth and death of God incarnate in Jesus Christ, the importance of being in a community of fellow believers, and committing to follow the commands of Christ and the Church, as stated in the New Testament (e.g., discipleship and selfless service). MacDonald may have been a Protestant, but he believed in Purgatory more than many Catholics. Chesterton and Tolkien may have been staunchly Catholic, but they did not hesitate to call Protestants "Christian," as well. Lewis may have been brought up to distrust Catholics, but he, nevertheless, entrusted his theological maturity to some of their claims in Chesterton and Tolkien, among others. They all agree on the basic tenets of Christianity, and as that agreement is enough for them, it is enough for our discussion of a shared philosophical perspective.

Chesterton asserts that Christian philosophy allows one to look through many windows instead of the one window by which other philosophies see the world (*Everlasting Man* 183), but it is clear that they did not agree with or even tolerate philosophies contrary to their own. Religious and philosophical toleration is beneficial for Hell, Screwtape claims during his toast, for a movement of religious toleration aids in the decline of Christianity because the movement is geared not simply at toleration but additionally at furthering belief in other religions from atheism to paganism ("Screwtape Proposes a Toast" 289). Lack of toleration for these philosophies, however, does not mean that these four authors did not engage with other philosophies. One of those philosophies, discussed throughout chapters 2–4 of this text, is that of naturalism (positivism or materialism), for which H. G. Wells advocated. Lewis, when referring to Wells as a naturalist, targets the hypocrisy of Wells and other naturalists' misanthropy. Their evolutionary and materialist view uses words like *ought* and *better* to describe nature and change, but these words have no meaning without a transcendental signified to declare what should be or what is good. Humanity, therefore, is not important to naturalist philosophy: "My idea is that they do forget. That is their glory. Holding a philosophy which excludes humanity, they yet remain human" (*Miracles* 333). Such misanthropy is not far from the "pessimistic fancy" of Swift, as Chesterton calls it in *The Everlasting Man* (14). Chesterton openly debated Wells, so much so that *The Everlasting Man* was his response to Wells's naturalist outline of the history of the world (7). In such materialist views, comments Lewis, humanity sees only notes about a poem, but Christianity, along with the notes, views the actual poem (*Miracles* 418).

More specific to the materialist view is atheism. Atheism, says Chesterton, finds its strength in the "perpetual fall" of humanity and the universe around humanity and the belief that, if God existed, then He would have been a savior to the world. Furthermore, He would be alive, and if He were not alive, then they would have watched Him die (*Everlasting Man* 163). The seeming lack of Providence is enough evidence for the atheist to discard the mystery and replace it with reasonable explanation: that there is no God. But, Lewis asserts that, while the atheist is forced to admit that all religions are a mistake of humanity, the Christian has the freedom to believe that pieces of truth may exist in any of them (*Mere Christianity* 39). Chesterton furthers the statement, arguing that atheism removes the possibility of purpose in life (*Everlasting Man* 162). Ironically, while materialist and atheistic views focus on external life and experience, the problem they cannot tackle is that of why humans exist. This problem of existence is evident beyond philosophies, for dreams, doubts, and even suicide are proof of humanity's need to understand why it exists (138). MacDonald admits that, if God is nonexistent, then words like *purpose* and *reason* have no more meaning than *cause* or *catalyst* for an effect or reaction: "we are willed upon, not willing; reeds, flowering reeds, it may be, and pleasant to behold, but only reeds blown about the wind; not bad, but poor creatures" (*Unspoken Sermons* 116). It is God who binds the universe together and gives it purpose (428): "If you do not believe in a personal God the question: 'What is the purpose of life?' is unaskable and unanswerable" (Tolkien, *Letters* 400). Suddenly, without purpose, philosophy has few questions to ask and no reason to ask them, which is why "philosophy is generally left to the idle; and it is generally a very idle philosophy" (Chesterton, *Autobiography* 96).

Contra to these dominant philosophies, these authors chose Christianity, in part, because it answers the questions that the other philosophies cannot or will not answer. Chesterton found Christianity engaging due to the attacks various philosophies made: "It looked not so much as if Christianity was bad enough to include any vices, but rather as if any stick was good enough to beat Christianity with. What again could this astonishing thing be like which people were so anxious to contradict, that in doing so they did not mind contradicting themselves?" (*Orthodoxy* 81–82) In the paradoxical humor typical of Chesterton, he responds to Lenin's calling religion "the opium of the people" with "This profound remark will readily explain the sleepy submission, the supine placidity, the dull and drowsy obedience of the Irish people as compared with the wild revolutionary frenzy, the incessant insurrection and revolt, the bloody riots and endless street-battles of the English people" ("The Opium of the People" 1). Certainly, each of the authors arrived at their Christianity in different ways. Flieger claims that Tolkien's theology is "manifestly tougher and darker" and "less hopeful" than Lewis's, and while Lewis arrived at his faith logically, Tolkien's beliefs are based on experience (*Splintered Light* xviii). Nonetheless, these authors can have common reasons for having faith in the Christian God. The question of purpose in life, according to Tolkien, is not entirely a human or moral question but a question of the universal. The question of purpose might inquire about how one uses the length of life one has or about why someone was created and given life. If the first question has an answer, then it will be answered as a result of the second question being answered (*Letters* 399). "We have all forgotten what we really are," writes Chesterton, "All that we call common sense and rationality and practicality and positivism means that for certain dead levels of our life we forget that we have forgotten. All that we call spirit and art and ecstacy only means that for one awful instant we remember that we forget" (*Orthodoxy* 46). When one recalls, first, that humans were made in the image of God and intended to be like God, Tolkien's questions are answered, for the purpose is to be like God and, therefore, one's life ought to be used to that purpose: to discover and be like God, partly, as Chesterton suggests, via spirit, art, and ecstasy. Lewis's conversion, accordingly, was due mostly to recognizing that Christianity completed something that was present but unrecognized to the mind of humanity ("Religion Without Dogma?" 389). As Chesterton suggests, what art reaches toward is what Lewis believes Christianity attains. MacDonald affirms this view; the objects of the material world are "shapes and manifestations in lower kind of the things that are unseen" and serve only as distractions from what is truly important (*Unspoken Sermons* 200). On the other hand, Chesterton lists several observations about practical things in life—temperate drinking, something personal about the whole of the universe, and that goodness is a remnant of some earlier ruin—which, without considering Christian theology, led him to understand how practical Christianity is; it simply makes sense (*Orthodoxy* 57).

Christianity is not simply a religion in which ritual is regularly observed; beyond the essential doctrines of Christianity, MacDonald, Chesterton, Lewis, and Tolkien embrace Christianity's outline for a lifestyle grounded in the belief that there is a purpose to each life and that each person ought to live in the light of the good. As we discussed in the framework of the Fall, these authors posit that evil is goodness gone awry, and "A good corrupted is no longer a good" (MacDonald, *Unspoken Sermons* 90). It can even arise from good intentions, such as may be seen in Boromir and Denethor's desire to obtain the Ring for protection[13] because, in the end, all evil is a perversion of good nature (Kreeft 177; Gaarden, "Cosmic and Psychological Redemption in *Lilith*" 25; Lewis, *Mere Christianity* 45; Tolkien, *Letters* 146). Good is "a remnant to be stored and held sacred out of some primordial ruin" (Chesterton, *Orthodoxy* 57). It was Boethius who first establishes that evil is simply the absence or unappreciation of good, while, on the other hand, Western thought has often believed that evil is real and present, even at war with goodness (Shippey, *The Road* 140). These authors seem to accept both views in that evil may have begun with goodness gone awry and continued, after its manifestation, to grow into something opposite but existent out of its war with good.

Two of the clearest ways of observing their Christian view of good and evil is in the motifs of light and darkness and of laughter. Flieger writes, "Images of light in all stages—brilliant, dim, whole, refracted—pervade the songs and stories of Tolkien's fictive world, a world peopled by sub-creators whose interactions with the light shape Middle-earth and their own destinies" (49). MacDonald's *The Light Princess* plays on the multiplicity of meaning in *light*: lighthearted, light body, and light, bright environment. Saffron Park, the opening scene of Chesterton's *The Man Who Was Thursday* is on "the sunset side of London, as red and ragged as a cloud of sunset" (9). It is a story born in the twilight, where light and dark, order and disorder, law and anarchy meet. Likewise, Lewis's earthly realm in *The Great Divorce* consists of a "subdued and delicate half-light," contrary to "the promise of dawn" in the heavenly realm (475). Both Primary and Secondary Worlds deal with the meeting of light and darkness, symbolic of good and evil. On one hand, light and dark are binary opposites; on the other hand, as with the linguistic sign, these binaries exhibit supplementation: a liminality and a spectrum from one end to the other. MacDonald expresses his view of the material world like Plato, with men in a cave watching shadows on the wall until, at the time of death, they see the sunshine (*Unspoken Sermons* 202). The torchlight is not the Sun, but the lesser signifies the greater. Darkness, likewise, has its signifiers, such as shadow. Wherever someone stands on the spectrum, the importance of the position lay in which direction she or he faces. For instance, during a conversation between a ghost visiting Heaven and a spirit in Heaven in Lewis's *The Great Divorce,* the ghost remarks of Earth, "You mean that the grey town with its continual hope of morning (we must all live by hope, must we not?), with its field for indefinite progress, is, in a sense, Heaven, if only we have eyes to see it? That is a beautiful idea." The spirit, however, responds, "We call it Hell" (484).

Laughter, in a similar spectrum, is a motif which demonstrates good and evil. Screwtape divides laughter into four categories: *Joy, Fun,* the *Joke Proper,* and *Flippancy* (Lewis, *The Screwtape Letters* 215). Laughter is one of the defining characteristics of the human being which sets it apart from the beast, as though the human creature knows a secret about the universe that not even the universe knows (Chesterton, *Everlasting Man* 36). As Lindvall writes, Chesterton is known for turning the world on its head to illicit truth and goodness "and the humorous ways of God. He entered Lewis's life as a kindly and gallant guardian angel—a giant, laughing cherub," for Chesterton casts a gigantic shadow over Lewis's landscape (31). But, "Laughter, like any other good gift bestowed by God, can be corrupted, bent, spoiled, and ruined. This happens when it exceeds the pleasant part of life it was meant to be and becomes life itself . . . sentencing the good, the virtuous, and the moral to endless mockery" (413). This mockery, in Lewis's terminology, is *flippancy* (*The Screwtape Letters* 215).

The spectrums of light and laughter can be separated into three phases: from light/void and joyful laughter to light/unlight and deceptive laughter to light/presence-of-darkness and evil laughter. Tolkien's work in *The Silmarillion* clearly demonstrates the growth of darkness—and its associative evil—in opposition to the light which existed in the beginning. The trees with the original light of the world of Eä are only contested by void, for they have no existing opposite. They are pure light, which cannot be recreated, like the Imperishable Flame of Ilúvatar[14] (16, 20, 78). Like Ilúvatar's

Imperishable Flame, pure light is of God, says MacDonald, and God is the source of life (Tolkien, *Silmarillion* 15; *Unspoken Sermons* 425).[15] Chesterton alludes to GMD's assertion when he claims, "The one created thing which we cannot look at is the one thing in the light of which we look at everything. Like sun at noonday, mysticism explains everything else by the blaze of its own victorious invisibility" (*Orthodoxy* 21).[16] Likewise, King explains how Lewis's poetry, "Noon's Intensity" in particular, depicts God's glory through the sunlight (292). To be right with the God of light, according to MacDonald, is also to be right with "the cherisher of joy, the lord of laughter" (MacDonald, *Unspoken Sermons* 479). Chesterton was known to laugh "robustly" at his own expense, "often howling with joy," perhaps not unlike the booming laughter Lewis's stepson found as a sign of Lewis's presence (Lindvall 39; Gresham 64). Lewis found Joyous Laughter to be the purest and the highest form of laughter (Lindvall 53). Perhaps the most joyous of the Valar is Tulkas, who is praised for his strength, deeds, and prowess, who has little concern for the past or future, and whose anger is like a powerful wind that separates clouds and darkness (*Silmarillion* 28–29, 35). Upon his entry into Middle-earth's Arda to fight in the First War against Melkor, Arda was filled with echoes of Tulkas's laughter (35). The scattering of darkness and the joy of pure laughter: Tulkas demonstrates, heroically, how laughter and light cannot coexist with what is impure.

The first recognition of darkness occurs when Ilúvatar hides the vision of Eä and its future, rightly at the end of Eru's explanation of the world, but the shift from light/void to light/unlight does not occur until the story is played out. When the Trees of Light are compromised by Melkor and Ungoliant,[17] the giant spider weaves webs of unlight until the unlight enveloped the roots of the Trees of Light, and the spider sucked all of the sap from the trees (*Silmarillion* 19, 74). The only remaining light of the trees survives in the elf-made Silmarils, three gems consisting of the original light, captured within.[18] Flieger writes that, when the trees are destroyed by Melkor and Ungoliant, "The darkness that descends on Valinor is itself a paradox; it is the felt presence of an absence—the absence of that light which has been the life of the Blessed realm" (*Splintered Light* 103). Darkness is not quite present, in that light is only opposed by unlight. Goodness has been twisted into something that is of but not goodness. Likewise, Fun Laughter and the Joke Proper can be related to Joyous Laughter, but they have the opportunity to be turned toward something else (Lewis, *The Screwtape Letters* 215–16). Certainly, they have the potential for good,

Joyous Laughter, but they also hold the keys to mocking, Evil Laughter. They are the gray area, which can be turned either way on the spectrum. For example, MacDonald's Anodos sees his White Lady at the time of the "setting sun," following her into the night, her cave, and into the light of a lamp, during which time she bellows "a low delicious laugh . . . the laugh of one who has just received something long and patiently desired—a laugh that ends in a low musical tone . . . [later] full of scorn and derision" (*Phantastes* 40–45). The White Lady turns out to be the dangerous Maid of the Alder who passes him off to his foe, the Ash-tree. Anodos's chosen path takes him from light, to half-light, and, eventually, to darkness. In the gray area, it is what the person makes of it. Anodos could have turned from the path he was walking, staying for the light of the Moon and the laughter of fairies, but he chooses to journey to darkness and the one with scornful laughter. Lewis, accordingly, places the words in MacDonald's mouth in *The Great Divorce:* "at the end of all things, when the sun rises here and the twilight turns to blackness down there, the Blessed will say 'We have never lived anywhere except in Heaven,' and the Lost, 'We were always in Hell.' And both will speak truly" (503).

After Ungoliant absorbs the light of the Trees of Light, the world of Eä first experiences the presence of darkness (*Silmarillion* 76). The two trees yield one last flower and fruit, which are made into the Sun and Moon. The Sun is a sign for the humans to awaken and for the elves to seek rest, while the Moon is a memorial of the elves (99). Tolkien terms the third phase, which understands the presence of darkness, as "the world under the sun" because it is not a divine symbol but only "a second-best thing," far removed from the divine Creator and symbolic of a Fallen world (*Letters* 148). This bottom phase, of light/presence-of-darkness, thus, is a place where true light is only signified. Whereas the Trees of Valinor were original light, the Sun and Moon signify what once was—though they are still light. Darkness, similarly, has signifiers of unlight, shadow, and ultimately, the presence of the absence of light and goodness. MacDonald writes that darkness cannot understand light any more than it can understand itself, "only the light knows itself and the darkness also" (*Lilith* 206). Hence, a Fallen Lilith, at times, will "writhe as in the embrace of a friend whom her soul hated, and laugh like a demon" while she is under the power of the Shadow (184, 203). Her laughter is no longer of Fun or the Joke Proper and is even farther from Joyous Laughter. She has entered into the realm of Fallen, or Evil Laughter. Paul de Man argues that, when one laughs at his Fallenness, he does not do so out of feelings of superiority but out of recognition of the opposite (Billone); that is, the laughter is self-deceptive of the Fallen state of their soul. Princess Makemnoit, for example, in *The Light Princess* genuinely has a sense of superiority, according to Amy Billone, which causes her to act evilly by trying to dominate others. Vis-à-vis the evil actions of Makemnoit to drain the lake, the Light Princess physically, emotionally, and spiritually experiences a Fall—finding her gravity in the time of her first tears. Simultaneously, the naive laughter of the Light Princess disappears, as she loses her childlike innocence and passes into adulthood. Darkness, sorrow, and Makemnoit's evil laughter have become fully present in the Light Princess's once innocent mind where she only knew light, cheeriness, and Fun Laughter. The twilight of Fun Laughter, which helped her to know joy, dissipated once she knew sorrow and darkness. Screwtape writes that "flippancy," or Evil Laughter, is far from joy because it corrodes the intellect instead of improving it, hurting also the relationship of those who use flippancy (Lewis, *The Screwtape Letters* 217). Lindvall adds, "The habit of flippancy blinds the eyes to goodness, even as its loud, unhappy laughter deafens the ears of truth" (415).

Ultimately, once the third phase has occurred, the binaries break down into good/evil, light/darkness, and Joyous/Evil Laughter. To these authors, it is significant for any philosophy to recognize the evolution of evil from twisted goodness. As Screwtape advises Wormwood, Hell requires that humanity fails to recognize a single good and a single evil; it thrives on the drive for relativism in which one good and one evil are not the same as another person's good and evil (*The Screwtape Letters* 236). These authors make it clear that good is good, evil is evil, and such clarity is observable in the nature of light and laughter. While Tolkien asserts that the Church is like the Sun on Earth, a signifier of the transcendental signified, MacDonald declares that the Bible is like "the moon of our darkness," reflecting the light of God (*Letters* 339; *Unspoken Sermons* 37). God may be "like the earth in spring, . . . like the sun at noonday," but Chesterton believes "There was some one thing that was too great for God to show us when He walked upon our earth; and I have sometimes fancied that it was His mirth" (*The Man Who Was Thursday* 168; *Orthodoxy* 154).

ATTRIBUTES OF GOD

To say there is light and dark is one thing, but to declare what the light is, is another. Goodness, as derived from God, is not something easily characterized except by its definition of being, simply, of God. Nonetheless, it is important to explicate the view of God presented by these authors in order to understand the Great Tower because it is the mysterious light by which they see the world from the tower roof and, therefore, essential to their *Weltanschauung*.[19] Lewis posits that the common understanding of God as an essay examiner or as an opponent in a bargaining match prevents a person from establishing a relationship with Him (*Mere Christianity* 120). MacDonald adds that too many people have attempted "to theorize concerning him rather than to obey him," which have caused others to have wrong or one-sided views of God (*Unspoken Sermons* 520). These authors believe that this unchanging but dynamic being, self-asserted as the "I am," has been misconstrued from what and who He is. "God changes not. Once God he is always God," but God works on humanity in more ways than one, including through nature, readings, and experience—whether the experience seems discouraging or encouraging of one's faith (MacDonald, *Unspoken Sermons* 158; Lewis, *Mere Christianity* 153). Hence, we will carefully follow what these authors declare as clear characteristics of God, but we will not go so far as to say that God can be described completely.

The first characteristic, in fact, is that God is mysterious. "God is by its nature a name of mystery," writes Chesterton, "and nobody ever supposed that man could imagine how a world was created any more than he could create one" (*Everlasting Man* 24). MacDonald believes that, throughout history, humanity has pieced a perception of God together from the way Christ taught Himself and, sometimes incorrectly, how humans have interpreted Christ (*Unspoken Sermons* 384–85). Seeing God demonstrate miracles to prove Himself would no more prove who He is completely than simply that He exists: "To say, *Thou art God*, without knowing what the *Thou* means—of what use is it?" (102) Tolkien asserts that we can answer some of the smaller questions of goodness and life, but to understand the whole, "that requires a *complete* knowledge of God, which is unattainable" (*Letters* 400). Jeremy Bentham's Flatland, cited by Lewis, is a common example of this view, in that God is a Trinity of Father, Son, and Holy Spirit, but God is incomprehensible in the way that the Flatland people are incapable of understanding a cube (*Miracles* 376). In agreement, Tolkien argues that one's view of God should not be limited by human understanding (*Letters* 339). Mystery becomes a vehicle by which the Christian finds clarity in a confusing world. Chesterton declares, "The Christian . . . puts the mystery into his philosophy. That mystery by its darkness enlightens all things" (*The Blatchford Controversies* 383).

The second characteristic is very close to the first: God is transcendent. God cannot be tied "to our measures of time," according to MacDonald (*Unspoken Sermons* 250–51). If time is considered a straight line, then God is the entire page the line is on, having no history or future, because both would mean not having part of reality (Lewis, *Mere Christianity* 139). This separation is something which should be rejoiced in, says Chesterton, because God is always present to love humanity, and humans are always present to love Him (*Orthodoxy* 125). Therefore, Ilúvatar is always present in the story of Eä, from beginning to end, but he is transcendent from the story, entering in only at certain moments like the creation of the dwarves, elves, and humans as well as the destruction of Númenor and reshaping of Middle-earth (Tolkien, *Silmarillion* 43–44; 278–79). Ilúvatar is seemingly removed but actively present. Chesterton argues that even paganism hints at what Christianity refers to as the absence of the presence of God, which is more like an empty chair than nonexistence, or, inversely, the presence of the absence of God, notable even in the incomprehensible sadness of pagan poetry[20] (*Everlasting Man* 92–93). God is transcendent, but He is present in His seeming absence. In *Miracles*, Lewis explains the ambiguous meaning of *nature* in modern language; however, nature is much easier to understand and much clearer once it is understood as a creature—something created. Then, many of the characteristics that people use to describe *nature* or even use *nature* for no longer fit, for those characteristics are characteristics not of nature but of God, the Creator (358).

Thus, the characteristics of mystery and transcendence are essential in understanding how these authors approach the fallibility of human language and, a priori, challenge the deconstructionist view of the transcendental signified. While God is both transcendent and definite, He remains mysterious in His being. He is unspeakable and indefinite by being "too definite" for language. Characteristics often applied to God misconstrue who God is, simply because any descriptions one can provide for God are metaphorical; this metaphorical language is representative of the life humans live: as metaphors of the true life found in God (Lewis, *Miracles* 381). Where deconstruction claims that the fallibility of the signifier/signified rests in the faulty belief of a transcendental signified, these authors argue that the transcendental signified is the only means by which language can be unified. Derrida seeks to remove the "presuppositions of metaphysics" from linguistics (21), but these authors recognize what Derrida does not: the transcendental signified is not static but dynamic and mysterious. Derrida argues that the transcendental signified—the Sun—must be removed in order to deconstruct the world with free play. The profound irony of these authors' view, however, is that the transcendental signified must be present in order to treat both sides of the binary equally. The Sun must be present in order for one even to see such binaries. Derrida would repeatedly change the transcendental signified to play, but the Christian, with God as the transcendental signified, understands that God is dynamic. The source of flawed language, then, is that humanity cannot accept all of God's characteristics at once, privileging one over another based upon a single characteristic of God as a transcendental signified. For example, both Christian and non-Christian have attempted to privilege one side of a binary over another, such as creation/destruction, depending on their chosen transcendental signified, such as peace. When the dynamic God is accepted as the ultimate transcendental signified, however, one realizes that God has also demonstrated war. The privileging of peace/war is not, therefore, accurate, so neither should creation/destruction be privileged by peace. God is the one who gives meaning to true language—in which signifier/signified are perfect and binaries are privileged only by a holistic understanding of God—so human language will show flaws because it does not understand God, the ultimate transcendental signified, fully.

The nearest to a perfect binary which can be reached in humanity's flawed language is that of good/evil; it is not perfect, however, because, as these authors argue, God can twist evil for good in the same way that evil is twisted goodness. Additionally, God's goodness is different from humanity's understanding of goodness, "not as white from black but as a perfect circle from a child's first attempt to draw a wheel" (Lewis, *The Problem* 568). Unlike Pantheism and Hinduism, which place God outside of good and evil, Christianity, Judaism, and Islam assert God's innate and total goodness (Lewis, *Mere Christianity* 39–40). Goodness is a characteristic of God, what Christ demonstrated in his life as a human (MacDonald, *Unspoken Sermons* 173). Chesterton admits that his conception of Sunday in *The Man Who Was Thursday* is an attempt to construct a new kind of optimism, grounded in the potential for minimum goodness even in nightmarish scenarios (*Autobiography* 106).

As Tolkien posited, it is the responsibility of the mythopoeic writer to reflect *evangelium*, the "good news" known as the *Gospel*, rendered from the Old English *gód spell* (Shippey, *The Road* 51). The goodness of the good news provides a guide for the paths and roads of the human journey. Goodness, or God-ness,[21] is the source of the virtuous signposts—selfless love, wisdom, justice, patience, mercy, hope, fortitude, and joy—and the means by which pity, fear, pleasure, and pain can be used appropriately. Any of these virtues and sensations are good when they are of God; they are evil when they are not and guide one on a path of *Bios* and bestiality.

Another challenge presented to the characterization of God and goodness is that God reveals Himself differently to different people. Christianity is a means of God revealing His nature, but at times, He reveals Himself in ways to some that He cannot to others because the person may be not be ready for Him. Like the Sun, without favoring one person over another, God is better reflected on a clean rather than a dusty mirror (Lewis, *Mere Christianity* 43, 135). The grandmother of MacDonald's *The Princess and the Goblin*, likewise, does not allow Curdie to see herself when Princess Irene tries to introduce them. Grandmother explains, "Curdie is not yet able to believe some things. Seeing is not believing—it is only seeing" (122–23); however, she concedes that, had she been in her workroom, Curdie would have seen her, but she decided to be by the fire in a different room (123). The different rooms may be likened to different aspects of her character: the workroom where she spins string to draw people to her and the fire room where she cleanses people and sends out pigeons that resemble angels in their actions (129). She would be unavoidably seen in the spinning room, but she can go unnoticed in the room where she cleanses those that see her or send angels only to those who are looking. Through Sunday in *The Man Who Was Thursday*, Chesterton illustrates many paradoxes, or binaries, of God. Each of the detectives perceives Sunday in a different way. Dr. Bull, for instance, notes Sunday as being "so fat and so light . . . [as] if an elephant could leap up in the sky like a grasshopper" (165). On the other hand, the secretary argues that Sunday is "a huge heap of a man, [yet] dark and out of shape" (166). Inspector Ratcliffe views Sunday as having an appearance where "everything seems in order; but he's absent-minded" (166–67) while Professor de Worms claims that Sunday's "face was so big that one couldn't focus it or make it a face at all. The eye was so far away from the nose that it wasn't an eye. The mouth was so much by itself that one had to think of it by itself" (167). Syme would say that the physicality of Sunday would confuse him as well: "But when I saw him from behind I was certain he was an animal, and when I saw him in front I knew he was a god" (169). Each detective observes Sunday as a different set of binaries where Sunday is fat yet light; shaped yet shapeless; both ordered and disordered; has a body part that is not a body part; and who is an animal yet a god. Perhaps the most profound of explanations comes from Gogol, who remarks that he cannot "think of Sunday on principle . . . any more than I stare at the sun on noonday" (167). Accordingly, the light of Ilúvatar in Middle-earth is observed differently by different people: as the Imperishable Flame, the Trees of Valinor, the Silmarillion, and the Sun and the Moon. As the original light has been retransmitted, it has been less pure; similarly, the people who see the light have been less pure. Galadriel, her husband, Celeborn, and Círdan the shipwright, in fact, are the only Children of Ilúvatar who saw the original light in the Trees of Valinor and who remain in Middle-earth until the end of the Third Age. Accordingly, when the full dominion of humans is underway, their time ends, and like the other elves, they pass into the West. A world under the Sun, alone, is the world of Middle-earth, no longer to be guided by those who have seen the original light.

Part of the difference of God's revealing is in the revelation of God through other people. Lewis writes, "Men are mirrors, or 'carriers' of Christ to other men. Sometimes unconscious carriers" (*Mere Christianity* 153). People and things of the physical world, what MacDonald calls "the world of showing," reveal what is part of "the world of being," or the metaphysical (*Unspoken Sermons* 200, 271). Tolkien writes to his son, Michael, "God cannot be limited . . . and may use any channel for His grace" (*Letters* 339). Sam, then, may be seen as a God-bearer to Frodo in *The Lord of the Rings*, for his relentless display of the cardinal virtues—wisdom, temperance, fortitude, and justice—along with three theological virtues—faith, hope, and love. All of these virtues may best be exemplified in the crowning moment on Mt. Doom as Frodo falters one last time before entering the mountain. A wise but just and fortuitous Sam, who temperately rationed food for the journey as best he could, picks up his fellow adventurer out of hope, love, and faith in his companion, declaring, "I can't carry it for you, but I can carry you and it as well. So up you get! Come on, Mr. Frodo dear! Sam will give you a ride. Just tell him where to go, and he'll go" (Tolkien, *The Return* 919). As Shippey says of the Eye of Mordor, "But once more ironically, it is what the Eye does not see that matters": not the visible sword and the heroic king but the tiny, courageous hobbits on the mountainside (*The Road* 166). Humans were meant, Chesterton asserts, to be statues "of God walking about the garden" (*Orthodoxy* 87).

Humanity, thus, is to bear God to the world around them. Chesterton notes another characteristic of God, the Trinity, repeated in "the pattern of the world," from father, mother, and child to the father, mother, and divine child to the Holy Father, Spirit, and Son (*Everlasting Man* 55). The dimension in which God exists allows three persons in one being, like a cube is six squares while being one cube (Lewis, *Mere Christianity* 133; *Miracles* 376).[22] God is humanly represented in Jesus, perhaps, best described in the relationship of father and son because it represents the love, delight, and respect present in this part of the Trinity (Lewis, *Mere Christianity* 55, 142; MacDonald, *Unspoken Sermons* 12; Chesterton, *Everlasting Man* 196; Tolkien, *Letters* 99). The problem, however, is that Jesus has been hidden by what Lewis calls "historical Jesus": as a liberal, humanitarian, Marxist, revolutionary, pagan-like hero, and moral teacher (Lewis, *The Screwtape Letters* 252; Chesterton, *Everlasting Man* 189, 252). In the same way that Tolkien admits he could not dare to capture God's incarnation in anything he wrote, Chesterton asserts that, because of the various perspectives that have been constructed out of the historical Jesus, "taken together they do suggest something of the very mystery which they miss" (Tolkien, *Letters* 237; Chesterton, *Everlasting Man* 197). Simply described by his teachings and the gospel books' characteristics, humility and meekness hardly match the "moral teacher" of history, for, if a person were to say the things Christ did while only being a human, then he would be considered a lunatic or a demon (Lewis, *Mere Christianity* 50).[23] The third part, the Holy Spirit, is that which connects the transcendent with the earthly (Tolkien, *Letters* 339). It is the active movement of God in the hearts and minds of humanity and throughout the world. Tolkien even characterized his creation of Ilúvatar and the Valar as resulting from a mind which believes in the Trinity (146). We, then, may assume that Ilúvatar is reminiscent of God and the Valar (along with their magic), of the Holy Spirit—much like Gandalf is reminiscent of Christ (Tolkien, *Letters* 237). The Holy Spirit is the part of the Trinity which is inside or in support of a person, working through an individual to share God's love (Lewis, *Mere Christianity* 143).

The primary presence of the Triune God in the physical realm is to be through the Christian Church, a further characteristic of God. The Church is the means by which the Spirit moves throughout the world, even if the

Church is often corrupting, reforming, and reviving (Tolkien, *Letters* 339). Accordingly, E. Humphrey Havard claimed that the Inklings were all Christians who were dissatisfied with the current state of the Church (Duriez, *Tolkien and C. S. Lewis* 83). MacDonald, likewise, demonstrates strong resistance to organized religion after being deposed from his church—so much so that he never accepted another role as a pastor, despite some strong financial offers. Chesterton admits that the Church was unfortunately shattered by the Reformation, letting vices run loose (*Orthodoxy* 22). Nonetheless, each of these authors supported the Church as the appointed presence of Christ on Earth, as Paul writes in 1 Corinthians 12.12–27. The Church, thus, is not a particular civilization or genetic line of people, but the union of those who serve God throughout the world (Chesterton, *Everlasting Man* 219). In writing *Mere Christianity*, Lewis hoped to have either aided in the reunion of the Christian Church or at least offered reasons why it should be reunited. Even the responses he received after the initial publication suggested to him that, at the center of most denominations, the same voice was being heard (8).

Although the Church fails to perfectly represent Christ on Earth, Chesterton reminds his readers, "It is not earth that judges heaven, but heaven that judges earth" (*Orthodoxy* 41). The Church may fail at times, but the God it serves is perfect. About God's perfection, Lewis quotes MacDonald that "God is easy to please, but hard to satisfy" (*Mere Christianity* 161). Lewis underlines in his copy of the first volume of MacDonald's *Unspoken Sermons*,[24] "Nothing is required of man that is not first in God. It is because God is perfect that we are required to be perfect" (MacDonald, *Unspoken Sermons* 6–7). Indeed, if goodness is of God, then God is perfect in goodness, so one who aspires to be good aspires not simply to be perfect but, ultimately, to be like God. As Ralph C. Wood remarks of Tolkien's theology as it is present in his creative works, only by the intervention of God can the world be set right—not by flawed humanity's deeds alone (Wood 161).

PURPOSE

Humanity's aspiration to perfection—to be like God—is of particular concern to MacDonald, Chesterton, Lewis, and Tolkien. The third and final approach to the overarching hypothesis is that of purpose. Chesterton writes that purpose is a "challenge and a fight. While it is deliberately broadened to embrace every aspect of truth, it is still stiffly embattled against every mode of error" (*Everlasting Man* 182–83). The purpose of Christianity is to battle and fight to be like Christ and to advocate for God to the world around it. By embracing the characteristics of God as the personal goals of the human journey, people act as God-bearers to others. Clearly, not every person aspires to follow God. Roland Hein coins the term *Doctrine of Becoming* to signify GMD's belief that individuals are always moving toward or away from God—becoming Godlike or beast-like (30). Hein further asserts that, while some scholars attribute the goblins, Irene, and the grandmother in *The Princess and the Goblin* to preceding Freud's theory of the tripartite psychological structure (id, ego, and superego, respectively), the likely use of these symbols is for MacDonald's Doctrine of Becoming, in which Irene moves toward being more goblin-like or more grandmother-like (34). MacDonald believed, according to Bonnie Gaarden, that salvation in God was achieved by a willful relationship with God, out of which relationship cleansing occurs ("Faerie Romance and Divine Comedy" 60).[25] Humanity, thus, was created with a purposeful story unlike the beasts; as Chesterton writes, human life is an adventure story in which "every man has forgotten who he is. . . . We have all forgotten our names. We have all forgotten what we really are. . . . All that we call spirit and art and ecstasy only means that for one awful instant we remember that we forget" (*Everlasting Man* 246; *Orthodoxy* 46).[26] The philosophies of life and differing perspectives of God, thus, inhibit humans from pursuing the perfect story designed by God, where each person is given a unique part in the drama. Because humans have redirected their search for purpose away from God, they have ruined their own story. The human story is separate from the divine story of which it was intended to be a part (*Everlasting Man* 246–47). Humans, therefore, have the opportunity of choice in their stories and, accordingly, in the divine story. Like actors in a divine metanarrative, humans may choose, as Melkor did, the way of disharmony, or as Manwë did, a way of service to the Supreme Being.

This point of "becoming" one way or the other is where these authors borrow most from MacDonald. Similar to humans in *The Princess and the Goblin*, the goblins control animals, but "in the case of these the human resemblance had greatly increased: while their owners had sunk towards them, they had risen toward their owners" (72). In other words, the goblins, although resembling humans, became beast-like; their pets, on the other hand, evolved to a more human-likeness yet were "incapable of

designs of their own, or of intentionally furthering those of their masters"
(73). Unlike their masters, the goblins' animals lack the ability to reason.
Therefore, as the goblins are a single step away from humans in their lack
of relationship with the Queen, the pets are another step away from being human because of their inability to reason. While the goblins are in
transition from human to beast, the animals of the goblins are completely
beast. In *The Princess and Curdie,* MacDonald explains the transition between beast and human more clearly: "All men, if they do not take care,
go down the hill to the animals' country; that many men are actually, all
their lives, going to be beasts" (219–20). MacDonald terms this devolution from humanity as "traveling beastward" (220).[27] MacDonald posits,
through the voice of Queen Irene, "Just so two people may be at the same
spot in manners and behavior, and yet one may be getting better and the
other worse, which is just the greatest of all differences that could possibly
exist between them" (220). Accordingly, Lewis, in the Preface to his text
George MacDonald, cites metaphysical process philosopher Alfred North
Whitehead as someone MacDonald "would obviously been more at home
with" theologically (xxxvi). The Doctrine of Becoming deconstructs existential metaphysics that privilege "being" over "becoming," and thus, the
Doctrine of Becoming claims that each person is on a path of "becoming" either toward God or toward evil (away from God). Lewis writes that
humans have a choice whether to accept the role of a Son or Daughter of
God. Addressing the reader through a persona of God, Lewis writes that,
if a person chooses to let God into his life, God will make him perfect. He
can choose to push God away out of his free will, but if he does not reject
God, God will drive him to improve toward perfection (*Mere Christianity* 161). Accordingly, one has a choice either to follow God's purpose to
perfection or not to do so; there is no neutral ground. As Camilla remarks
to Jane in *That Hideous Strength,* no one can choose to be neutral; a non-
answer to God is a decision to play on the opposing team (113).

Hence, as Chesterton claims in *The Everlasting Man,* the human life is
an adventure story (246). We return to the path and road motif, as one's
choice of fate may lead one to be more like God, as we have characterized,
or more like the beast. MacDonald believes that one's sole ambition should
be to rise above oneself to be Godlike; all other ambitions are of the devil
and must be forgiven by God so that He "sweeps away a path" (*Unspoken
Sermons* 54, 220, 265). The human journey is, in a sense, like a play that
God planned to be perfect, but, says Chesterton, He allowed "human ac-

tors and stage-managers, who had since made a great mess of it" (*Ortho-doxy* 71). The *Bios* and *Zoe* makes the human like Ransom in *Perelandra,* a piebald: pale on one side and sunburned on the other. Downing asserts that these two halves demonstrate the war within Ransom, which is why the two-tone mostly fades when he decides to fight the Un-man (*Planets in Peril* 113–15). According to Tolkien, humanity always has the ability to "slowly turn Men and Elves into Orcs," no matter how successful one may be at eliminating the clearer evils in the world (*Letters* 78). Insofar as no human is perfect, no human is made perfectly evil nor irredeemable (Tolkien, *Letters* 90, 243; Kreeft 178). A Christian, then, is not a person who never makes a mistake but one who has the ability given him to rise up when he falls because Christ enables him to do so, helping him to improve, repair, and live a life and death as Christ did (*Mere Christianity* 59). Being a Christian is not simply making a statement or a single commitment, but "a permanent indefinitely repeated act . . . which must go on—so we pray for 'final perseverance'" (Tolkien, *Letters* 338). God presses the Christian "on, or up, to a higher level: putting him into situations where he will have to be very much braver, or more patient, or more loving, than he ever dreamed of being before" (Lewis, *Mere Christianity* 162). As Farsight in *The Last Battle* repeatedly calls, "Further up and further in!" or Vane describes in *Lilith,* "farther in, higher up" (Lewis, *The Last Battle* 761; MacDonald, *Lilith* 231).

Christianity, although it means placing oneself as second to God and others, does not mean an abandonment of oneself. D. Williams characterizes Lewis, Tolkien, and Chesterton's view of the selfless side of Christianity as something like sonship or daughterhood, and by accepting one's role as the child of God, one becomes fully human (105). Lewis borrows from MacDonald's Grandmother in *The Princess and the Goblin* when he writes, "The only things we can keep are the things we freely give to God. What we try to keep for ourselves is just what we are sure to lose" (*Mere Christianity* 168).[28] One's greatness is measured not in one's pride or abilities but "that of a great instrument in God's hands—a mover, a doer, even an achiever of great things, a beginner at the very least of large things" (Tolkien, *Letters* 9). The *imago Dei,* or the image of God, is humanity's highest calling in the journey and the ultimate guide to each person's path, for "He wants to make us in his own image, *choosing* the good, *refusing* the evil. . . . God gives us room *to be;* does not oppress us with his will; 'stands away from us,' that we may act from ourselves, that we may exercise the pure will for good" (MacDonald, *Unspoken Sermons* 117). It is the only religion which

Chesterton found dared to reach into the depths of the self; it is the belief which led him to realize that humanity does not fit into the world because it is a monstrosity—something both better and worse than all other things on Earth (*Autobiography* 334; *Orthodoxy* 72–73). Christianity does not call for self-abandonment; on the contrary, it is not until a person has given herself up to Christ that she finds her real self: "Give up yourself, and you will find your real self. Lose your life and you will save it" (Lewis, *Mere Christianity* 176).[29] God wants a world of people who are united in Him but distinctly themselves (*The Screwtape Letters* 207).

A key to the Christian journey, then, is obedience to God—what GMD calls "the one key to life" (*Unspoken Sermons* 226). Obedience provides true self-discovery and the ability to overcome "inadequacies and sins" for human growth, albeit through "a painful purification often assisted by the difficulties and trials" (Gaarden, "Faerie Romance and Divine Comedy" 60). As Lewis reiterates of John Henry Newman's view of obedience, humans are imperfect creations who need improvement, "rebels who must lay down our arms" (*The Problem* 602). Obedience is not always perfect, but it is an attempt to be perfect (MacDonald, *Unspoken Sermons* 399). Tolkien certainly demonstrates how obedience can be misplaced, especially when wrongly demanded like with the Entwives and Denethor, but good things happen on the journey when obedience to the rightful master occurs, as with Sam to Frodo, men to Aragorn—for Gollum takes steps toward goodness, and the men begin servitude to the rightful king (*The Return* 837, 857; *The Two Towers* 464, 604). Although Sam greatly wishes to see Bywater again, he knows that he must help Frodo to the final step of his journey, trusting in the order of obedience from Gandalf to Frodo to himself: "Well, if that is the job, then I must do it" (*The Return* 913).

Abstractly, then, the Christian acts obediently to God and His commands, but practically for these authors, Christianity forces them to obediently question key aspects of one's worldview: including language, literature, humanity, civilization, and history. Their purposes on the paths they chose were to steer their readership in the right direction: to disciple them. Their beliefs cannot allow a word like *religion* to confound society. As Screwtape declares, religion, as modern culture knows it, will fuel Hell's fires until the day it disappears from the Earth (Lewis, "Screwtape Proposes a Toast" 296). The word *mine* truly has no meaning, except temporally, but if society believes one's earthly lifetime is all there is, then those members of society, ultimately, will discover that nothing, including their souls, ever belonged to them; rather, it belonged to Hell all along (*The Screwtape Letters* 246–47). Such confusion has seeped from language into culture, philosophy, and literature, damning the progression of human history and civilization to digression, for, says the demon Screwtape, "Everything has to be *twisted* before it's any use to us. . . . Nothing is naturally on our side" (249). Hence, these authors impressed upon their readers clear definitions of words like *good, justice, mercy, love, fortitude* and *courage, pity* and *fear,* and *wisdom* and *prudence.* These words—all of them attributes of God that have been twisted by human use—are the signposts that should guide humanity, but signs are not of much good if they do not signal the correct action or if they are isolated from the others.

In these authors' minds, the origination of language rests in the one true language of the one true God. God is the only true and the ultimate Transcendental Signified, alive, dynamic, and unrestricted by binaries of human design because He can fit into both sides of a binary. His justice is merciful and His mercy is just. As Chesterton writes in *The Everlasting Man,* the words of Christ have the ability to compare three levels of goodness at once. Thus, although one can prize a good peace over a good war, a good war may be more appealing than a bad peace (201). Lewis, similarly, views language in "the highest possible view: language is a metaphysical reality with a transcendent origin. From another point of view, he sees that it is, in this sublunary world, subject to severe constraints" (Ward 151). Humans are forced, by human language's constraints, to use metaphorical language because we cannot explain beyond the senses (Lewis, *Miracles* 364). Therefore, Lewis contends, based on an assertion by Barfield, that metaphorical and literal aspects of language have always been a part of language; metaphor did not begin as a means of explaining fiction (*Miracles* 369). As MacDonald asserts, someone may "discover truth in what he wrote" because he was wrestling with concepts "that came from thoughts beyond his own" ("The Fantastic Imagination" 9). McGrath, in the tradition of disparity in worldview, posits that Lewis and Tolkien differed in their view of creating a fantastic world. He admits that their creative inspiration for the Narniad and *The Hobbit* similarly form out of mental images, "Yet Lewis did not really see himself as 'creating' Narnia. As he once commented, 'creation' is 'an entirely misleading term.' Lewis preferred to think of human thought as 'God-kindled,' and the writing process as the rearrangement of elements that God has provided" (264). One may recall, however, Tolkien's reflections that much of what he wrote was not from his own mind, hinting at divine inspiration—God-kindled, as one might say. Tolkien had this realization about his own work when asked if he had written *The Lord of the Rings* on his own: "I have never since been able to suppose so. An alarming conclusion for an old philologist to draw concerning his private amusement" (*Letters* 413). Tolkien's experiment in language turned to divine inspiration through sub-creation. *Mythopoeia,* by Tolkien's definition, is to "reflect splintered fragments of the true light" of God (Carpenter, *J. R. R. Tolkien: A Biography* 151). Such creation is "of the likeness of man's work to the work of his maker" (MacDonald, "The Imagination" 3). Accordingly, Chesterton can assert that the philosopher or literary critic seeks hidden truth in Plato or Shakespeare, but "The man who lives in contact with what he believes to be a living Church is a man always expecting to meet Plato and Shakespeare tomorrow at breakfast. He is always expecting to see some truth he has never seen before" (*Orthodoxy* 148). The critic, then, has reason to pursue adventure and discovery through art and the artist's perspective because he or she may discover deep truth hidden beneath the surface of human language or human image.

At the root of all Christianity is "that God was a creator, as an artist is a creator," but in the same vein, the artist lets the work go after creation is completed: "Even in giving it forth he has flung it away. This principle that all creation and procreation is a breaking off is at least as consistent through the cosmos as the evolutionary principle that all growth is a branching out. . . . All creation is separation. Birth is as solemn a parting as death" (70). That is, the canvas God created is always in decay because that which He painted destroys His creation. Tolkien pinpoints his Christianity as the source of his view of history as a "long defeat" despite "glimpses of final victory": "This is a fallen world. . . . The world has been 'going to the bad' all down the ages. The various social forms shift, and each new mode has its special dangers" (*Letters* 46, 255). Some philosophies argue that God enslaved the world when He made it, but Christianity views the act as His setting the world free (Chesterton, *Orthodoxy* 70–71). The Fall is humanity's doing, not God's. By free will, humanity has sought explanation, understanding, invention, and production: all characteristics of what may be called *civilization.* Indeed, Chesterton asserts that Christianity is not the result of a barbaric time but one that was too civilized, for when God sent Christ to set the world right, all those who stood around the cross should have recognized "the great historical truth of the time; that the world could not save itself. Man could do no more" (*Everlasting Man*

209–10, 216). As long as humanity believes that it can do what is divine on its own, the less divine humanity will be (204); the *Bios* wins over the *Zoe*.

The power of transformation rests in the individual, not in civilization. Individuals like Sam, Frodo, Aragorn, Faramir, Legolas, Gimli, and Gandalf are the catalysts by which civilization can reform. The individual is more significant than civilization for two reasons: the individual outlasts civilization in the Christian view,[30] and the individual is the means by which civilization and history can be transformed. Lewis writes in *Mere Christianity* that civilization will never be saved if civilization is to be the main focus. On the contrary, Heaven must be the main focus of humanity's salvation; with Heaven as the focus, the truly good things of the Earth will be part of the journey (112). Humanity must recognize that progress is not the answer and that we must "return to the king" (Chesterton, *Everlasting Man* 69). Even if only temporarily focused on God, the decay may be halted like during the rule of Aragorn.[31] At least, out of the decay humanity can realize its need for something greater than itself: "The whole history is a divine agony to give divine life to creatures. The outcome of that agony, the victory of that creative and again creative energy, will be radiant life, whereof joy unspeakable is the flower" (*Unspoken Sermons* 301).

Humanity and civilization must get back to their origin. Tolkien writes that Chesterton once advocated for humanity to be patriotic toward the world it lives in, but that idea is no longer sufficient; rather, "Gandalf added" that, since one cannot choose the era of her or his birth, one must seek to improve and fix the era one is born into (*Letters* 402). His *The Lord of the Rings*, hence, demonstrates what happens in a time prior to the courtly love discussed in Lewis's *Allegory of Love* with all its pretenses; the culture of Middle-earth during *The Lord of the Rings* is "more primitive," "less corrupt," and "nobler" (*Letters* 324). From there, Chesterton posits that humanity became more tyrannical as it became increasingly civilized—perhaps more tyrannical in order to be more civilized (*Everlasting Man* 68). The only remedy is to go backward in order to go forward. Humanity continues to move forward, despite its mistakes, and, instead of relocating to the right path, of going back to go forward, it presses on (Lewis, *Mere Christianity* 33–34).[32] Chesterton says there are two ways of getting home. One can either stay home, or he can walk all the way around the world to get back to the same place he began (*Everlasting Man* 9). Since civilization clearly has not stayed home, it must travel around the world to get back to its origin.

Death is one means of going around the world to get home. Lewis writes that it is a sort of safety net for Fallen humanity, which prevents humanity from becoming an unredeemable fiend, a principle which, I believe, may be extended to include the Armageddon of civilization (*Miracles* 417). Perhaps, the end of the world is the only way for the mass of civilization to be cut off from unredemption, but individuals have the choice to return to unity with their Creator, their origin; in effect, they also carry the responsibility to disciple others—their civilization—to return to unity. MacDonald, Chesterton, Lewis, and Tolkien explicated that the brokenness of language reveals something behind it, that the greatest art should reveal truth which is further up and further in, that humanity's journey should guide them in goodness to goodness, and that a fragmented civilization is not the means to healing. They attempted to restore unity to the individual and the cultures they affected. As Meilaender writes of Lewis, he emphasized the fullness of oneself in God and community—not in community alone (52). He and Tolkien practiced unity in their community of Inklings who, not coincidentally, wrote about community.[33] Each of these authors embraced a sense of community—whether with like-minded individuals or those they disagreed with. MacDonald's circles extended from Mark Twain, with whom he agreed to write a book, to Charles Dodgson to Matthew Arnold to John Ruskin; Chesterton debated with George Bernard Shaw and H. G. Wells when he was not having tea with Henry and William James or at the pub with his fellow news-writers and Belloc; before the Inklings, Tolkien shared in the TCBS and Lewis engaged in various clubs with both the student body and the professoriate. In his *Autobiography*, Chesterton overturns modern society's belief that one must develop their own ideas apart from other people, for people, like flowers, grow better in a garden than in the wilderness (333). As Lewis claims in *The Four Loves*, friendship is the nearest thing to Heaven that one can obtain on Earth, and that friendship produces better results than if each one were alone, especially since each person sees and communicates about God in a different way (62). Like the Blessed Trinity and the aim of the Church, individuals need to work together in community to reach unity with their origin in God. The diverse civilization was met with unity at the birth of Christ—which brought astrologers, philosophers, commoners, and kings to the feet of God again—but as Chesterton asserts, that birth was the death of strictly human history. The birth of Christ meant a new start to the world; God entered into the Earth again as He did in the Garden of Eden (*Everlasting Man* 213). Clearly, as these authors posit, civilization has continued to separate in such a way that the *Zoe* dissipates, but as God did with the birth of Christ and as the Church is expected to do in its work, humanity is to be brought back to unity with its Creator.

Although we begin with linguistic fallibility, broken humanity on the wrong path and at the center of a hierarchy, and a discontented, lost civilization, the bleak perspective turns on an overarching hypothesis that each of these aspects can be redeemed in God. "The real argument about religion turns on the question of whether a man who was born upside down can tell when he comes right way up," claims Chesterton (*Orthodoxy* 151). Language and art can reveal truth if the critical viewer searches beneath the surface; humanity can be restored in its journey if it sees the higher goal of unity with God; and civilization can find hope if it strives obediently, on the level of the individual, to be like God—good, loving, merciful, just, and the like. Each fragment or flaw, then, is restored by looking back to its origin in God as a way of moving forward. As the earliest of these authors asserts, "The whole system of the universe works about this law—the driving of things upward towards the centre" (*Unspoken Sermons* 133).

Conclusion

Drawn from his address to the Oxford Socratic Club entitled "Is Theology Poetry?" Lewis's quote on the stone in Poets' Corner reads: "I believe in Christianity as I believe that the Sun has risen, not only because I see it but because by it I see everything else" (qtd. in Westminster Abbey 4). The passage, clearly borrowed from Chesterton's clarifying "sun at noonday" (*Orthodoxy* 21), reflects also MacDonald's letter to his fiancé and future wife, Louisa Powell, on 12 May 1849: "Is God's sun more beautiful than God Himself? Has He not left it to us as a symbol of His own life-giving light? But I cannot now explain all that I mean . . ." (qtd. in Greville MacDonald, *George MacDonald and His Wife* 112). Tolkien makes a similar claim about the light of the Sun and Moon for one to see by (*Letters* 339). These authors grounded their *Weltanschauung* in their understanding of God, the accompanying Christianity, and the mythopoeia which evidences it. MacDonald, Chesterton, Lewis, and Tolkien's literary pursuits were not so much about themselves. Certainly, their essays, lectures, and stories contain elements of their worldview, but as Chesterton writes, "if a man would make his world large, he must be always making himself small. . . . Towers that vanish upwards above the loneliest star are the creations of humility. For towers are not tall unless we look up at them. . . . All this gigantesque imagination, which is, perhaps, the mightiest of the pleasures of man, is at the bottom entirely humble" (*Orthodoxy* 23). Throughout this analysis, we have examined the foundations, levels, and structures of their tall tower in order to understand their worldview. Ironically, insofar as the parts of the Great Tower of Elfland have been explained, these authors would undoubtedly argue that the view—not the structure or the builders—is the most important part, for by this view, they can glimpse the Sun and the sea.

Though many texts attempt to structure literary, philosophical, and cultural opinions based upon their theological premises, my intention was to explicate their unified opinions about language, literature, criticism, humanity, civilization, and history without prejudice by examining their theological assumptions. Although elements of their Christian worldview are peppered throughout the text, the purpose of the structure was to appeal to elements of a worldview that may be shared by Christian and non-Christian, alike. Their views of language, literature, criticism, humanity, the Fall, fate, free will, *wyrd,* virtues, vices, civilization and its downfalls, loss of morality, and human corruption over the course of history are all points in which any individual is able to appreciate and even accept, regardless of the reader's religious opinion. The difference, for these authors, is that these elements of the worldview are all grounded in their humble faith—the unifying, overarching hypothesis, which I approached last to demonstrate how the branches come back to the root. In the same way that Chesterton believes that the reason for the stark contrast of worldviews between George Bernard Shaw and himself is solely due to "religious difference; indeed I think all differences do" (*Autobiography* 220), many people will find themselves in agreement with some elements of the herein-expressed worldview. I would surmise that those people who do not are not of the same perspective because their theological position is what grounds their opinions on everything else. As Freud says, that is what a *Weltanschauung* is. These authors differ from one another, certainly. As Ward comments, Lewis and Tolkien need to be able to attempt their own pursuits in different ways and to be assessed in their own right, for "Lewis is not Tolkien quickened any more than Tolkien is Lewis prolonged" (10). Are these men and their worldviews mimetic? No. But, they must be understood as two men with a common mythopoeic goal who went about it in different ways, not unlike their agreement to pursue two different mythopoeic directions at the same time: one in space travel and the other in time travel. As P. Zaleski and C. Zaleski remark, "Tolkien's mythology was deeply Christian and therefore had an organic order to it; and Lewis's Christian awakening was deeply mythopoeic," their work ultimately leading to a "revitalization of Christian intellectual and imaginative life" (510). Their Christianity is central to their mythopoeia; all else is collateral and concomitant but, in many places, in agreement, for as Shippey believes, Tolkien, Lewis, and MacDonald—to which we can add Chesterton—each in his own way, attempt to express their firm beliefs in "traditional, if sometimes unorthodox, Christianity" ("Liminality and the Everyday in *Lilith*" 19).

Through mythopoeia, these authors conveyed the Christian worldview and its effects. They understood, as Chesterton asserts via the thesis of *The Everlasting Man,* that Christ does not stand side by side with other myths or religions, but myth can be a means by which one touches "original truth that was behind all the mythologies like the sky behind the clouds"—the same message about "splintered fragments of the true light" spoken by Tolkien that helped Lewis to convert to Christianity (Chesterton, *Everlasting Man* 7, 211; Carpenter, *Inklings* 43). Many of their stories deal with not only one's immediate life but also one's eternal life, including Tolkien's Undying Lands and Niggle's final journey, Lewis's Aslan's country, Chesterton's Sunday's house, and MacDonald's glimpse of Heaven in *Lilith.* Fairyland, as Hein asserts, is an intermediate, liminal realm between the Primary World and humanity's "ultimate destination," the Final World (142–43). In "Liminality," Shippey asserts a common belief of Tolkien, Lewis, and MacDonald—to which list we may add Chesterton: "[T]his present world, *le monde mundain,* is relatively unimportant *sub specie aeternitatis;* and yet it is in a sense vitally important in that behavior here determines one's fate on the far greater stage of eternity; and that true success on that greater stage depends on an ability to close one's eyes to the apparently obvious rewards offered and punishments threatened in this one. And one had to take all this on faith" (19).

The liminality of the Primary World and Final World occurs in the Secondary World. The Secondary World helps one to progress, via imagination, from the Primary to the Final World when one realizes that the Secondary World elicits deep truth. Without the Secondary World's liminality, grounded in Christianity, the human mind would never be unified; the dreaming and the calculating lobes would function separately. As a result, says Chesterton, a person would dream of the impossible in one part of the brain and calculate endlessly in the other (*Everlasting Man* 248). The Secondary World is, for these authors, intended to deal with the spiritual world—what Screwtape admits to be the true reality (Lewis, *The Screwtape Letters* 274). MacDonald, Chesterton, Lewis, and Tolkien each felt his part in the story of human history to be one of passing Christian myth on. The Great Tower of Elfland was not for them, alone. Adam in *Lilith* passes responsibilities on to Vane to save Lilith, her daughter, and others. GKC's *Manalive* husband and wife demonstrate what it means to make life an adventure to those around them. Lewis's Narniad children pass the Secondary

World down the line from Digory to the Pevensies and beyond (though, perhaps, inadvertently). And the story of the Ring of Power is passed down from Bilbo to Frodo to Sam. Myth is to be shared. It is only when someone stops believing in the power of myth and imagination, as Susan Pevensie does—essentially losing the faith of a child—that one's salvation for the next life is endangered.

Specifically, what occurs within myth and true fairy-story is what these authors believe leads most to salvation: joy. Chesterton writes that it is the greatest secret of the Christian (*Orthodoxy* 153). It is not simple happiness but a taste of something which leads to longing. This joy "is consolation for every true heart . . . [and] it stands on the border of the kingdom, about to enter into ever fuller, ever-growing possession *of the inheritance of the saints in light*" (MacDonald, *Unspoken Sermons* 606). Tolkien uses the same words, *joy* and *consolation,* to describe eucatastrophe ("On Fairy-Stories" 153). He admits that his discovery of eucatastrophe came with the revelation that it produces "a sudden glimpse of Truth, your whole nature chained in material cause and effect, the chain of death, feels a sudden relief as if a major limb out of joint had suddenly snapped back" (*Letters* 100). Fallen humanity, thus, has a chance at being pushed back into place—of salvation for eternity. If the story has what Tolkien deemed literary truth in the Secondary World, then the story of humanity contains the same kind of truth in the Primary World where the supreme eucatastrophe occurred in the resurrection of Christ, producing the necessary emotion of "Christian joy which produces tears because it is qualitatively so like sorrow, because it comes from those places where Joy and Sorrow are at one, reconciled, as selfishness and altruism are lost in Love" (100). Hence, were all the world to be tossed aside or placed on the verge of collapse—humanity, civilization, and all that we know in the Primary World—there is still eucatastrophe: a consolation which leads to a powerful joy and a sudden turn of events, even on the individual level. That is the target of their work: to bring about eucatastrophe for their readers, to pass on the mythopoeic vision which transformed them. Lewis writes that such events were always known to be contrary to "the natural course of events; we know still that if there is something beyond Nature, they are possible. Those are the bare bones of the question; time and progress and science and civilisation have not altered them in the least" (*Miracles* 343). Therefore, it is on this Great Tower of Elfland, upon the foundation of Christianity, that these authors perceive time, progress, science, and civilization and write with the hope of creating eucatastrophe and joy in the human spirit.

Notes

1. My intention is not to tear down the entirety of Sammons's work, though I feel her argument is hyperbolic. When broken into small details, certainly, incongruities are bound to appear, as will happen even when a ceramic varies slightly from one mold cast to another of the same variety. My intention here, rather, is to show how, even in explicating "war" between Lewis and Tolkien, a scholar cannot forego admitting that the two meet in unity in more than a few ways.

2. It is, nonetheless, ironic that the same CSL who rebutted Wain in the early 1960s wrote an invitation to Williams in March 1936, advertising only two informal requirements of Inkling membership: authorship and Christianity (Zaleski and Zaleski 238).

3. My choice of Freud's definition is not arbitrary. Kant's use of *Weltanschauung* seems, generally, to focus on a person's will, whether morally, religiously, or epistemologically motivated (see Richard Kroner's *Kant's Weltanschauung*, trans. John E. Smith), and Hegel considers these motivations within phenomenology (see his *Phenomenology of Mind* or, alternatively titled, *Phenomenology of Spirit*). Probably due to his psychoanalytic approach, Freud's definition is focused more on the internal source of one's worldview than Hegel's approach and is interested more in the motivation of the will than Kant's postulate. Because this text deals with moral, religious, epistemological, and phenomenological perspectives before espousing the overarching hypothesis, Freud's definition effectively characterizes the concept of the *Weltanschauung* herein described; furthermore, his definition is not only precise but also clear and concise, unlike the implied and lengthy explanations by Kant and Hegel.

4. For example, see *Letters*, pp. 28, 71, 72, 76, 79, 80, 81, 83, 103, 122, 184, 362, and 366.

5. The TCBS is an early literary group of which Tolkien was a part before entering into World War I.

6. I mean no offense here. Though *hypocrite* reportedly comes from a word meaning "actor" in its classical form, *hypocrite*, after all, contains the prefix *hypo-*, meaning "below," and roots *kritēs* and *kritikos*, from *critic*, or one with discerning judgment according to a set of standards ("Critic"; "Hypo-"; "Hypocrite"). Tolkien, in relation to his own literature, is a critic, I believe, whose judgment is subpar, so much so that he does not, at times, realize his failure to apply his standards for other literatures to his own. Tolkien even admitted that he was not a critic (*Letters* 126).

7. The most convincing argument to the contrary comes from Eric Seddon's article, "*Letters to Malcolm* and the Trouble with Narnia: C. S. Lewis, J. R. R. Tolkien, and their 1949 Crisis." Seddon makes many astute observations and necessary clarifications, such as debunking the "completely erroneous" assertion that Lewis embraced the Roman Catholic doctrine all but in name (74). On the contrary, Seddon argues that the "professional jealousy, artistic narrowness, and even personal complexity . . . seem unconvincing when considered in the broader context of their friendship and careers" (62). Seddon believes theological differences between the Anglican Lewis and Roman Catholic Tolkien created the divide between the once-close friends, particularly after Lewis's *Letters to Malcolm*, which makes jabs at Catholic beliefs on prayer and sainthood. Seddon's view, however, is complicated in many ways, not least by the "subjectivism" he attributes to Lewis and the "objectivism" he attributes to Tolkien on spiritual matters (67). It is clear that both were subjective in their views, but, ironically, it was Lewis who attempted to be objective in his theological approach, demonstrated most clearly in his publication of a denomination-less Christianity in *Mere Christianity*. Furthermore, though Tolkien appears to have been upset with Lewis's spiritual writings, Lewis would continue to write in the 1950s about how his trust in Catholics changed with Tolkien, attributing a key time of his spiritual development to his friendship with Tolkien (*Surprised by Joy* 209). Given the Catholic influences Lewis admits in his life—Tolkien, Chesterton, and Bede Griffiths, to name a few—it is hard to believe that the falling-out in their friendship is attributable to Lewis's subjectivity. The more likely conclusion is that, while Tolkien expected that his views receive Lewis's respect, Tolkien was unwilling to respect Lewis's views, causing Tolkien's withdrawal.

8. For example, 6–8 March 1941, Tolkien writes about how a man can be purely physical, friendly, or a lover in a relationship with a woman, but the sexual instinct is present in all instances, whether acknowledged or unacknowledged. Such problems with the sexual instinct result from living in a fallen world (*Letters* 48). He closely parodies Lewis's views in *Mere Christianity*, bk. 3, ch. 5 and in *The Screwtape Letters*, where Lewis posits that a relationship, recognized or not, is established whenever a man and a woman have sexual relations, and they will have to embrace or suffer the eternal ramifications of that relationship (237). Perhaps such similar views were one reason why Lewis dedicated *The Screwtape Letters* to Tolkien; Tolkien admittedly did not know why (*Letters* 342).

1. Language and Literature

1. McGrath claims that Lewis, likewise, may have traded apologetics for "fiction and symbol" after reportedly losing a debate to Katherine Anscombe in 1948 (260).

2. In *The Screwtape Letters,* Lewis writes from the perspective of the demonic Wormwood to his nephew, Screwtape, that the human should hypocritically demand every one of his statements be interpreted for the precision of his words, while he judges others' statements on intention, tone, and context (192).

3. Lewis demonstrates his concern for context throughout his fiction and didactic work. In *English Literature in the Sixteenth Century Excluding Drama,* he notes the modern misconception of the words *puritan* and *humanist.* While the modern understanding of *puritan* means "ascetic" and *humanist* means the opposite of *puritan,* the Elizabethan puritan sought, as radical Protestants, to reform the Church of England, and the humanist's aim was to apply the principles learned by studying Greek and Latin; Puritanism and Humanism, Lewis says, were not in opposition (17–18).

4. Tolkien referred to the difficult study of asterisk-words as "star-spangled grammar" in his "Valedictory Address" (237).

5. W. H. Auden called MacDonald's use of laws in fairyland "dream-realism," for they did not agree with the laws of reality but functioned consistently within themselves (Reis 89).

6. Eärendil is a man who, after recovering one of the three Silmarils, journeys to the land of the Valar, where he is given a ship to fly around the skies with the Silmaril. Those in Middle-earth could see the ship in the sky, calling it "Gil-Estel, the Star of High Hope" (Tolkien, *Silmarillion* 250).

7. Tolkien quipped at this kind of tagline to a fairy-story, though he made the argument that fairy-stories are for all ages ("On Fairy-Stories" 129).

8. Lewis further divides castle-building into two categories, egoistic and disinterested. Egoistic castle-building asks the daydreamer to be the hero and see the world like the hero; disinterested castle-building asks the daydreamer simply to observe the hero but not to be the hero or even present in the story (*An Experiment in Criticism* 52).

9. This passage is marked by Lewis in his copy of *Unspoken Sermons* at the Wade Center, Wheaton College.

10. As *The Everlasting Man* was a significant book for Lewis, it is not surprising that the theme of the virgin ride appears in *The Magician's Nephew* as well as *The Horse and His Boy.*

11. Please note that this wish-fulfillment differs from Lewis's concern of castle-building. Escape wish-fulfillment is to be taken into another world entirely—the world of the author—whereas castle-building has a set of psychological demands and Primary World laws that are expected to be fulfilled—much more a world of the reader than the author.

12. For clarification, I mean *real* not in the sense of *material.* One can point to stories, for instance, that reveal real problems and real solutions as clearly—or, perhaps, more clearly—than in the Primary World. Working with Coleridge's definition of the Primary and Secondary Imaginations, I would go so far as to say that Christ used the Secondary Imagination to illustrate truth through parables because truths were not as easily taught in the Primary World. Tolkien, Lewis, Chesterton, and MacDonald used the escape of fairy-stories in much the same way: to illustrate pieces of God's truth.

13. Lewis asserts that if, in fact, one's sense of adventure and fantasy is childish, then humanity need not engage in what he calls "chronological snobbery," or disapproval of things from an earlier time, because we should preserve imagination, the suspension of disbelief, and the readiness to pity, to wonder, and to admire (*An Experiment in Criticism* 72).

14. Adding to the concepts of fantasy and recovery, Lewis saw a bear named Bultitude at a zoo on the day he declares he found his salvation in Christianity; the bear at the zoo is adapted to *That Hideous Strength*'s bear, Mr. Bultitude (Green and Hooper 116).

15. Lewis, admittedly, created allegory with *The Pilgrim's Regress,* but he did not believe that fairy-stories or myths were allegories.

16. In evaluating MacDonald's mythopoeia, Richard H. Reis provides three categories of symbols, which, I add, inexplicably apply to Tolkien but which he would have resisted: traditional symbols, arbitrarily assigned through history (e.g., water, earth, air, and fire); natural symbols, assigned by apparent or linguistic context (e.g., Greek *psyche* means both "sun" and "butterfly"); and private symbols, assigned by the author's personal significance (108–11).

17. See Letter 131, a 1951 letter to Milton Waldman. Tolkien writes that he does not like intentional allegory, but an explanation of myth or fairy-story requires the use of allegorical language (*Letters* 145).

18. John Garth suggests that Tolkien's dragons, orcs, and balrogs, among other creations—I would add the Wolfhead, Grond, to the list—resemble the tanks and new armored vehicles of the Great War, which he notes were referred to as jabberwocks, Leviathans, and other "mythical monsters" by one diarist of the war (220–21).

19. "The subject-matter of literary criticism is art, and criticism is evidently something of an art too. . . . There is another reason why criticism has to exist. Criticism can talk, and all the arts are dumb" (Frye 3–4).

20. Here, Tolkien borrows a phrase from Friedrich Max Müller's *The Science of Language* in the lecture "Metaphor," cited by Lewis in "The Empty Universe," p. 82.

21. For a clearer understanding of Tolkien's view of the entanglement of *Lit* and *Lang,* see his "Valedictory Address," where he posits a study of literature is a study of language, for literature is composed of language. Hence, in his mind, English degrees should only be in "English Language," not in "English Language and Literature."

22. It is worth mentioning that the authors did not pursue a psychobiographical approach in literature, as Lewis is clearly against it in "The Genesis of a Medieval Book" (38). The idea is to appreciate and understand the artist's world, not the author. Peter Shakel comments that the poet, for Lewis, is "an abstraction constructed after the fact," for the biography and world of the author is only important insofar as it helps to create the text (113). As McGrath notes, a poem is to be read for what the poet sees, not what the readers sees of the poet (190).

23. Tolkien, here, warns CSL that Lewis the critic gets in the way of Lewis the writer but concedes that Lewis is "a born critic" and "teacher," the former of which Tolkien, self-admittedly, is not (*Letters* 126).

24. Arnold, *A Note on the Verse of John Milton*. The text is available at the Marion E. Wade Center at Wheaton College.

25. Lewis categorizes readers into literary and unliterary, explaining the pros and cons of both types. See particularly *An Experiment in Criticism,* pp. 28–53.

26. Lewis echoes this sentiment strongly in "Screwtape Proposes a Toast," pp. 293–96.

27. *Favoring* and *appreciating* should not be confused here. MacDonald, Chesterton, Lewis, and Tolkien encourage the audience to *appreciate* the view of the artist via *logos* and *poiema*, although they may not *like* it according to their taste. Lewis writes that the true reader immerses his entire self into each text, making himself as open to the text as possible (11). For the artist to attempt to meet the reader's taste would do what Tolkien regrettably did with *The Hobbit* in trying to meet some audiences halfway.

28. Their shared concept of the fairy-story fits into myth, as defined here.

29. Lewis disagrees with Frye's simple definition of *myth* as when the hero is superior to other humans (*Anatomy of Criticism* 33).

30. Tolkien believes that readers can sometimes misattribute the numinous experience to technicalities: for myth to touch them on a deeper level yet to believe the effect was due, somehow, to the poetic form or artistic style ("Beowulf: The Monsters" 14–15).

Joseph Campbell claims there are four essential functions of occidental mythology: to create the numinous experience (to use Lewis's term); to create a cosmology out of the numinous and mysterious divinity; to support social order; and to facilitate individual psychological development (519–21). Campbell's view of myth is simpler and focused more on the relation of myth to the Primary World; however, the only point of disagreement is that Lewis et al. rejected myth as a mode of cultural change or order (though it can express or record such changes).

31. Chesterton was referring to the imagination of W. B. Yeats.

32. Duriez notes that Bombadil's character is drawn from a name given to a Dutch doll of Tolkien's son, Michael (*Tolkien and C. S. Lewis* 62).

33. Haldane, similarly, says Dante and Milton struggled to reconcile science with theology in their times, and "Lewis finds it impossible" (16). Lewis responds that his science does not need to be correct in his fiction, but Haldane's history should be correct in his essay. Dante was aware, for instance, of the astronomy

NOTES TO PAGES 39–48

of the time—Ptolemy's *Almagest*—and the roundness of the Earth—Vincent of Beauvais's *Speculum Naturale* ("A Reply to Professor Haldane" 70–71).

34. If my theory is at all true, then it makes sense that Tolkien would claim he was a hobbit in every way except his size, followed by a list of hobbit-like qualities with which he sympathizes (*Letters* 288).

35. It is worth noting that Barfield's view of imagination differed from Lewis and the others. As P. Zaleski and C. Zaleski suggest, Barfield thought the imagination was a means to acquire objective truth, whereas Lewis and Tolkien—and I would add Chesterton and MacDonald—felt that the imagination "pointed toward truth but could not disclose it directly" because fairy-stories only subtly "reflect religious truth" in ways unlike the Primary World (114, 125).

36. See Chesterton, *Orthodoxy*, p. 43.

37. Tolkien believes his position on imagination diverges from Coleridge's, but as Flieger claims, Tolkien's views are largely indebted to Coleridge (*Splintered Light* 22–23). The real difference, says Flieger, is that Tolkien understood imagination and fancy as differences only in degree rather than separation (24). Coleridge writes, "Fancy and Imagination were too distinct and wildly different faculties, instead of being, according to the general belief, either two names with one meaning, or, at furthest, the lower and higher degree of one and the same power" (54). For Tolkien, the Primary Imagination is "God's creative Logos—the Word—in the mind" while the Secondary is an echo of the Primary, more human and less Godlike; fancy is giving a sense of reality to ideal, imaginary creations: fantasy. By combining imagination and fancy, then, the sum is sub-creation (Flieger, *Splintered Light* 25).

38. Tolkien says a glimpse of divinity via religion sometimes occurs in mythology ("On Fairy-Stories" 124).

2. ALL THAT IS HUMAN

1. Borrowing, says Oser, from Swift's 1725 letter to Pope (10–11).

2. The Huorns exemplify his contemplation in that Merry believes they are Ents that appear to have devolved into trees, something strange and "wild" (Tolkien, *The Two Towers* 551).

3. Roderick McGillis, in his "Explanatory Notes" to *The Princess and the Goblin / The Princess and Curdie*, interprets the soft goblin feet to signify their lack of souls—another attribute necessary to be hnau (349).

4. Indeed, *The Princess and the Goblin* and *The Princess and Curdie* may be grounded in MacDonald's meditation on Romans 8.1–17, which discusses the dichotomy between focus on flesh and spirit, life and death, and adoption by God.

5. See ch. 5, under the heading "Attributes of God" (page 136), for a discussion of how reason is found in the God figure.

6. Lewis, no doubt, draws upon Genesis 1.26–27: "Then God said, 'Let us make humankind in our image, according to our likeness; and let them have dominion

over the fish of the sea, and over the birds of the air, and over the cattle, and over all the wild animals of the earth, and over every creeping thing that creeps upon the earth. So God created humankind in his image, / in the image of God he created them; / male and female he created them" (NRSV).

7. *Bios* is not innately evil. As Lewis writes in *The Problem of Pain*, biological matter can not only hold people apart but also bring people together. Humans are able to have an external self and internal self, physical body and metaphysical spirit, an appearance and a being (563). The problem occurs when the *Bios* is privileged above the *Zoe*.

8. See ch. 3 for further discussion on fate.

9. There is, perhaps, a further sense of the Medieval in Lewis's view, for as Edmund, Lucy, and Eustace peer at a distance at the End of the World into Aslan's country, it is through a wall of water at the end of the world, something like the Medieval view of the Empyrean outside Earth's atmosphere. Whereas modern society believes it looks outward at the Empyrean, the Medieval person looked inward at something greater and more wonderful than the realm within Earth's limits (*The Voyage of the* Dawn Treader 539–40; "Imagination and Thought" 59).

10. The presence of evil in the hierarchy will be discussed further in ch. 5.

11. In context of ch. 3, the pony's ability to select a good path is like that of guiding his master to a good fate.

12. It is worth noting that Tolkien warns that beasts are not to be valued over humans. When humans feel more for animals than for other humans, the necessary hierarchy is disregarded, and humans fail to value the divine more than the bestial ("Beowulf: The Monsters" 160).

13. Galadriel hints at the power of the will when she talks with Frodo and Sam after their view into the Mirror of Galadriel: "Did not Gandalf tell you that the rings give power according to their measure of each possessor? Before you could use that power you would need to become far stronger, and to train your will to the domination of others" (*The Fellowship* 357).

14. The Fall, in fact, is throughout Lewis's space trilogy. In *Out of the Silent Planet*, Ransom observes the Fall on Malacandra (Mars), examines the mythology of Thulcandra's (Earth's) Fall, and hears of the Silent Planet's, Thulcandra's, corrupt Oyarsa who rebelled against Maleldil. *That Hideous Strength* is the culmination of these events, where the interplanetary—or, shall we say, heavenly—rebellion is brought to the forefront.

15. Civilization and its corruption will be further discussed in ch. 4.

3. THE JOURNEY

1. P. Zaleski and C. Zaleski note that *Anodos* is "a Platonic term for the ascent to truth" (85).

2. To complicate things further, Tolkien claims that Frodo lost control of himself. Frodo could not choose to avoid his doom; he would fail in his quest, give into

temptation, and break under the pressure of Sauron's will, regardless of any choice or desire to do otherwise (*Letters* 233). See also, *Letters,* pp. 251, 326.

3. Along these lines, Pippin notes that the group should not follow a particular path because it was made by trolls (200). The maker of the path, therefore, seems significant as to whether one should follow it, not unlike one's life choice to follow a good or evil person, a compassionate person or a thieving criminal.

4. Neither the earlier judgment of fate nor the imposed judgment of *wyrd* seem necessarily to impact the result of death, as one dwarf reportedly made it to the right of Aslan (Lewis, *The Last Battle* 751).

5. Recall, from ch. 1, that *eucatastrophe* is Tolkien's term for the sudden turn of events that leads to a happy ending, an essential element of the fairy-story ("On Fairy-Stories" 153).

6. Chesterton demonstrates this kind of fear with ch. 5, "The Feast of Fear" in *The Man Who Was Thursday,* as the men have a healthy fear of the nightmarish God-character, Sunday.

7. See also *Letters,* pp. 234, 253.

8. Fear and pity, as we have discussed, are also signs along the way, but fear is not a traditional virtue, despite being a means by which one demonstrates the virtue of courage, or fortitude. Thus, for the sake of brevity, I have not expounded further on courage, as it was covered already in the discussion of overcoming unhealthy fear. Pity, however, will be discussed further in terms of mercy.

9. Chesterton writes, "The virtues have gone mad because they have been isolated from each other and are wandering alone" (*Orthodoxy* 22).

10. In fact, Lewis thanks Tolkien in the Preface to *The Allegory of Love* for reading and commenting on the first chapter, from where the following claims are extracted.

11. McGrath offers a reason why courtly love was problematic for Lewis when he asserts that Lewis participated in courtly love with Mrs. Moore. Lewis saw his love for her as "a noble and honourable code of conduct by which a young man might 'leap up on errands' or 'go through heat or cold, at the bidding of one's lady'" (97).

12. Lewis's copy of *Unspoken Sermons* at the Wade Center, Wheaton College, has much of this passage underlined with a side mark to note its significance.

13. To be accurate, Frodo does not actually go to an eternal life in Valinor. His stay in Valinor will only be to the end of his life—a kind of purgatory to help cleanse him before his passing into death (Tolkien, *Letters* 198–99, 205).

14. GMD here is referring to one who has seen a sign of death and has a longing for new life.

15. Lewis writes vis-à-vis the demon, Screwtape, that humans are subject to pride even in their humility, for the moment the person recognizes their own humility, their pride may surface to praise how humble they are (*The Screwtape Letters* 224).

16. A further discussion on the problem of evil is in ch. 5.

17. GMD's opinion on Hell was not shared by the group; however, his view that good can come out of evil is present in this opinion.

4. Civilization and Origination

1. Other similar terms are *presentism* and what Richard D. Altick and John J. Fenstermaker call the *anachronistic fallacy:* "either attributing present-day attitudes to a past society or of reproaching that society for *not* sharing our values" (153). The difference between Altick and Fenstermaker's term and Lewis's term, *chronological snobbery,* is that Lewis suggests such snobbery extends beyond a reproach of a past society to a complete discredit of a past society or belief. See also: Lewis, *An Experiment,* 73.

2. Lewis may very well be reflecting on a section of Chesterton's *The Everlasting Man* in which Chesterton explains that savage in modern times could not be like a primitive savage because the modern is not primitive—in the same way that an ancient is not modern. Primitive humans had certain experiences and contexts that shaped them in the same way that modern people are shaped by context and experience (57).

3. At first glance, it may appear that GMD is privileging royalty as civilized and the goblins as savage people, but the assignment of *civilized* to the royal garden is arbitrary in its description of humanity. The wildness of the mountain as the goblin home, however, is intentional because the goblins truly are bestial and uncivilized in their lack of humanity.

4. One might argue that the examples of artistic creations used here were ultimately evil. Agreeably, I submit that Fëanor's creation of the Silmarils led to selfish, un-hnau-like actions such as his rejection of the Valar; however, he created out of his hnau nature, and by embracing the creative side of his nature, he created in a pure way. It was his response after creating the product that corrupted his path. Similarly, the rings of power were created naively by elves who thought Sauron their friend. While their motives of artistic creation were pure, Sauron's clearly were not.

5. Chesterton refers to *realism* as occurring when truth is applied to everyone else except oneself (*Autobiography* 325). Lewis, likewise, differentiates among the meanings of *realism* in *An Experiment,* where he explains that *realism,* in logic, refers to what is nominal, but, in metaphysics, *realism* refers to the opposite of idealism. A third meaning (more of a connotation than a definition) appears in politics, which uses *cynicism* to describe *realism* when an opponent is realistic or which uses *realism* as a positive term when the favored party uses it (57).

6. Chesterton writes, "The greatest disaster of the nineteenth century was this: that men began to use the world 'spiritual' as the same as the word 'good'" (*Orthodoxy* 146).

7. For instance, Lewis fronted an attempt, with Neville Coghill, Frank Hardie, and Henry Yorke (penname Green) to send mock Eliot-like verse to the *Dial* or *Criterion* under the names of an incestuous brother and sister, Rollo and Bridget Considine, in hopes it would be published as serious poetry (Green and Hooper 89; Carpenter, *Inklings* 21).

8. It is on this basis that GKC claims Jesus was either a madman or exactly who he said he was. Lewis borrows this claim in *The Problem of Pain*, p. 558.

9. MacDonald studied chemistry and natural philosophy at King's College, but he would write to his father that he had doubts whether or not he should study chemistry. Raeper believes that GMD's "poetic yearnings" directed him in one way while "common sense and sound economics" encouraged him in another path (44).

If one were to consider the modern scientific String Theory, then Lewis and MacDonald's claims are all the more factual. The idea that all things are connected by tiny strings is conceptually reminiscent of how many religions have viewed the world: as a world connected by spirit. Perhaps the first time since the Age of Reason, many popular theologians have begun to recognize the similarities of scientific findings to the beliefs of Christianity. For example, see Rob Bell's film *Everything Is Spiritual* or Louie Giglio's *Indescribable*.

10. For example, Wheelwright suggests three main human liminal thresholds that affect language: time, otherness (other-than-self perspectives), and upward (vertical growth; e.g., heavenward, religion) (19–31). Humanity cannot process all of these thresholds completely, as we are trapped within time, othered in too many ways to be calculated, and we have limited knowledge of the upward journey.

11. Recall the definition of *civilization* since its inception in the Age of Reason: "human cultural, social, and intellectual development when considered to be advanced and progressive in nature" (*OED*).

12. I do not mean *bestiality* in the common, modern, and sexual understanding of the word, though this form of bestiality very well demonstrates the point about how virtues could not naturally arise from such behavior; nonetheless, I mean *bestiality* in its traditional understanding: to refer to what is beast-like.

13. The human creation as a creator will be discussed further in ch. 5.

14. The creation of Eä by Ilúvatar's word, *Eä*, in *The Silmarillion* is an example of what John describes at the beginning of his gospel: "In the beginning was the Word, and the Word was with God, and the Word was God. He was in the beginning with God. All things came into being through him, and without him not one thing came into being. What has come into being in him was life, and the life was the light of all people. The light shines in the darkness, and the darkness did not overcome it" (John 1.1–5, NRSV). Additionally, the word, *Eä*, means, "it is," a copula usage simply to demonstrate existence, much like Moses's experience with God at the burning bush in Exodus 3.14: "I AM WHO I AM. . . . Thus you shall say to the Israelites, 'I AM has sent me to you'" (NRSV).

15. This passage is another example of Tolkien's adoption of Lewis's philosophical discussion in texts of which he disapproved. Lewis writes in *Mere Christianity, good* could not mean *good* unless something deemed it *good,* and the moment someone declares what *good* is, a third thing comes into play aside from *good* and *evil:* a law, standard, or rule that determines what fits within the category of *good.* Accordingly, whoever or whatever determines the rule is

above the rule, and though others can try to establish *goodness,* the determining being is ultimately God (44).

16. One might recall Herman Melville's *Typee* and the narrator's stark contrast of Polynesian to British women; both were as stately and beautiful as the other, if the former was not moreso attractive. They simply had different standards of appearance.

17. Kreeft cites *Macbeth* V.5, where Macbeth articulates a view of history which sees no purpose in life and certainly no story.

18. Lewis reiterates Chesterton's comments in *The Abolition of Man,* pp. 721–23.

19. The egoistic belief that the will is the means to power is counter to the *Tao,* which is concerned for the individual; ironically, says Chesterton, Nietzsche denied his own egoistic philosophy simply by preaching it: "To preach egoism is to practice altruism" (*Orthodoxy* 30). The problem with the modern revolutionist is that, "In his book on politics he attacks men for trampling on morality; in his book on ethics he attacks morality for trampling on men. Therefore the modern man in revolt has become practically useless for all purposes of revolt. By rebelling against everything he has lost his right to rebel against anything" (34).

20. In maintaining the musical quality of morality, Meilaender notes how the dance becomes an image for Lewis to demonstrate community among humanity and God, as with the King and Queen of Perelandra (49–50).

21. Compare to Genesis 16.12.

5. The Overarching Hypothesis

1. Clearly enough, Lewis was an Irish Protestant (which Tolkien criticizes him for); MacDonald was a bridge between Protestantism and Catholicism; Chesterton was a Protestant-to-Catholic convert who still held strong to some Protestant principles (although he certainly would not admit to them as being Protestant); and Tolkien was an avowed Catholic, arguably due to a sad family history.

2. Shippey notes, "It seems very likely that Lewis and Tolkien co-operated in their analysis of Christian essentials" (*The Road* 236).

3. The pun is intended here, for each author certainly had stories to tell, though each part of this chapter represents a storey, or floor, in the Great Tower of Elfland. Coincidentally, *storey* is, perhaps, drawn from Late Middle English and a special usage in Anglo-Latin, which referred to "a tier of painted windows or sculptures" representing something historical on the front face of a building ("Storey"). The stories of this tower no less represent the tales of these authors' lives alongside the tales they wrote than they represent the artifacts that make up their *Weltanschauung.*

4. Campbell calls original myths *occidental myths* and subdivides them into religious (divinity judges humanity) and humanistic (humanity judges divinity) (4).

5. Purtill notes that creating an original myth today would be nearly impossible because the belief would make the myth rather than the other way around (5–6).

6. See Wheelwright, *The Burning Fountain* 33–34, for a Gestalt-like approach in which he elucidates four imaginations that fit into both Primary and Secondary imaginations: confrontative (intensifies and particularizes an object), stylistic (distances and stylizes the object), compositive (unifies separate elements), and archetypal (object viewed in larger context).

7. Lewis footnotes this passage with a clarification that *myth* means something that may be factual as well as fictional. He wants the reader to know that *myth* does not, as in Dr. Niebuhr's definition, necessarily symbolize nonhistorical truth (593).

8. For example, see Lewis, *Surprised by Joy* 150–51; Tolkien, *Letters* 235; Carpenter, *J. R. R. Tolkien: A Biography* 130.

9. Positivism, empiricism, and materialism may serve as modern equivalents to what Lewis terms *naturalism,* all of which decenter humanity in the universe.

10. Lewis explains the liminality of reality in that other types of nature may not be restricted to the temporality of the Primary World. Though he does not use the term *dimension,* his explanation hints at a philosophy that liminality is the space between "Other Natures," or dimensions, which would not otherwise synchronize. Their only relation is that they come from the same Creator: God (*Miracles* 309).

11. Anodos of *Phantastes,* likewise, is another of MacDonald's characters who demonstrates liminality between Primary and Secondary Worlds. Though his name is "pathless," he does find a path: one which extends between worlds.

12. In agreement with Chesterton's later claim, MacDonald writes of imagination, "The word itself means an *imaging* or a making of likenesses. The imagination is that faculty which gives form to thought—not necessarily uttered form, but form capable of being uttered in shape or in sound, or in any mode upon which the sense can lay hold" ("The Imagination" 2).

13. Tolkien, likewise, explains that if Gandalf had become the master of the Ring—the only one capable of overpowering Sauron's will—he would have been worse than Sauron because his righteousness would have turned into self-righteousness. While Sauron's rule maintained a distinction between good and evil, Gandalf's rule would have made good seem evil (*Letters* 332–33).

14. Yavanna has the ability to sing life into the world, and like Ilúvatar whose note, *Eä,* puts the Ainur's song into physical existence, Yavanna sings life and light into the world via the Two Trees of Valinor (Tolkien, *Silmarillion* 38).

15. Furthermore, as Flieger notes, the dispersing of elves (Quendi) from Valinor, where light originates, symbolizes the fragmentation of light. The elves who journey to Valinor earn the prefix *tar* to be Tareldar, "High Elves." Those who do not go are the Avari, the Unwilling/Refusers. The Quenya language of the Avari changes over time. The Tareldar later become known as the Calaquendi, Elves of Light—*kal-* meaning "shine" (*Splintered Light* 73). The elves who stay in Middle-earth instead of going to Valinor earn the *mor-* prefix, meaning "dark." *Moreldar* is the name given to the Avari by the Tareldar, though not called such by the Avari themselves. The Calequendi are literally named "Speakers of Light"; the Moriquendi, the "Speakers of Darkness" (74).

16. Lewis echoes GKC in *Miracles* when he claims that a person believes the sun is in the summer sky at noon not because one has stared at the sun but because one can see the world around them (400).

17. Ungoliant is the ancestral spider of Shelob in *The Two Towers*.

18. The Silmarils acquire their name from the word *silmarilli,* which means "radiance of pure light" (Tolkien, *Letters* 148).

19. For the sake of focus and brevity, I have chosen to discuss only what may be considered some of the main characteristics of God affecting the *Weltanschauung* categories as we have observed in this text rather than present an extensive catalogue of agreed-upon adjectives for the divine.

20. Lewis and Tolkien note this same quality of pagan poetry in their view of *Northernness.* Lewis, in particular, would refer to this sadness as part of *Northernness* in *Surprised by Joy* (69).

21. The *OED*'s etymology actualizes the connection between *good* and *god,* as *good* is traced through Old English *gód,* Old Norse *góð,* and Germanic root *gôd-,* which may be a variant of *gad,* "to bring together, to unite," but *good* implies a standard which requires "having an adequate degree those properties which a thing of the kind ought to have" and as a noun, "Whatever is good in itself, or beneficial in effect" ("Good").

22. *Perichoresis* is the term in vogue to characterize the Trinity: "The interrelationship or interpenetration of the Persons of the Trinity; the manner in which the three Persons are regarded as conjoined or interlinked without each one's distinct identity being lost" (*OED*).

23. Chesterton discusses how Christ could be viewed as either insane or divine (*The Everlasting Man* 192–93, 202–06, 270).

24. On p. 9 of Lewis's copy of MacDonald's first volume of *Unspoken Sermons* at the Marion E. Wade Center.

25. Gaarden argues that MacDonald rejected the Reformation's idea of salvation as a pardon for sin; instead, GMD returned to the old Catholic doctrine iterated in Dante: the individual in union with God like St. John's image of Christ married to the Church ("Faerie Romance and Divine Comedy" 60).

26. To unpack this statement, in the context of art as the highest mode of human creation and one of the crucial ways in which humans may be like God—sub-creators—Chesterton is saying that when humans create, we come into contact with part of that spiritual nature. When one creates art, one may come into contact with the most Godlike aspect of the human for "one awful instant."

27. McGillis, in the "Explanatory Notes" to *The Princess and the Goblin / The Princess and Curdie,* claims GMD's doctrine of becoming is a "revisionary reading of Darwin" where physical and spiritual states undergo change (345).

28. See MacDonald, *The Princess and the Goblin* 13, 84.

29. See also: MacDonald, *Unspoken Sermons* 29; Lewis, *The Screwtape Letters* 222.

30. Lewis writes in *Mere Christianity* the significance of the individual over civilization. A person may only live seventy years as compared to a culture or

civilization that may last for millennia; however, according to Christianity, the individual's soul will last far beyond a civilization because the soul will exist for eternity (69).

31. After the rule of Aragorn, all of Middle-earth resumes its progressive decay, so much so that Tolkien says he could have written a thriller—what he believed was not worth writing (*Letters* 344).

32. Chesterton uses the same phrase in his *Autobiography* that he must go backward in his story in order to go forward (109).

33. Carpenter believes this theme of community and male companionship is found also in the writings of Chesterton (*J. R. R. Tolkien: A Biography* 148).

Works Cited

Ahlquist, Dale. "Lecture 6: *The Napoleon of Notting Hill.*" Chesterton.org. *The American Chesterton Society* (2012). Web. 19 Feb. 2014.

Altick, Richard D., and John J. Fenstermaker. *The Art of Literary Research.* New York: Norton, 1993.

Arnold, Matthew. *A Note on the Verse of John Milton. Essays and Studies,* Vol. XXI. N.p.: N.p.,1936.

Attebery, Brian. "High Church versus Broad Church: Christian Myth in George MacDonald and C. S. Lewis." *New York Review of Science Fiction* 18.3.207 (2005): 14–17.

Billone, Amy. "Hovering between Irony and Innocence: George MacDonald's 'The Light Princess' and the Gravity of Childhood." *Mosaic: A Journal for the Interdisciplinary Study of Literature* 37.1 (2004): 135–48. *LION.* Web. 4 Mar. 2012.

Burns, Marjorie. *Perilous Realms: Celtic and Norse in Tolkien's Middle-Earth.* Toronto: U of Toronto P, 2005.

Campbell, Joseph. *The Masks of God: Creative Mythology.* New York: Viking, 1965.

Carpenter, Humphrey. *The Inklings.* London: HarperCollins, 1997.

———. *J. R. R. Tolkien: A Biography.* New York: Houghton, 2000.

Chesterton, G. K. *The Autobiography of G. K. Chesterton.* San Francisco: Ignatius, 2006.

———. *The Ballad of the White Horse.* Mineola, NY: Dover, 2010.

———. *The Ball and the Cross. The Collected Works of G. K. Chesterton.* Vol. VII. San Francisco: Ignatius, 2004. 37–258.

———. *The Blatchford Controversies. The Collected Works of G. K. Chesterton.* Ed. David Dooley. Vol. I. San Francisco: Ignatius, 1986. 367–95.

———. *The Everlasting Man.* San Francisco: Ignatius, 2008.

———. "Fools and Facts." N.d. MS-19. Marion E. Wade Center, Wheaton, IL.

———. "George Macdonald [sic]." *SEVEN: An Anglo-American Literary Review* (2011): 4–7. PDF file.

———. "George Macdonald [sic] and His Work." *SEVEN: An Anglo-American Literary Review* (2011): 8–10. PDF file.

———. "GKC on Fairy Tales." Ca. 1889. MS-121. Marion E. Wade Center, Wheaton, IL.

———. *Heretics. The Collected Works of G. K. Chesterton.* Ed. David Dooley. Vol. I. San Francisco: Ignatius, 1986. 39–207.

———. "Man." Ca. 1900. MS-123. Marion E. Wade Center, Wheaton, IL.

———. *The Man Who Was Thursday: A Nightmare.* Ed. Kingsley Amis. Harmondsworth: Penguin, 1986.

———. "Misc. Notes and Sketches." N.d. MS-26. Marion E. Wade Center, Wheaton, IL.

———. *The Napoleon of Notting Hill. The Collected Works of G. K. Chesterton.* Vol. VI. San Francisco: Ignatius, 1991. 215–379.

———. "The Opium of the People." N.d. MS-36. Marion E. Wade Center, Wheaton, IL.

———. *Orthodoxy.* Mineola, NY: Dover, 2004.

———. "Preachers from the Pew—'Vox Populi, Vox Dei.'" TS (MS-61). Marion E. Wade Center, Wheaton, IL.

———. "The Psychological Man." N.d. MS-42. Marion E. Wade Center, Wheaton, IL.

Christopher, Joe R. *C. S. Lewis.* Boston: Twayne, 1987.

"Civilization." *The Oxford English Dictionary.* Oxford UP, 2014. Web. 9 Mar. 2014.

Coleridge, Samuel Taylor. *Biographia Literaria.* Ed. John Calvin Metcalf. New York: MacMillan, 1926.

Collins, Robert A. "Liminality in *Lilith.*" *Lilith in a New Light. Critical Explorations in Science Fiction and Fantasy.* Ed. Lucas H. Harriman. Vol. 10. Jefferson, NC: McFarland, 2008. 7–14.

"Critic." *Oxford Dictionaries.* Oxford UP, 2015. Web. 30 Dec. 2015.

Derrida, Jacques. *Of Grammatology.* Trans. Gayatri Chakravorty Spivak. Baltimore: Johns Hopkins UP, 1976.

Downing, David C. *Planets in Peril: A Critical Study of C. S. Lewis's Ransom Trilogy.* Amherst: U of Massachusetts P, 1992.

———. "Sub-Creation or Smuggled Theology: Tolkien contra Lewis on Christian Fantasy." C. S. Lewis Institute.org. *C. S. Lewis Institute,* n.d. Web. 1 Apr. 2012. http://www.cslewisinstitute.org/.

Dryden, John. "The Author's Apology for Heroic Poetry and Heroic License." Preface to *State of Innocence. The Works of John Dryden.* Ed. Sir Walter Scott. Vol. 5. Edinburgh: Archibald Constable, 1821. *Google Books.* 105–18. PDF file.

Duriez, Colin. *The Oxford Inklings: Lewis, Tolkien, and Their Circle.* Oxford: Lion, 2015.

———. *Tolkien and C. S. Lewis: The Gift of Friendship.* Mahwah: HiddenSpring, 2003.

Edwards, Bruce. "Toward a Rhetoric of Nineteenth-Century Fantasy Criticism." *The Victorian Fantasists: Essays on Culture, Society, and Belief in Victorian Mythopoeic Literature.* Ed. Kath Filmer. London: MacMillan, 1990. 69–81.

Flieger, Verlyn. *Green Suns and Faërie: Essays on J. R. R. Tolkien.* Kent, Ohio: Kent State UP, 2012.

———. "Myth, Mysticism, and Magic: Reading at the Close of *Lilith.*" *Lilith in a New Light. Critical Explorations in Science Fiction and Fantasy.* Ed. Lucas H. Harriman. Vol. 10. Jefferson, NC: McFarland, 2008. 39–45.

———. *Splintered Light: Logos and Language in Tolkien's World.* Grand Rapids, MI.: Eerdmans, 1983.

Freud, Sigmund. "Lecture XXXV: The Question of a *Weltanschauung.*" *The Freud Reader.* Ed. Peter Gay. New York: Norton, 1989. 783–95.

Frost, Robert. "The Road Not Taken." *Bartleby.com. Bartleby,* 2014. Web. 21 Feb. 2014.

Frye, Northrop. *Anatomy of Criticism.* Princeton, NJ: Princeton UP, 1957.

Gaarden, Bonnie. "Cosmic and Psychological Redemption in *Lilith.*" *Lilith in a New Light. Critical Explorations in Science Fiction and Fantasy.* Ed. Lucas H. Harriman. Vol. 10. Jefferson, NC: McFarland, 2008. 111–27.

———. "Faerie Romance and the Divine Comedy: God Marries His People in George MacDonald's Heather & Snow." *Scottish Studies Review* 7.2 (2006): 58–78. PDF file.

Gabelman, Daniel. "Two Essays on George MacDonald by G. K. Chesterton." *SEVEN: An Anglo-American Literary Review* (2011): 1–3. PDF file.

Garth, John. *Tolkien and the Great War.* Boston: Houghton, 2003.

Glyer, Diana Pavlac. *The Company They Keep: C. S. Lewis and J. R. R. Tolkien as Writers in Community.* Kent, Ohio: Kent State UP, 2007.

"Good." *The Oxford English Dictionary.* Oxford UP, 2014. Web. 14 Mar. 2014.

Green, Roger L., and Walter Hooper. *C. S. Lewis: A Biography.* New York: Harcourt, 1974.

Gresham, Douglas H. *Lenten Lands: My Childhood with Joy Davidman and C. S. Lewis.* New York: HarperSanFrancisco, 2003.

Haldane, J. B. S. "Auld Hornie, F. R. S." *Shadows of Imagination: The Fantasies of C. S. Lewis, J. R. R. Tolkien, and Charles Williams.* Ed. Mark R. Hillegas. London: Southern Illinois UP, 1979. 15–25.

Hardy, Elizabeth Baird. *Milton, Spenser, and the Chronicles of Narnia: Literary Sources for the C. S. Lewis Novels.* Jefferson, NC: McFarland, 2007.

Hein, Rolland. *The Harmony Within: The Spiritual Vision of George MacDonald.* Grand Rapids, MI: Christian UP, 1982.

Hetzler, Leo A. "George MacDonald and G. K. Chesterton." *Durham University Journal* 37 (1976): 176–82.

Holmes, John R. "Tolkien, Dustsceawung, and the Gnomic Tense: Is Timelessness Medieval or Victorian?" *Tolkien's Modern Middle Ages (The New Middle Ages).* Ed. Jane Chance and Alfred K. Siewers. New York: Palgrave, 2009. 43–60.

"Hypo-." *Oxford Dictionaries.* Oxford UP, 2015. Web. 30 Dec. 2015.

"Hypocrite." *Oxford Dictionaries.* Oxford UP, 2015. Web. 30 Dec. 2015.

"Joy." *The Oxford English Dictionary.* Oxford UP, 2014. Web. 9 Mar. 2014.

King, Don W. "Topical Poems: C. S. Lewis's Postconversion Poetry." *C. S. Lewis: Life, Works, and Legacy.* Vol. 2. Westport: Praeger, 2007. *EBSCOhost.* Ebook. 8 Apr. 2015.

Knoepflmacher, U. C. "Introduction." *The Complete Fairy Tales.* By George Mac-Donald. Ed. U. C. Knoepflmacher. New York: Penguin, 1999. vii–xx.

Kreeft, Peter. *The Philosophy of Tolkien: The Worldview Behind the Lord of the Rings.* San Francisco: Ignatius, 2003.

Levi-Strauss, Claude. *Myth and Meaning.* New York: Schocken, 1979.

Lewis, C. S. *The Abolition of Man. The Complete C. S. Lewis Signature Classics.* New York: HarperOne, 2007. 689–738.

———. *The Allegory of Love: A Study in Medieval Tradition.* New York: Oxford UP, 1958. Print.

———. "The Death of Words." *On Stories and other Essays on Literature.* Orlando, FL: Harvest, 1982. 105–07.

———. "De Audiendis Poetis." *Studies in Medieval and Renaissance Literature.* Cambridge: Cambridge UP, 1966. 1–17.

———. "Democratic Education." *Present Concerns.* Ed. Walter Hooper. San Diego: Harvest, 1986. 32–36.

———. "The Empty Universe." *Present Concerns.* Ed. Walter Hooper. San Diego: Harvest, 1986. 81–86.

———. *English Literature in the Sixteenth Century Excluding Drama.* Oxford: Clarendon UP, 1965.

———. "Equality." *Present Concerns.* Ed. Walter Hooper. San Diego: Harvest, 1986. 17–20.

———. *An Experiment in Criticism.* Cambridge: Cambridge UP, 1961.

———. *The Four Loves.* Boston: Mariner, 2012.

———. "The Genesis of a Medieval Book." *Studies in Medieval and Renaissance Literature.* Cambridge: Cambridge UP, 1966. 18–40.

———. "God in the Dock." *The Collected Works of C. S. Lewis:* The Pilgrim's Regress, Christian Reflections, God in the Dock. New York: Inspirational, 1996. 462–65.

———. *The Great Divorce. The Complete C. S. Lewis Signature Classics.* New York: HarperOne, 2007. 463–541.

———. *The Horse and His Boy. The Chronicles of Narnia.* New York: HarperCollins, 2001. 199–310.

———. "Imagination and Thought in the Middle Ages." *Studies in Medieval and Renaissance Literature.* Cambridge: Cambridge UP, 1966. 41–63.

———. "Is English Doomed?" *Present Concerns.* Ed. Walter Hooper. San Diego: Harvest, 1986. 27–31.

———. *The Last Battle. The Chronicles of Narnia.* New York: HarperCollins, 2001. 665–767.

———. *The Magician's Nephew.* New York: HarperCollins, 2001. 7–106.

———. *Mere Christianity. The Complete C. S. Lewis Signature Classics.* New York: HarperOne, 2007. 2–177.

————. *Miracles. The Complete C. S. Lewis Signature Classics.* New York: Harper-One, 2007. 297–462.

————. "Modern Man and His Categories of Thought." *Present Concerns.* Ed. Walter Hooper. San Diego: Harvest, 1986. 61–66.

————. "Myth Became Fact." *The Collected Works of C. S. Lewis:* The Pilgrim's Regress, Christian Reflections, God in the Dock. New York: Inspirational, 1996. 341–44.

————. "On Obstinacy in Belief." *The Sewanee Review* 63.4 (1955): 525–38. *JSTOR.* PDF file.

————. *Out of the Silent Planet.* New York: Scribner, 2003.

————. *Perelandra.* New York: Scribner, 2003.

————. Preface. *George MacDonald.* Ed. C. S. Lewis. London: HarperCollins, 2001. xxiii–xxxix.

————. *A Preface to Paradise Lost.* London: Oxford UP, 1942.

————. *The Problem of Pain. The Complete C. S. Lewis Signature Classics.* New York: HarperOne, 2007. 543–646.

————. "Religion Without Dogma?" *The Collected Works of C. S. Lewis: The Pilgrim's Regress, Christian Reflections, God in the Dock.* New York: Inspirational, 1996. 387–98.

————. "A Reply to Professor Haldane." *On Stories and other Essays on Literature.* Orlando, FL: Harvest, 1982. 69–79.

————. *The Screwtape Letters. The Complete C. S. Lewis Signature Classics.* New York: HarperOne, 2007. 179–277.

————. "Screwtape Proposes a Toast." *The Complete C. S. Lewis Signature Classics.* New York: HarperOne, 2007. 279–96.

————. *Surprised by Joy.* Orlando, FL: Harcourt, 1955.

————. *That Hideous Strength.* New York: Scribner, 2003.

————. "Three Kinds of Men." *Present Concerns.* Ed. Walter Hooper. San Diego: Harvest, 1986. 21–22.

————. "Unreal Estates." *On Stories and Other Essays on Literature.* Orlando, FL: Harvest, 1982. 143–53.

————. *The Voyage of the* Dawn Treader. *The Chronicles of Narnia.* New York: HarperCollins, 2001. 419–541.

Lindvall, Terry. *Surprised by Laughter.* Nashville: Nelson, 1996.

MacDonald, George. "The Fantastic Imagination." *The Complete Fairy Tales.* Ed. U. C. Knoepflmacher. New York: Penguin, 1999. 5–10.

————. "The Golden Key." *The Complete Fairy Tales.* Ed. U. C. Knoepflmacher. New York: Penguin, 1999. 120–44.

————. "The Imagination: Its Function and Its Culture." *A Dish of Orts.* Whitehorn, CA: Johannesen, 1996. 1–42.

————. *The Light Princess. The Complete Fairy Tales.* Ed. U. C. Knoepflmacher. New York: Penguin, 1999. 15–53.

————. *Lillith.* Grand Rapids, MI: Eerdmans, 1981.

————. *Phantastes.* Grand Rapids, MI: Eerdmans, 2000.

————. *The Princess and Curdie. The Princess and the Goblin / The Princess and Curdie.* Ed. Roderick McGillis. Oxford: Oxford UP, 1990. 169–342.

————. *The Princess and the Goblin. The Princess and the Goblin / The Princess and Curdie.* Ed. Roderick McGillis. Oxford: Oxford UP, 1990. 1–167.

————. *Unspoken Sermons: Series I, II, III.* Whitehorn, CA: Johannesen, 2011.

————. *The Wise Woman, or the Lost Princess: A Double Story. The Complete Fairy Tales.* Ed. U. C. Knoepflmacher. New York: Penguin, 1999. 225–303.

MacDonald, Greville. *George MacDonald and His Wife.* New York: Dial, 1924.

Manlove, Colin. "The Logic of Fantasy and the Crisis of Closure in *Lilith.*" *Lilith in a New Light. Critical Explorations in Science Fiction and Fantasy.* Ed. Lucas H. Harriman. Vol. 10. Jefferson, NC: McFarland, 2008. 46–58.

McConnell, Frank. *Storytelling and Mythmaking.* New York: Oxford UP, 1979.

McGillis, Roderick, ed. *The Princess and the Goblin / The Princess and Curdie.* By George MacDonald. Oxford: Oxford UP, 1990.

McGrath, Alister. *C. S. Lewis—A Life: Eccentric Genius, Reluctant Prophet.* Carol Stream, IL: Tyndale, 2013.

Meilaender, Gilbert. *The Taste for the Other: The Social and Ethical Thought of C. S. Lewis.* Grand Rapids, MI: Eerdmans, 1978.

Mendelson, Michael. "*Lilith,* Textuality, and the Rhetoric of Romance." *Lilith in a New Light. Critical Explorations in Science Fiction and Fantasy.* Ed. Lucas H. Harriman. Vol. 10. Jefferson, NC: McFarland, 2008. 21–38.

Milbank, Alison. *Chesterton and Tolkien as Theologians: The Fantasy of the Real.* New York: Clark, 2009.

Moorman, Charles. "'Now Entertain Conjecture of a Time'—The Fictive Worlds of C. S. Lewis and J. R. R. Tolkien." *Shadows of Imagination: The Fantasies of C. S. Lewis, J. R. R. Tolkien, and Charles Williams.* Ed. Mark R. Hillegas. London: Southern Illinois UP, 1979. 59–69.

Noel, Ruth S. *The Languages of Tolkien's Middle-earth.* Boston: Houghton, 1980.

Oser, Lee. *The Return of Christian Humanism: Chesterton, Eliot, Tolkien, and the Romance of History.* Columbia: U of Missouri P, 2007.

"Perichoresis." *The Oxford English Dictionary.* Oxford UP, 2014. Web. 18 Mar. 2014.

Purtill, Richard L. *J. R. R. Tolkien: Myth, Morality, and Religion.* San Francisco: Harper, 1984.

Raeper, William. *George MacDonald.* Tring, IL: Lion, 1987.

Reis, Richard H. *George MacDonald.* New York: Twayne, 1972.

Rosebury, Brian. *Tolkien: A Cultural Phenomenon.* 2nd ed. New York: Palgrave, 2003.

Rossi, Lee Donald. *The Politics of Fantasy: C. S. Lewis and J. R. R. Tolkien.* Diss. Cornell U., 1972. Ann Arbor, MI: Xerox U. Microfilms, 1975.

The Saga of the Volsungs. Trans. Jesse L. Byock. New York: Penguin, 1999.

Sammons, Martha C. *War of the Fantasy Worlds: C. S. Lewis and J. R. R. Tolkien on Art and Imagination.* Santa Barbara, CA: Praeger, 2010. *EBSCOhost.* Ebook. 8 Apr. 2015.

Seddon, Eric. "*Letters to Malcolm* and the Trouble with Narnia: C. S. Lewis, J. R. R. Tolkien and Their 1949 Crisis." *Mythlore* 26.5 (Fall/Winter 2007): 61–81. *EbscoHost.* 13 May 2015. PDF file.

Shakel, Peter J. *Reason and Imagination in C. S. Lewis: A Study of* Till We Have Faces. Grand Rapids, MI: Eerdmans, 1984.

Shelley, Percy Bysshe. *A Defense of Poetry.* Ed. Albert S. Cook. Boston: Ginn, 1890. *Google Books.* 1–46. PDF file.

Shippey, Tom. "Liminality and the Everyday in *Lilith.*" *Lilith in a New Light. Critical Explorations in Science Fiction and Fantasy.* Ed. Lucas H. Harriman. Vol. 10. Jefferson, NC: McFarland, 2008. 15–20.

———. *The Road to Middle-earth: How J. R. R. Tolkien Created a New Mythology.* Boston: Houghton, 2003.

"Storey." *Oxford Dictionaries.* Oxford UP, 2016. Web. 6 Jan. 2016.

Sydney, Sir Philip. "The Defense of Poesy." Ed. Albert S. Cook. Boston: Ginn, 1890. *Google Books.* PDF file.

Tolkien, Christopher. Preface. *Tree and Leaf.* Ed. Christopher Tolkien. London: HarperCollins, 2001. v–ix.

Tolkien, J. R. R. "Beowulf: The Monsters and the Critics." *The Monsters and the Critics and Other Essays.* London: HarperCollins, 1997. 5–48.

———. *The Fellowship of the Ring.* Boston: Houghton, 1994.

———. *The Hobbit.* Boston: Houghton, 1997.

———. "Leaf by Niggle." *Tales from the Perilous Realm.* Illus. and afterword by Alan Lee. Ed. Tom Shippey. London: HarperCollins, 2008. 283–312.

———. *The Letters of J. R. R. Tolkien.* Ed. Humphrey Carpenter. Boston: Houghton, 2000.

———. "Mythopoeia." *Tree and Leaf.* Ed. Christopher Tolkien. London: HarperCollins, 2001. 85–90.

———. "On Fairy-Stories." *The Monsters and the Critics and Other Essays.* London: HarperCollins, 1997. 109–61.

———. "On Translating *Beowulf.*" *The Monsters and the Critics and Other Essays.* London: HarperCollins, 1997. 49–71.

———. *The Return of the King.* Boston: Houghton, 1994.

———. "A Secret Vice." *The Monsters and the Critics and Other Essays.* London: HarperCollins, 1997. 198–223.

———. *The Silmarillion.* Ed. Christopher Tolkien. 2nd ed. Boston: Houghton Mifflin, 2001.

———. "Smith of Wootton Major." *Tales from the Perilous Realms.* London: HarperCollins, 2008.

———. *The Two Towers.* Boston: Houghton, 1994.

———. "Valedictory Address." *The Monsters and the Critics and Other Essays.* London: HarperCollins, 1997. 224–40.

"The Victorian Age." "Introduction." *The Norton Anthology of English Literature.* Ed. M. H. Abrams, Stephen Greenblatt et al. Vol. 2. 7th ed. New York: Norton, 2000. 1043–65.

Ward, Michael. *Planet Narnia: The Seven Heavens in the Imagination of C. S. Lewis.* Oxford: Oxford UP, 2008.

Westminster Abbey. *A Service to Dedicate a Memorial to C S Lewis Writer, Scholar, Apologist.* London: Barnard, 2013. PDF file.

Wheelwright, Philip Ellis. *The Burning Fountain: A Study in the Language of Symbolism.* Bloomington: Indiana UP, 1968.

Williams, Donald T. *Mere Humanity: G. K. Chesterton, C. S. Lewis, and J. R. R. Tolkien on the Human Condition.* Nashville: B&H, 2006.

Wood, Ralph C. *The Gospel According to Tolkien: Visions of the Kingdom in Middle-earth.* Louisville, KY: Westminster John Knox, 2003.

Wright, Marjorie Evelyn. "The Cosmic Kingdom of Myth: A Study in the Myth-Philosophy of Charles Williams, C. S. Lewis, and J. R. R. Tolkien." Diss. U of Illinois–Urbana, 1960.

Zaleski, Philip, and Carol Zaleski. *The Fellowship.* New York: Farrar, Straus, and Giroux, 2015.

Index

Ainur, 20, 51, 53, 62, 113, 114. *See also* eldila; Valar

Alcuin, 124, 126

Alighieri, Dante, 119, 120, 160–61n33, 168n25

allegory, 27–28, 120, 159n15, 159n17

altruism, 77, 110–11, 114, 155, 166n19

anachronistic fallacy, 47, 164n1. *See also* chronological snobbery

anarchy, 70–71, 101, 125, 131

angels, 20, 52–56, 60, 94, 114, 121, 139. *See also* Ainur; eldila; Valar

animal nature, 44, 88–89

animals. *See* beasts

arche-writing, 16, 109

Aristotle, 36, 76–77

Arnold, Matthew, 28, 35, 42, 150

art: and audience, 34; and creation, 29, 33, 51, 122, 160n22; and criticism, 159n19; and escape, 25; fairy-story, 41; and fantasy, 23; government, 101; and history, 33–34; and humanity, 12, 29–41, 50–52, 94, 130, 143, 168n26; and imagination, 4, 32; and Inklings, 3; literature, 31–32; and the Machine, 122; myth, 42; poetry, 37; and Primary and Secondary Worlds, 121–22; and science, 102; and truth, x, 27–41, 121, 148, 150–51. *See also* creation

atheism, 18, 97, 128–29

Attebery, Brian, 6, 38, 122

Auden, W. H., 35–36, 158n5

Augustine, 60, 80

Austen, Jane, 96

barbaric, 12, 91–95, 97, 148. *See also* savage

Barfield, Owen: on imagination, 161; as

Inkling: xi, 1, 6–7; on language, 147; on Modernism, 91

beasts: beast-like, 48, 52, 64, 143–44; beast-mastering, 54–59, 61, 94; beastward, 57–59, 144; definition, 44; and goblins, 47, 93; and hierarchy, 52–54; and hnau, 43, 45, 52–57, 59, 64, 161n3; and humans, 44–59, 63, 64, 105, 132, 139, 144, 162n12; and knowledge, 55; and love, 45; and mystery, 45; and mysticism, 108; personification of, 44; and pride, 45; and virtues, 165n12

beauty: in fairy-stories, 9, 21, 102; and God, 152; and imagination, 24; and law, 22; natural, 43

Belloc, Hilaire, 99, 101, 150

Bentham, Jeremy, 136

The Bent One, 54, 110

Beowulf, 9–10, 13, 31–32, 34, 36–37, 72–73, 120, 126

Billone, Amy, 135

Bios, 47–48, 60, 63, 64, 88, 122, 124–25, 139, 145, 149, 162n7

Blake, William, 11, 114, 120

Boethius, 131

Brady, Charles A., 1–2

Browning, Elizabeth Barrett, and Robert Browning, 12, 36, 96

Bultitude, 26, 45, 56, 159n14

Burns, Marjorie, 3–4, 6, 99

Camus, Albert, 91

Carpenter, Humphrey: on the Inklings, 2–4, 40, 169n33; on Tolkien, 6, 8–10, 126

catharsis, 76–79

Cecil, David, 1

178